PROVERB MASTERS

PROVERB MASTERS

Shaping the Civil Rights Movement

Raymond Summerville

University Press of Mississippi / Jackson

The University Press of Mississippi is the scholarly publishing agency of
the Mississippi Institutions of Higher Learning: Alcorn State University,
Delta State University, Jackson State University, Mississippi State University,
Mississippi University for Women, Mississippi Valley State University,
University of Mississippi, and University of Southern Mississippi.

www.upress.state.ms.us

The University Press of Mississippi is a member
of the Association of University Presses.

Any discriminatory or derogatory language or hate speech regarding race,
ethnicity, religion, sex, gender, class, national origin, age, or disability that has
been retained or appears in elided form is in no way an endorsement
of the use of such language outside a scholarly context.

Copyright © 2024 by University Press of Mississippi
All rights reserved

∞

LCCN 2024931666
Hardback 9781496852489
Trade Paperback 9781496852557
ePub Single 9781496852564
ePub Institutional 9781496852571
Web PDF Single 9781496852588
Web PDF Institutional 9781496852595

British Library Cataloging-in-Publication Data available

For Wolfgang Mieder, professor, mentor, and friend

CONTENTS

Acknowledgments ix
Foreword by Patricia A. Turner. xiii
Introduction: Proverbs and Social Justice 3
Chapter One: "Eternal Vigilance Is the Price of Liberty":
    The Proverbs and Proverbial Sayings of Ida B. Wells-Barnett 12
Chapter Two: "Literature Is the Expression of Life": Sayings,
    Proverbs, and Proverbial Expressions of Charles W. Chesnutt 48
Chapter Three: "Winning Freedom and Exacting Justice":
    A. Philip Randolph's Use of Proverbs and Proverbial Language 74
Chapter Four: "Words Are but Wind": The Proverbs and Proverbial
    Sayings of Bob Dylan. 97
Chapter Five: "Each One, Teach One": The Proverbs and
    Proverbial Expressions of Septima Poinsette Clark 110
Chapter Six: "You Can't Hate the Roots of a Tree and Not Hate
    the Tree, You Can't Hate Africa and Not Hate Yourself":
    The Important Proverbs, Sayings, and Proverbial Expressions
    of Malcolm X 136
Chapter Seven: "Black Power" and Black Rhetorical Tradition:
    The Proverbial Language of Stokely Carmichael 154
Conclusion: Proverbs Shaping Legacies 197
Notes 205
Works Cited 207
Index 219

ACKNOWLEDGMENTS

There are some very important peremiologist for whom without this book would not have been possible, Wolfgang Mieder and Sw. Anand Prahlad. Mieder communicates the story best of how he was drawn to proverb studies in his preface for *American Proverbs: A Study of Texts and Contexts* (1989). Mieder says: "Almost twenty years ago I came in contact with a most inspiring professor of German and Folklore at Michigan State University. This man was Stuart A. Gallacher (1906–77), himself a former student of Archer Taylor, America's greatest proverb scholar. Stuart A. Gallacher introduced me to the study of proverbs in a seminar on German folklore in 1969, and thus I owe my fascination with this intriguing subject matter to him. He inspired me to write my dissertation on proverbs, and I have now tilled the field of proverbs myself for many years. During this time, I have never forgotten what my former teacher did for me by kindling my interest in proverbs" (Mieder 1989).

Decades ago Mieder taught Prahlad when Prahlad was a graduate student at the University of California at Berkely. In 1980, at the age of thirty-six, Mieder was invited to Berkely to teach as a guest professor by the late world-renowned folklorist Alan Dundes. I asked Mieder about the experience, and he said that it was "a great honor for me. Out of this came our edited volume *The Wisdom of Many: Essays on the Proverb* (1981). Prahlad was in my graduate student seminar on proverbs during that spring 1980 term. I have very fond memories of that."[1] I am extremely grateful that Dundes made that move, because I would later learn a tremendous amount from them both. Like Mieder, Prahlad also wrote his dissertation on proverbs, and it was published as *African American Proverbs in Context* (1996). It arguably is the earliest and most important book on proverb use in African American culture. Later, Prahlad introduced me and several other lucky folklore graduate students to the vast field of paremiological scholarship during my very first semester of graduate study at the University of Missouri–Columbia. Fall semester of 2010 was the first and only time that Prahlad taught a graduate seminar specifically on proverbs, even though, by the time that I had enrolled, he had already published several important books and articles on the subject. Later, at an American Folklore Society Conference, Prahlad introduced his graduate students to Mieder, who encouraged us to continue to work on making our own contributions to the field. *Proverb Masters* certainly would not have been possible without all of the knowledge and expertise that they eagerly share with students like me. Likewise, it would have been equally impossible without their encouragement.

It is impossible for me to name everyone who has contributed to this project either directly or indirectly, but I would like to thank several. First, I would like to thank Katie E. Keene, senior acquisitions editor at the University Press of Mississippi, who six years ago read and shared my initial book proposal and showed immense support for the project from the very start. I am grateful to Mary Heath, the associate editor who read earlier drafts of the manuscript and offered very important comments and suggestions. I would like to thank design manager Todd Lape and his team for the creative and artistic cover design and for obtaining permission to use the photo. I would like to thank project editor Corley Longmire and copyeditor Peter Tonguette, who read several final drafts of the manuscript, although I take full responsibility for any errors which may exist. I would like to thank the new editors of *Proverbium*, Melita Aleksa Varga and Hrisztova-Gotthardt at the University of Croatia, for converting the journal into an invaluable digital resource for folklorists. They also granted permission for several essays to appear in this volume. I am grateful to all my former colleagues and former professors at North Carolina Agricultural and Technical State University who always showed me much support. I am also indebted to all my friends, former colleagues, and former professors at the University of Missouri–Columbia, especially Elaine J. Lawless and Sw. Anand Prahlad whose careful guidance and training in folkloristics made me feel confident and well prepared. I am extremely appreciative to all my friends and colleagues at Fayetteville State University, for their unwavering support, especially Ji Young Kim, Brooksie Harrington, and Nicole A. McFarlane. I would like to thank Patricia A. Turner for years of encouragement and for writing an excellent forward. I am also grateful to Katherine Mellon Charron at North Carolina State University, who did her master's thesis and dissertation on Septima Clark. Charron's book *Freedom's Teacher: The Life of Septima Clark* (2009) informed much of chapter five. Without Charron's scholarly efforts so much information about Clark's life would have either remained unknown or would have simply been forgotten. Professor Charron was both kind and gracious in answering any questions I had regarding Clark and the movement. The Davis Library and the Harold Schiffman Music Library at the University of North Carolina at Greensboro house many rare and difficult-to-find texts that I needed. Schiffman is a virtual goldmine for finding information on folk music, blues music, and works on Dylan. I also spent ample time at Davis Library and the Sonja Haynes Stone Center for Black History and Culture at the University of North Carolina, and together they represent one of most extensive Black studies collections in the state. I would also like to thank Jordan Lovejoy at the Center for the Study of the American South at the University of North Carolina for the amazing work that she does. I am also grateful to Perkins and Bostock libraries at Duke University, two extraordinary facilities that house extensive works by folklorists. SNCC Digital Gateways is another resource which was very helpful. It is also facilitated by Duke University libraries' partnership with the SNCC Legacy Project and the Center for Documentary Studies, and it is one of the largest digital collections on civil rights (https://snccdigital.org/). I found many rare images, interviews, and historic documents and more through this amazing state-of-the-art resource. I am grateful to Bluford Library at North Carolina Agricultural and Technical State University, which has archived an extensive collection of A. Philip Randolph's *Messenger* magazine and other titles important to the movement. I extend thanks to all the experts at Charles W. Chesnutt Library at Fayetteville State University. I would also like to thank Durham Public Libraries. I am grateful to the Auburn Avenue Research Library in Atlanta, Georgia, for sending me documents from their Bond Collection quickly and on short notice. I am extremely grateful to the American Folklore Society (AFS) and the Western States Folklore Society (WSFS) for continuing to provide folklorists with spaces to collaborate and exchange ideas. I would also like to extend a very special thanks AFS president Marilyn M. White, who is always willing to share her own personal experiences with others and for organizing and encouraging so many other Black folklorists at AFS. She is truly an inspiration. Without both important organizations, this project simply would not have been possible. Lastly, I would like to thank Crystal Good, founding editor of *Black By God: The West Virginian* (http://blackbygod.org), who is keeping Stokely Carmichael and Ron Karenga's vision of Pan Africanism and Kwanzaa alive by covering important news and events effecting all Black people in the United States and in Africa.

FOREWORD

Raymond Summerville's *Proverb Masters: Shaping the Civil Rights Movement* comes to students, teachers, and all manner of people interested in Black culture, folklore, and history not a minute too soon. The past few decades have offered precious little on the study of African American proverbs. The esteemed paremiologist Wolfgang Mieder has supplied several full-length texts that delve into the repertoires of noted political figures, including Frederick Douglass (*"No Struggle, No Progress": Frederick Douglass and His Proverbial Rhetoric for Civil Rights* [Peter Lang, 2001]), Martin Luther King Jr. (*"Making a Way Out of No Way": Martin Luther King's Sermonic Proverbial Rhetoric* [Peter Lang, 2010]), and Barack Obama (*"Yes We Can": Barack Obama's Proverbial Rhetoric* [Peter Lang, 2009]) and is scrupulous in including African American examples in his many more general books about proverbial usage. But, as Mieder would be the first to acknowledge, given the density of proverb use in Black verbal culture, far more attention is warranted.

It was different in the early days of African American folklore research. While the field was never choked with scholars, most folklorists serious about documenting Black traditions made sure to consider proverbs. As Alan Dundes notes in his comprehensive *Mother Wit from the Laughing Barrel* (University Press of Mississippi, 1973), J. Mason Brewer, Langston Hughes, Zora Neal Hurston, Guy B. Johnson, Arna Bontemps, and others documented and analyzed African American proverbs. But by the time Anand Prahlad came forward with *African American Proverbs in Context* (University Press of Mississippi, 1996) and *Reggae Wisdom in Jamaican Music* (University Press of Mississippi, 2001), few scholars were engaged in this important work.

While Summerville can't make up for all of the neglected terrain in one volume, *Proverb Masters* makes a significant contribution. By probing the proverb use of African American public figures whose spheres of influence span from the late nineteenth century, with the exacting discourse of Ida B. Wells, to a half-century or more later, with the witty rhetorical wisdom of

Stokely Carmichael, he enables the reader to measure what tropes remain the same and which ones shift. Although his subjects include more men than women, he does provide gender diversity by accounting for Wells and the much too understudied Septima Clark. Importantly, he explores figures such as Clark and Charles W. Chestnutt, who, while well-known to serious students of African American history, have received far too little academic attention. Summerville also looks to the lyrics of white singer-songwriter Bob Dylan for evidence of the impact of Black proverbial discourse beyond the race.

Proverb Masters not only has much to offer to folklorists; it also has a great deal to offer to students and scholars of the civil rights movement. In so many volumes penned in this field, the writers are clearly unaware that the proverbial language that they draw attention to is, in and of itself, a field of study and is informed by Black traditional language preferences. Future scholars delving into Malcolm X, A. Philip Randolph, and others in this book would do well to familiarize themselves with Summerville's cogent arguments.

My fondest hope for this volume is that it reaches a large swath of young folklorists who recognize the value embedded in the study of Black proverbs and set themselves to the task of their own paremiological pursuits.

Patricia A. Turner
Los Angeles, California

PROVERB MASTERS

Introduction

PROVERBS AND SOCIAL JUSTICE

The purpose of this book is to illustrate the extent that proverbs, sayings, and proverbial expressions are connected to issues surrounding social justice in America. It is focused on important figures of the long civil rights era. The term "long civil rights era" was coined by historian Jacquelyn Dowd Hall (2005).[1] As Dowd explains, it encompasses most of the 1900s to the present because important leaders were concerned with procuring social justice and equality for Black people long before such efforts evolved into what we now recognize as the civil rights movement. Important leaders of the long civil rights era addressed in this book include Ida B. Wells-Barnett, Charles Waddell Chesnutt, Asa Philip Randolph, Bob Dylan, Septima Poinsette Clark, Malcolm X, and Stokely Carmichael. This book explores the powerful influence that their words have on people due in part to their use of proverbial language. It is important to note at the outset that this is not a chronologically organized account of their lives or an attempt to document every single proverb or proverbial expression that they have ever used, but it does cover a great deal of ground. Studies of this nature were most recently initiated by paremiologist and folklorist Wolfgang Mieder, who defines a proverb as "a short, generally known sentence of the folk which contains wisdom, truth, morals, and traditional views in a metaphorical, fixed and memorizable form and which is handed down from generation to generation" (Mieder 2004: 3; Mieder 2008: 11). Mieder's scholarship on proverbs illustrate several important things: first, Mieder's scholarship proves that folklore, paremiology, and American history can be used in tandem to reexamine important people, places, and events. In fact, proverbs, sayings, and proverbial expressions often mark important events in history, functioning as mnemonic devices (Bowden 1996: 442), reminding us of the monumental accomplishments of important Americans. Second, Mieder's scholarship demonstrates that these disciplines may be used together to better understand the important values, beliefs, and worldviews of significant leaders, some of whose important ideals are in accord with basic principles under which the United States was founded. Third, Mieder's work is the first to demonstrate that the lens of paremiology offers scholars a unique way to study the civil rights era, because several important leaders use proverbs and proverbial expressions to communicate important messages about themselves and the movements that they serve. Fourth, works of this nature illustrate that examining the proverbial language of different leaders from the same movement offers scholar's differing perspectives and angles of perception for evaluating important events. Fifth, examining multiple viewpoints may ultimately lead to a greater awareness of what some of these historical events mean for us in the present. Mieder's works on this subject include *"No Struggle, No Progress": Frederick Douglass and His Proverbial Rhetoric for Civil Rights* (2001), *"Yes We Can": Barack Obama's Proverbial Rhetoric* (2009), *"Making A Way Out of No Way": Martin Luther King's Sermonic Proverbial Rhetoric* (2010), *"Keep Your Eyes on the Prize": Congressman John Lewis's Proverbial Odyssey for Civil Rights"* (2014), *"Right Makes Might": Proverbs and American Worldview* (2019), *The Worldview of American Proverbs* (2020), and *Proverbial Rhetoric of Four Civil Rights Heroes: Frederick Douglass, Martin Luther King, Jr., John Lewis, and Barack Obama* (2020). Mieder's pioneering paremiological scholarship establishes a strong foundation on which other folklorist, historians, and paremiologist may build.

Another important contribution to the field of peremiology comes from folklorist Anand Prahlad. In his groundbreaking text *African-American Proverbs in Context* (1996), he contends that proverbs may be understood on many different levels including grammatical levels, situational levels, social levels, and symbolic levels (Prahlad 1996: 23). Furthermore, he argues the possibility that more levels of meaning have yet to be discovered. Prahlad also coins the term "proverb master," from which this work has its namesake, and describes some of the proverb master's underlining characteristics. For Prahlad, proverb masters are those certain individuals whose use of proverbs and proverbial expressions are deeply connected to their personal identity (Prahlad 1996: loc 1644). Additionally, Prahlad asserts that proverb masters may think about proverbs in ways that transcend any one field of meaning, saying that for the proverb master "the proverb is perceived as a doorway through which philosophical introspection, contemplation, and emotional growth lie, a reference marker containing layer upon layer of meaning" (Prahlad 1996: loc 1769) and "the recall or application of most proverbs triggers associative memories that are invariably linked to strong symbolic meanings, and these tend to color many of the proverbs in [their] repertoire and . . . inform(s) . . . choice, use, and function" (Prahlad 1996: loc

1769). Furthermore, the proverb master derives "psychological comfort and pleasure" from using proverbs (Prahlad 1996: loc 1821).

The idea that one can become a proverb master and the notion that proverbs, from a historical standpoint, have been instrumental to issues surrounding social justice in America are fundamental ideas that are of utmost importance to this study. Likewise, it is important to realize that the proverb masters chosen for this study all share one key trait which made their proverb usage much more likely: they were all highly literate people who read widely and indiscriminately for most of their lives. This is not to say that one must be literate to become a proverb master, but literacy does increase one's chances of becoming one due to the frequency that proverbs are shared through literature. For instance, as a point of comparison, some early blues artists were either illiterate or admitted to having a very limited amount of formal schooling. Of course, this is due largely to circumstances beyond their own control, but it remains a significant fact nonetheless. In fact, folklorist Michael Taft[2] explores proverb frequency in blues and documents the extent that proverbs are used in blues to describe biological and emotional needs. In the following passage, Taft poses his overarching question: "Partly through its formulaic structure, the blues replays and plays with the fundamental concerns of African American society: The blues is like a discourse that comprises the 'already said' of Afro-America. In such a discourse, would not the proverb serve to describe the 'basic human experiences and emotions' (once again to borrow Mieder's words) which the singer tried to convey to the blues audience?" (Taft 1994: 230). While Taft's research does yield a response that leans towards the affirmative, he also discovers proverbs in blues to be rather sparse, saying that blues singer's "use of proverbs ... [is] comparatively limited," and that "among all the proverbs available to blues singers, only a few became ... apart of the storehouse of phrases which singers relied upon in the composition of their songs" (Taft 1994: 234).

In addition to attaining high levels of literacy, often at early ages, some of the proverb masters discussed in this book also had knowledge of one another or worked alongside some of the same people during the civil rights movement. This is a reality that may have contributed to them thinking about social justice in similar ways, and it may have also influenced the proverbs that they chose to use, share, and have in common. One need only imagine the political ideas and folk knowledge that may have been exchanged as Wells and Chesnutt collaborated in establishing the inaugural chapter of the National Association of Colored People (NAACP), or when A. Phillip Randolph first learned about Highlander Folk Center and then later sent his young protégé, Dr. Martin Luther King Jr., there to master the fundamentals of nonviolent direct action from teachers like Myles Horton and Septima Clark. (Highlander is addressed more fully in chapter five.) As asserted in chapter four, Highlander is also the very same institute where Bob Dylan once strummed tunes for young civil rights activists who wanted to create their own brand-new forms of protest music. Dylan would later share a stage with Randolph and King at the 1963 March on Washington for Jobs and Freedom as he performed with Joan Baez. Likewise, Stokely Carmichael received counsel and instruction from Septima Clark at Highlander. Carmichael also sought out and received guidance from Malcolm X, who would sometimes share political advice in the form of proverbial wisdom with Carmichael and other members of the Student Nonviolent Coordinating Committee (SNCC). Additionally, Malcolm X and Carmichael both spent time in Africa with Ghanian president Kwame Nkrumah and Guinean president Ahmed Sékou Touré to get a fuller understanding of Pan-Africanism and to learn ways to connect African political struggles, with American civil rights struggles, and the political struggles of Black people around the globe. Later in life, Carmichael would write a speech for the grand opening of Malcolm X Liberation University in Durham, North Carolina. Whether they knew it then or not, their legacies would become intertwined because they helped change the way that race and class would be viewed in America. The study of these leaders and their proverb use provides some insight into the kinds of ideas that they exchanged with one another and the extent that they supported and contributed to one another's causes.

The first chapter, "'Eternal Vigilance Is the Price of Liberty': The Proverbs and Proverbial Sayings of Ida B. Wells-Barnett,"[3] explores some of the important life experiences that made Wells who she was as a person, and as a political and social activist. She was dubbed the "mother of the Black club movement," because she helped initiate dozens of Black clubs and nonprofit organizations devoted to helping Black people in need, some of which are still in existence today (e.g., Head Start programs and the National Association of Colored People [NAACP]). Wells is widely known as the very first African American female sociologist and investigative journalist because she single-handedly investigated scores of lynchings to uncover a new truth for the world to see: that the Black people being lynched were not the simple-minded brutes and savages that white presses made them out to be. Wells demonstrated a masterful use of proverbs and proverbial language as she made efforts to speak and write truthfully and realistically about racial violence, and as she engaged in the political and social struggles which were necessary for bringing attention to the movements and causes that she cared most deeply about, including the antilynching movement, the temperance movement, and the women's suffrage movement.

The second chapter, "'Literature Is the Expression of Life': Sayings, Proverbs, and Proverbial Expressions of Charles W. Chesnutt," will discuss some of the most important developments in Chesnutt's early life and career which contributed to him becoming the first African American writer of fiction. Some of Chesnutt's diary entries reveal that at an early age he was extremely hurt and saddened by encounters he had with racist white people growing up in Fayetteville, North Carolina, and this was a major impetus for him having the seemingly lofty goal of becoming a fiction writer. This monumental decision was also made, in part, in response to the absence of Black writers in the 1800s. Furthermore, African American characters who were included in the works of white fiction authors during Chesnutt's lifetime were routinely portrayed in unrealistic and unflattering ways. Chesnutt realized that harmful Black stereotypes in American popular fiction had the power to greatly influence public opinion and policies, thus impacting Black lives on epic scales. Chesnutt wrote tirelessly against pernicious representations of Black people while simultaneously writing in support of new antiracist legislation and new nonprofit organizations designed to help Black people thrive (many of whom were newly freed slaves, or one generation removed from slavery). Throughout some of Chesnutt's carefully crafted fiction, insightful speeches, and heartfelt personal correspondences, he demonstrates an uncanny ability to make important statements on life, race, and American culture using proverbs and proverbial expressions. Furthermore, some of the sayings which Chesnutt coins himself, for instance the chapter's namesake, "Literature is the expression of life," have also become proverbial over time.

The third chapter, "'Winning Freedom and Exacting Justice': A. Philip Randolph's Use of Proverbs and Proverbial Language,"[4] examines the life and times of Randolph and in the process explores some of the reasons why he is such an important figure in American history. Randolph's untiring efforts in trying to establish social, economic, and political, equality in American society is unparalleled. This chapter discusses ways that Randolph's early life lessons and experiences influenced his decision to devote his entire life to championing for equality and justice for all people. It also illustrates ways that proverbs, proverbial expressions, and sayings were used by Randolph as instrumental political weapons as he fought against forces of white supremacy to accomplish monumental feats such as establishing the nation's first Black labor union, the Brotherhood of Sleeping Car Porters (BSCP). He also founded one of the first organizations in American history to garner enough support to gain national political leverage, the March on Washington Movement (MOWM). Through this organization, Randolph was able to win several important concessions on behalf of Black people, such as executive orders from the president to extend access to equal employment and equal pay in American defense industries and in transportation industries. One of the biggest highlights of Randolph's political career (and an event which has been used by many scholars to define his legacy) was his planning and execution of the 1963 March on Washington for Jobs and Freedom, in which over 250,000 people descended onto the steps of the White House lawn to demand equality. Randolph was a very influential politician due to his legal knowledge, his persistence, and his ability to persuade others through his masterful use of proverbial wisdom.

Chapter four, "'Words Are but Wind': The Proverbs and Proverbial Sayings of Bob Dylan,"[5] will examine some of the important roles that Dylan played during the civil rights movement (1954–68) and how his implementation of proverbs, proverbial expressions, and sayings inspired others and even helped the movement to gain traction. The 1960s marks a time of turmoil, confusion, and distrust in American politics because of racial injustice at home and the Vietnam war abroad. Dylan's music filled a huge void for millions of young people looking for something righteous to believe in even amongst all of the chaos. There is no questioning the fact that Dylan has gained countless numbers of followers, supporters, and fans throughout his career as a folk artist, and he has done so without making claims to being either a political activist or a prophet. In interviews, Dylan has consistently rejected both of those labels. Nevertheless, from the start of his career to the present, Dylan has baffled audiences with his mysterious ability to create ingenious songs filled with critical social and political commentary. The proverbs in the memorable lines and compelling leitmotifs found in Dylan's music moved people to political action. Chapter four will explore some of the proverbial social and political critique found in Dylan's music. There is ample scholarship on Dylan's life that proves that he was one of the more dominant and authoritative voices of the 1960s and 1970s, so much so that his music still helps to define the civil rights era for those of us who did not experience it.

Chapter five, "'Each One, Teach One': The Proverbs and Proverbial Expressions of Septima Poinsette Clark,"[6] explores ways that proverbs and proverbial language helped Clark to connect to people and to communicate important values, beliefs, and pedagogical philosophy as she worked as an educator of the rural poor. Today, Clark's legacy is still celebrated at Highlander Folk School and in the South Carolina communities that she served, but as historian Katherine Mellon Charron illustrates, Clark has largely gone ignored by civil rights historians, and her impact on the movement has been mostly understated. Chapter five illustrates that the philosophy found in Clark's proverbial language closely reflects her life work. Clark's career began in South Carolina in 1910, when at sixteen years of age, she taught Black children of all ages in an unfurnished, ramshackle, one-room wooden shack. She didn't even have the convenience of using grade-level distinctions among her students who were the children of former slaves and members of the Gullah Geechee community. For Clark, the experience was disheartening due to the unfair pay and horrible working conditions that all of the Black educators faced, but rather than deter her, the experience helped to motivate her to continue to educate the rural poor and to work on behalf of eradicating disparities in education for the rest of her life. Clark became well-known for her work at Highlander Folk Center, where she was very instrumental in helping Myles Horton establish one of the first and only places in America where the poor and disfranchised could learn together without any regard to race, color, or creed. Highlander became a successful endeavor despite the backlash that it received for breaking the nation's segregation laws. At Highlander, Clark taught adult literacy courses and citizenship classes which covered civic fundamentals including how to pass complicated voter registration tests designed to deter Black people from ballot boxes. Many Black people who entered Highlander were illiterate, due in part to segregation and a widespread lack of adequate public schools for Black people, but when they completed Clark's programs, they had become both literate and much more independent. In fact, many of Clark's students at Highlander went on to seek higher education and to even run for public offices themselves. Largely due to Clark's efforts, the teaching of literacy, civics, life skills, and nonviolent direct action was offered to thousands of poor people across the South who would otherwise have never been afforded opportunities to learn anything aside from menial labor. Clark had her literacy programs down to a science, and this made her programs easily reproducible. While most were only concerned with gaining the right to vote, Clark believed that only educated voters could affect meaningful change. Thus, her well-known philosophy in the form of proverbial wisdom, "Each one, teach one," is one of the reasons why Clark has been dubbed "the grandmother" of the civil rights movement. Chapter five explores the philosophy behind this proverb and others that she frequently used as she taught throughout the Deep South.

Chapter six, "'You Can't Hate the Roots of a Tree and Not Hate the Tree, You Can't Hate Africa and Not Hate Yourself': The Important Proverbs, Sayings, and Proverbial Expressions of Malcolm X," examines the multifaceted use of proverbs, proverbial expressions and sayings in the speeches and writings of Malcolm X, who worked as a minister in Harlem and as a spokesperson for the Nation of Islam (NOI) before founding his own organizations, the Muslim Mosque Incorporated (MMI) and the Organization for Afro-American Unity (OAU). During the civil rights movement, Malcolm X's teachings were very important to many people. Malcolm X was a shining example of what one could accomplish with education. He motivated many poor Black urban youth to take pride in themselves and in their communities despite the unfair obstacles and challenges they faced such as job discrimination, housing discrimination, and police brutality. Malcolm X was extremely vocal regarding these problems. Malcolm X was not a politician, nor was he running for any kind of public office, but his opinions on race and politics in America were sought out by major news outlets throughout the country. Furthermore, he was invited nearly one hundred times to give public talks at major universities where he would enthusiastically engage in friendly exchange with professors, students, and members of the general public who wanted to understand his views on the most effective ways to create positive change in America. During his lifetime, Malcolm X went from being the fiery mouthpiece of the Nation of Islam (NOI) to being a free and independent thinker who embraced all people regardless of race or religion. Chapter six aims to demonstrate that Malcolm X's proverb use reflects his unique upbringing on rural midwestern farmland and his unique philosophies and worldview.

Chapter seven is entitled "'Black Power' and Black Rhetorical Tradition: The Proverbial Language of Stokely Carmichael."[7] Carmichael is widely known as being that memorable and outspoken leader of the Student Nonviolent Coordinating Committee (SNCC) who is responsible for popularizing the saying "Black power." During the civil rights movement, the "Black power" mantra became a rallying call for the social, economic, and political independence of Black communities. What some people do not know is that long before "Black power" became a well-known saying, proverbs, proverbial expressions, and sayings were already a very important part of Carmichael's life. Carmichael learned very important lessons as a child from the proverbial wisdom of his parents and grandparents. Carmichael would also internalize the popular proverbs, proverbial expressions, and sayings that he encountered as a young student roaming the halls and dormitories of Howard University. Later in life, when Carmichael expatriated and embraced Pan-Africanism, he even obtained proverbial knowledge from two important individuals who would become his close mentors and future namesake: Guinean president Ahmed Sékou Touré and Ghanian president Kwame Nkrumah. Both African presidents would impart lessons on life and leadership to Carmichael (Kwame Turé). The brief and memorable sayings which they easily communicated to him (despite slight language barriers) are dispersed throughout his speeches and writings where Carmichael also reflects on their complex meanings. Chapter seven will examine some of the aphorisms which were most influential to Carmichael's thinking.

This work illustrates that proverbs are easily used to make covert statements, and when one applies paremiological evidence a range of possible meanings become exposed to interpretation, and each possible meaning is worth exploring. In some cases, through the act of contextualizing proverbs, proverbial expressions, and sayings, one may realize that some proverbial statements may be sentiments that the speaker may not have wanted to divulge explicitly—a decision that was most often influenced by a fear of backlash. Thus, covert political statements in the form of proverbs were a lot more common during the Jim Crow era than they are today. Today, many people from all walks of life have no fear of making bold political statements using absolutely no discretion at all. This is illustrated daily on social media platforms such as Facebook, Twitter, TikTok, and YouTube. However, making overt political statements during the Jim Crow era could have very easily meant the difference between life and death, making proverb use a necessity in some cases. Even though racial violence in America still exists, some historians would agree that it has consistently decreased in frequency and intensity over the past couple of centuries. An overarching theme in this book is that any decrease in racism or racial violence in America is due in large part to the work of those discussed in this study and others like them who spent most of their lives drawing the world's attention to social justice issues. I hope that *Eternal Vigilance* helps their stories to become better known, and that their proverbial wisdom may influence future generations.

Chapter One

"ETERNAL VIGILANCE IS THE PRICE OF LIBERTY"

The Proverbs and Proverbial Sayings of Ida B. Wells-Barnett

Ida B. Wells-Barnett (July 16, 1862–March 25, 1931) is an important figure in American history for several reasons. She initiated and was at the forefront of the antilynching movement and women's suffrage movements respectively. She also fought for the civil rights of all people. She is regarded as one of the first African American female sociologist and the very first Black female investigative journalist. During her life, she played many different roles. She was affectionately known as "Joan of Arc," "the mother of the club movement," and also "the princess of the Black press." Wells displays what historian Patricia A. Schechter identifies as *visionary pragmatism*, which can be defined as "a distinctive blend of religious and political commitments involving African American Christianity and a particular understanding of Reconstruction's unfinished business in the United States" (Schechter 2001: 9). She is also what historian Paula J. Giddings refers to as a "radical interracialists," or an African American woman who was "determined to enter the mainstream" (Terborg-Penn 1998: 119). In *A Red Record* (1895), her longest antilynching publication, Wells writes: "Virtue knows no color line, and the chivalry which depends upon complexion of skin and texture of hair can command no honest respect" (Harris 1991: 147; Bay and Gates 2014: 155). As a long-lasting testament to her radical interracialist ideals, the proverb "virtue knows no color line" would become one of her most well-known sayings (Harris 1991: 147; Bay and Gates 2014: 155). Wells embarked on fairly new territory when she became one of the first African American women to run for public office when she unsuccessfully sought a senate seat in the state of Illinois the year before her death. However, the most significant and inspiring label that Wells wore proudly was given to her by her many detractors—that of "race agitator."

In fact, at one point the Military Intelligence Division considered Wells to be "a far more dangerous agitator than Marcus Garvey" (Giddings 2008: 575). As a teen in the late nineteenth century, Wells was the first African American woman to attempt to sue a railroad company, which even precedes the landmark railway car discrimination case *Plessy v. Ferguson* (1892) (which resulted in the expansion of Jim Crow laws across the country). Wells's case also precedes the successful campaigns against the racially bias employment practices of railroad companies led by Asa Phillip Randolph (1889–1979) throughout the mid and late twentieth century. Even though she was always willing to confront racism early in her life, Wells became a "race agitator" when her writings began to awaken America's conscience regarding lynching.

There is an old riddle that goes, "If a tree falls in the woods and no one is around to hear it fall, does it make a sound?" Wells would become that sound for countless numbers of Black lynching victims throughout her lifetime—victims whose deaths would go unnoticed otherwise. During the Reconstruction era (1865–77) in the decade following the Civil War (1861–65), lynching became common practice in the South and continued to happen well into the twenty-first century. The Tuskegee Institute recorded nearly 5,000 lynchings that took place between 1882 and 1968. Lynching often involved the apprehension of unsuspecting victims and then hanging them from trees or light posts. Additionally, lynch mobs burned their victims alive and filled their lifeless bodies with bullets. Victims were also mutilated by incensed crowds and photos, and small pieces of their charred flesh, teeth, and articles of clothing were often distributed as souvenirs. Some victims were lynched under the assumption that they had committed a criminal offense, and the lynchings generally took place whether the actual offense was committed by an accused individual or not. The most popular excuses provided for lynching Black victims was often the sexual assault or rape of white women or stealing, but victims were also murdered for standing up to their white employers, and crimes as petty as being "sassy" to whites. Investigations of these crimes generally ended with the superficial determination that the murder(s) took place "at the hands of parties that are unknown." For over a century, lynching was a widespread practice that often went uncontested and lynch mobs were hardly ever brought to justice.

Ida B. Wells was one of the first to publicly contest this practice, and she began to do so after three of her closest friends, Thomas Moss, Calvin McDowell, and Will Stewart, were lynched in 1892. Each of the victims were known to be successful, law-abiding, upstanding citizens. Devastated, angry, and heartbroken, Wells religiously and vigilantly began to use the Black press to make the world aware of the deceptive and fraudulent nature of lynch law in the US. She went to the physical locations where crimes took place and gathered specific details from eyewitnesses and others involved. In all the articles and pamphlets that she would feverishly produce following her friends' murders, such as *Southern Horrors* (1892), *A Red Record* (1895), *Lynch Law in America* (1900), and many others, she questioned the validity of the practice of lynching, proving in many of the cases that victims were not guilty of any crime at all. In fact, most of the time, as in the case of her close friends, the victim's only crimes had been their very own success. Wells's friends ran a successful grocery store in Memphis called the People's Grocery Company, which began to infringe on the profits of a neighboring white-owned store. Furthermore, two of the three victims were postmasters, a government appointed position that was generally viewed as being reserved for whites only. Through her painstaking investigative work, journalistic talent, and public speaking engagements, she revealed repeatedly that racial hatred and jealousy were the underlying causes of most lynchings. By openly contesting the false accusation of rape that preceded most lynchings of Black men, she helped to open America's eyes to the gendered politics of southern racism and ultimately motivated law makers to pass more antilynching legislation even though the actual enforcement of such legislation would take even longer to achieve. Wells devoted her entire life to advocating for Black people and her far-reaching social, cultural, and political influence is still felt today. Unfortunately, her work is sometimes overlooked and ignored, but she certainly deserves to be in the very same conversation as other American political heroes and pioneers of the Reconstruction and civil rights eras, such as Abraham Lincoln (1809–65), Frederick Douglass (1818–95), Asa Phillip Randolph (1889–1979), and Martin Luther King Jr. (1929–68), due to the immeasurable global impact that she had and continues to have nearly a century after her death.

Wells made a conscious effort to incorporate traditional language in her work. By "traditional," I am referring to her use of proverbs and proverbial language. Her subjects are very serious, and in turn, she uses adages and proverbial expressions to make very serious-minded observations. For instance, Wells grew very concerned when racial tensions began to escalate in Chicago in 1919. After witnessing the deaths of nearly 300 African Americans in the East Saint Louis race riots of 1917, Wells begged the city of Chicago to intervene. When she and her delegates were turned away from the mayor's office on two separate occasions, Wells sent an open letter to the *Chicago Tribune* editor dated June 30, 1919. The letter was subsequently published on July 7, 1919, and it urged government officials to take action. She closed her letter by saying: "An ounce of prevention is worth a pound of cure. And in all earnestness I implore Chicago to set the wheels of justice in motion before it is too late, and Chicago be disgraced by some of the bloody outrages that have disgraced East St. Louis" (Thompson 1990: 123; McMurry 1998: 325). Nearly forty people would die in the Chicago race riots, which began on July 27 and lasted seven days, but had Mayor William Hale Thompson heeded Wells's bit of proverbial wisdom and "set the wheels of justice in motion," dozens of lives might have been saved in East St. Louis.

Wells also incorporated traditional language from some of America's most sacred and well-known texts to shed more light on the deadly southern rite of passage. In doing so, she simultaneously emphasized that the practice of lynching contradicts all the values and principles on which the nation was founded. In a speech entitled "Lynch Law in All Its Phases" delivered at Tremont Temple in Boston on February 13, 1893, Wells incorporated sayings from the Declaration of Independence (1776), the Gettysburg Address (1863), and "The Star-Spangled Banner" (1814). She said:

> And yet, the observing and thoughtful must know that in one section, at least, of our common country, a government of the people, by the people, and for the people, means a government by the mob; where the land of the free and home of the brave means a land of lawlessness, murder and outrage; and where liberty of speech means the license of might to destroy the business and drive from home those who exercise this privilege contrary to the will of the mob. Repeated attacks on the life, liberty and happiness of any citizen or class of citizens are attacks on distinctive American institutions. (Bay and Gates 2014: 77)

The first saying, "a government of the people, by the people, and for the people," is from Lincoln's Gettysburg Address. The second saying, "land of the free and home of the brave," is from "The Star-Spangled Banner." Wells's references to "life, liberty and happiness" allude to the Declaration of Independence. All these sayings are easily recognized by her audience as being derived from distinctly American texts. Wells employs this rhetorical strategy on several separate occasions throughout her career. In "Afro-Americans and Africa" (1892), Wells says: "In no other country but the vaunted 'land of the free and home of the brave' is a man despised because of his color. As Irish, Swede, Dutch, Italian and other foreigners find this 'sweet land of liberty,' the Afro-American finds it the land of oppression, outrage and persecution"

(Bay and Gates 2014: 47). In "Our Country's Lynching Record" (1913), Wells writes:

> Civilization cannot burn human beings alive or justify others who do so; neither can it refuse a trial by jury for black men accused of crime, without making a mockery of the respect for law which is the safeguard of the liberties of white men. The nation cannot profess Christianity, which makes the golden rule its foundation stone, and continue to deny equal opportunity for life, liberty and the pursuit of happiness to the black race. (Bay and Gates 2014: 287)

In "The East St. Louis Massacre: The Greatest Outrage of the Century" (1917), Wells says:

> The race prejudice of the United States asks Americans of black skins to keep an inferior place and when the Negroes ask an equal opportunity for life, liberty, and the pursuit of happiness, they are lynched, burned alive, disfranchised and massacred! Wherever a black man turns in this land of the free and home of the brave—in industry, in civic endeavor, in political councils in the ranks of Christians (?)—this hydra headed monster confronts him; dominates, oppresses and murders him! (Bay and Gates 2014: 311)

In "The Arkansas Race Riot" (1920), Wells writes about a group of Black men sentenced to death for defending themselves from a vicious mob. She says:

> The other white man mentioned in the record, Clinton Lee, met his death next day while he and hundreds of other white men were chasing and murdering every Negro they could find, driving them from their homes and stalking them in the woods and fields as men hunt wild beasts. They were finishing up the job they began the night before. As a group of Negroes ran before the mob two shots were fired from a rifle one of them carried, and Clinton Lee fell dead. For his death five of the twelve men sentenced are awaiting death by electrocution. Yet no man in this "land of the free and home of the brave" will say that a man is not justified in firing back on other men who are after him armed with shotguns to take his life! (Bay and Gates 2014: 318)

According to historian Angela D. Sims, statements like these that incorporate American proverbial rhetoric may serve two distinct purposes: "She wanted to promote a collective positive self-definition of African Americans in the public sphere and 'at the same time arouse the conscience of the American people to a demand for justice to every citizen, and punishment by law for the lawless'" (Sims 2010: 41–42). Wolfgang Mieder asserts that American quotations that have become proverbial can easily serve as a "guidepost for humankind" by reminding everyone that "we are tied together globally in a network of mutuality," and this was certainly one of Wells's intentions (Mieder 2019: 298).

It is well-known that proverbs and proverbial language are a defining feature in American and African American political rhetoric. It is well-documented by paremiologist and folklorist Wolfgang Mieder, who asserts that "traditional proverbs are indeed a living part of all political discourse. They play a significant role in the speeches and writings of major politicians, who employ them both positively and negatively to reach their political goals" (Mieder 2019: 35). Mieder has written about the proverbs and proverbial sayings of famous political figures, and his scholarship illustrates that proverbs have and always will be an integral part of American history and the American political scene. Furthermore, Mieder's work provides ample evidence that the study of proverbs and proverbial language may highlight essential aspects of leaders' lives, such as the ways that social and political injustices have influenced them. In many cases, the proverbial utterances of leaders encapsulate their reactions to sociopolitical wrongs. Paremiological evidence demonstrates that many important politicians and leaders have benefited in a multitude of ways from the use of proverbs. Likewise, an examination of the work of Wells illustrates that they were an important component of her communication style. She used them in her public speeches, private writings, correspondences, and in her many publications. Sometimes proverbs and proverbial sayings were spoken or written about her by others, and she was, in turn, responsive to them. This also illustrates that proverbs were a popular and meaningful aspect of her life.

Proverbs may be defined as "concise traditional statements of apparent truths with currency among the folk" (Mieder 2004: 4). They generally originate from people who communicate an idea using a concise and memorable phrase. The phrase is then used by others, which often results in variation. In addition to oral transmission, the process of dissemination is abetted by literature and other forms of media. Despite being recognized and understood by ordinary people or "the folk," proverbs should not be regarded as absolute truths, but they are used precisely because they sound "true." According to folklorist Barbara Kirshenblatt-Gimblett, "Neat symmetries and witty convergences of sound and meaning, tight formulations of logical relations, highly patterned repetitions, structural balance, and familiar metaphors encapsulate general principals and contribute to the feeling that anything that sounds so right must be true" (Kirshenblatt-Gimblett 1981: 111–12). On the contrary, it is widely accepted that proverbs such as "if the shoe fits, wear it" and "good fences make good neighbors" should be understood according to the context in which they are used. As Mieder emphasizes, "proverbs are apparent truths about experiences and each proverb does not have universal applicability. In special situations . . . any proverb will express some short wisdom of sorts that comments or reflects on a given situation, even though the truth of it could be put into question when looked at from a larger philosophical framework. Proverbs are context-bound, and so is their wisdom, no matter how minute that kernel of truth may be" (Mieder 2019: 267).

Wells may have acquired proverbs and proverbial expressions that she uses from several different sources. These sources may include, but are not limited to, her family and friends, preachers and political figures that she often listened to, and the vast amount of literature that she was exposed to as a young child and throughout her lifetime. There is also evidence that Wells may have been a folklorist at heart, habitually recording proverbs and proverbial sayings that she encountered as she traveled. In one of her diary entries, marked Thursday July 8, 1886, Wells writes, "Have been in the city four days and this is the first opportunity I've had to record the sayings & doings of the people whom I've met and the impressions of the country I've received" (DeCosta-Willis 1995: 86). This was written when Wells was twenty-four years old as she was traveling to Topeka, Kansas, with friends for a National Education Association conference. The city that she is referring to is Kansas City, Missouri, which they stopped at along the way. If it exists this document of "sayings and doings" has not yet been recovered by historians, but if it is found, it could possibly reveal new or previously unrecorded proverbs while also shedding more light on the origins of some proverbs and sayings that are still in circulation.

Since Wells did not leave behind a record of sayings, as she expressed an interest in doing, one must rely on historical background information and her writings to contextualize the proverbs and proverbial expressions that she uses. Wells's life story is compelling by any standard. Ida B. Wells was born enslaved in Holly Springs, Mississippi, on July 16, 1862, to enslaved parents, James "Jim" Wells and Elizabeth "Lizzie" Warrenton, three years before the end of the Civil War and a mere three days before Abraham Lincoln, the sixteenth president of the United States, would reveal his intentions to end slavery to a few select members of his cabinet. When Lincoln finally announced his Emancipation Proclamation on September 22, Ida B. Wells was two months old, but it would not go into effect until January 1, 1863 (Davidson 2007: 12–13). It was the Dred Scott decision of 1857 that ultimately determined, by way of the Supreme Court, that "the black man had no rights which the white man is bound to respect" (Davidson 2007: 15). This decision was not reversed until April 1866 when Congress passed the Civil Rights Act. It was followed by the ratification of the Fourteenth Amendment in June 1868 which "put the guarantee of citizenship into the constitution and added the promise of due process of law" (Davidson 2007: 20). While African Americans were technically and legally free, they were reminded repeatedly that they were not full-fledged citizens. The enactment of Black Codes, vagrancy laws, and later Jim Crow laws would limit the freedoms and movements of African Americans for more than one hundred years.

Wells's father, James "Jim" Wells, was born enslaved in 1840 in Tippah County, Mississippi in an area known as Hickory Flats. He was the son of a wealthy slave master, Morgan Wells, and an enslaved woman named Peggy, who arrived at the Morgan estate earlier that very same year. It was a very common and unquestioned practice during the antebellum era for slave owners to father children with their own slaves. Morgan Wells never had any children with his lawful wife, "Miss Polly," and possibly for this reason he may have placed a considerable amount of value on James. In the mid-nineteenth century, cotton, or "King Cotton" as it was sometimes called, was the primary cash crop in Mississippi, and for plantation owners, it made slave labor a necessity. Most slaves worked in the fields from "can see" to "can't see," and endured scorching heat and unbearable working conditions. Morgan made sure that his only child was educated and skilled in the trade of carpentry. James would remain a carpenter for twenty years. He worked for seven years while still enslaved and then he worked for another thirteen years as a carpenter after gaining emancipation (Sims 2010: 36). By being a skilled tradesman, James was afforded opportunities that most enslaved African Americans were not. The most important benefit of being a carpenter was being "hired out" to neighboring towns and cities, and thereby evading the dehumanizing treatment that often accompanied backbreaking field labor. At eighteen years of age, James was apprenticed to Spires Bolling in Holly Springs. In the Bolling household, James Wells would meet his future wife Elizabeth "Lizzie" Warrenton (1844–78), who was a very skilled cook. Holly Springs, also known as "the City of Flowers," was a bustling township that was growing at an exponential rate. In 1840 the population of Holly Springs was 17,536, which included 8,260 slaves and 8 free African Americans. Twenty years later, in 1860, the population grew to nearly 29,000, which included 1,295 slave owners who collectively owned 17,439 slaves. The free

Black population remained at eight during this two-decade time span and did not include James Wells. However, being skilled in a trade was the very next best thing to having complete freedom (McMurry 1998: 3–5).

Wells's mother, Elizabeth Wells, did not enjoy any of the protection or comforts that often came along with being the offspring of a slave master. Elizabeth was one of ten children born to slaves in Virginia. She could easily remember being separated from her parents and two sisters at the auction block. Although she tried to relocate them years later, she was unsuccessful and would never see them again. According to family members, Elizabeth never forgot the many beatings that she endured. When Morgan Wells died, Miss Polly immediately ordered Peggy to be stripped of her clothing and beaten severely, which was then carried out by slaves. This is something that Miss Polly knew that her husband Morgan would never allow had he still been living. Despite such extenuating circumstances, James and Elizabeth Wells married while both were still in bondage. However, they would marry again, officially, shortly after being freed (McMurry 1998: 3–5). Growing up listening to her parents talk about their lives under bondage would provide young Wells with her first glimpse into the racialized and gendered politics of slavery which she would spend her entire life trying to change.

Ida B. Wells would inherit many values and beliefs from her parents. They instilled in her the importance of work ethic, family, and education. They also helped to shape her political and religious views. James, as a freedman, was what many at the time would call a "race man," meaning that he maintained an active civic life and was committed to procuring equal rights and political power for African Americans. He was a Freemason, also known as the Masons, and he was also a member of a very secretive organization called the "4-L's," which stood for Lincoln's Legal Loyal League. This group, which started holding meetings at some point before the end of the Civil War, was organized by people from northern states that had relocated to Holly Springs. It was a private and guarded organization that incorporated an intricate system of "passwords, special knocks, and signs." There were branches of the 4-L's organization all over the South (Davidson 2007: 21). James Wells knew the significance of the ballot for Black people, and he stayed well informed about politics by having young Ida read the newspaper aloud to him. In fact, she would recount later in interviews that she was reading at such a young age that she could not even remember ever being taught. It is unclear if her father James knew how to read himself, but the evidence certainly leans toward the affirmative. He made it known that the education of all African Americans was very important to him. It is also a cause that Wells would later champion herself. James was elected to the board of trustees at Shaw

University in Holly Springs, a new school for Blacks that Ida would later attend for some time. The name was later changed to Rust College.

Elizabeth Wells also shared many of the same values as her husband. She taught Ida at a very young age how to prepare food, wash clothes, and clean house—essential skills that would make her more independent as a young woman. Many people believe that Ida learned and developed the strong work ethic that she would exhibit later in life from her parents. Much like her husband, Elizabeth Wells also valued learning. In the South, it was a misdemeanor or punishable offense to teach slaves how to read. Some slaves would learn by secretively watching their master's children as they were learning to read. This was a very risky practice that one must assume that Elizabeth was not willing to try. However, she longed for the opportunity and made it a priority to learn upon gaining her freedom. In fact, she accompanied her young daughter Ida to school until she had learned enough to read the Bible on her own. Elizabeth encouraged Wells to read everything that she could. In fact, in her autobiography Wells writes, "I used to sit before the blazing wood fire with a book in my lap during the long winter evenings and read by firelight. I had formed my ideals on the best of Dickens's stories, Louisa May Alcott's, Mrs. A. D. T. Whitney's, and Charlotte Brontë's books, and Oliver Optic's stories for boys" (Duster 1970: 21). Despite Wells's insatiable enthusiasm for literature, on Sundays Elizabeth would only allow the reading of the Bible, which Wells read in its entirety. There is no doubting that Wells's parents were a strong influence on her, although she would benefit from having them for only sixteen years of her life. Both James and Elizabeth Wells would die within twenty-four hours of one another of Yellow Fever during the epidemic that hit Holly Springs, Mississippi in 1878. Wells would find out about this tragedy while away in Tippah County helping her grandmother Peggy in the cotton fields. Upon receiving the news of her parents' deaths, she returned home.

When Wells arrived, she was informed that the Masons (also her father's closest friends) planned to split her six siblings up to help ease the financial burden. However, Wells vehemently objected to this idea, insisting instead that her parents would "turn over in their graves" if their family were to be separated. As an alternative solution, Wells requested that the Masons' help her to find a teaching position, so that she could afford to take care of her siblings on her own. The Masons were obliged and were able to make arrangements for her to teach at a small country school nearby for a salary of $25 a month. It was difficult for Wells, but her mother had taught her how to manage a household. She would also receive help from another friend of the family, Rachel Rather, who would look after the children during the week as she taught. Every Friday, Wells would return home, traveling six miles on the back of a mule to prepare the children's food and clothing for the week (McMurry 1998: 17). In 1880, the two boys were able to be apprenticed as carpenters, requiring them to move and become independent. After a few years, Wells was invited along with her two younger sisters to move to Memphis to live with an aunt. Her disabled sister, Eugenia, who was paralyzed from the waist down from spinal meningitis, was invited to live with another aunt who had a small farm nearby. In the year 1884, at the young age of nineteen, Wells was already becoming acclimated to life as an adult, and she was also adapting to life as a teacher. Wells enjoyed living in Memphis and had many friends. Living with her aunt in Memphis allowed her to maintain two teaching positions, one with Memphis city schools and another in Woodstock. She would often make the two-hour commute by train (McMurry 1998: 17).

Wells did not particularly enjoy teaching, because schools for Black children were often small and kept in very poor condition. Furthermore, classes were also overcrowded. She would sometimes teach as many as seventy students at a time. The terrible conditions would only contribute to the restlessness and unruly conduct of some of her pupils. Wells did not like this aspect of the job, but she continued to teach out of necessity. She had no way of knowing it at the time, but her true calling was journalism. She would make this discovery inadvertently after a life altering occurrence during one of her commutes to Woodstock.

In 1881, Tennessee passed new Jim Crow laws requiring railway companies to make Black and white passengers travel in separate cars. The car for whites, also referred to as "first-class" or "the ladies' coach," was upscale and comfortable, while the car designated for Black passengers could be considered a health hazard. The colored car was located directly behind the loud engine which would billow huge plumes of black smoke that easily reached passengers. It was often overcrowded and allowed drinking, smoking, and gambling. Furthermore, the loud and boisterous passengers would use the floor as opposed to the spittoons to discard tobacco juice. Sometimes exceptions to the rule requiring segregation would be made. For instance, Black midwives traveling with pregnant or nursing white women were allowed to stay in the ladies' coach and white men were permitted if they were chaperoning a woman. Well-dressed African American women were also often permitted to stay in first-class if no white person objected to their presence.

On May 4, 1884, Wells read quietly to herself as she traveled to Woodstock in the ladies' coach. However, at some point during her trip she was interrupted by the conductor who informed her that she would have to move to the colored car. Wells objected, and the conductor attempted to remove her by force. Wells reacted by sinking her teeth into his hand, causing him to bleed. Realizing that he could not force her to move on his own, the conductor went to get two other workers to help him. This only made Wells even angrier. She braced herself by placing both of her hands and feet on the seat in front of her, forcing the workers to use all their strength to pry each of her limbs loose one at a time, tearing off the sleeve of her jacket in the process. After the men removed her from her seat, she was left on the platform with her bags. Ironically, she still held on to her first-class ticket throughout the entire ordeal (Fadin 2000: 20–23; Davidson 2007: 64–75).

Wells, at twenty-one years of age, would decide to file a lawsuit against the Chesapeake and Ohio Railroad company. On December 24 the circuit court judge, who was also a former Union soldier, ruled that the railway company acted unlawfully when they forced her to move. She was awarded $500 in damages. Unfortunately, having the satisfaction of knowing that she confronted racial prejudice and won would be her only reward. The railroad company unsuccessfully attempted to settle with Wells out of court for several hundred dollars, and when Wells did not accept this offer, they decided to appeal the case with the Tennessee State Supreme Court. This time, C&O won. The State Supreme Court determined that Wells was merely trying to harass the railroad company and ordered her to pay $200 in damages. She was crushed by this unfair decision, but it would ultimately propel her towards a life of activism (Fadin 2000: 34; Davidson 2007: 64–75).

Many texts that relate the life of Wells mark this point in her life as a major turning point because it is when she became devoted to confronting racial injustices. It is also when she started writing about it. Wells began to keep a journal in 1885, and also as a young adult, she edited and wrote for the *Evening Star* (which was the newspaper of the Lyceum, a popular literary club that she was a member of), and a Black church weekly called the *Living Way* (Fradin 2000: 26–27). Due to the direct and unapologetic tone of her work, her keen eye for details, and her entertaining writing style, her work quickly became popular among the local Black public. Subsequently, she would grow to become a prolific journalist, and examining some of the writings that she generated, one can clearly see that proverbs and proverbial language were always an important part of the way that she expressed her ideas. For instance, upon learning of the Tennessee State Supreme Court decision to rule in favor of the railway company, Wells writes in her diary:

> I felt so disappointed, because I had hoped such great things from my suit for my people generally. I have firmly believed all along that the law was on our side and would, when we appealed to it, give us justice.

I feel shorn of that belief and utterly discouraged, and just now if it were possible would gather my race in my arms and fly away with them. O God is there no redress, no peace, no justice in this land for us? Though hast always fought the battles of the weak & oppressed. Come to my aid at this moment & teach me what to do, for I am sorely, bitterly disappointed. Show us the way. (Fadin 2000: 34–35)

The important message and somber tone of this brief diary entry may easily represent the trajectory of her future writings. Wells frequently expressed the emotional pain that she felt in witnessing racial injustices, and she often incorporated figurative language in the process. For instance, she says that she trusted that the "law was on our side," and because this time the justice system had failed her, as it did for so many other Black people in the South, she wants to "gather the race in [her] arms and fly away" (Fadin 2000: 34–35). This is an appropriate metaphor that illustrates that she not only anticipated victory for herself but for the entire race. It also foreshadows the migrations that Black people in southern regions would embark on due to the increasingly hostile racial climate. For Wells, they are only lines in her diary, but they still show that she was thinking far ahead of her time, at least from an ideological perspective. More importantly, it illustrates that even as a young woman she had a genuine desire to improve conditions for Black people in the South.

Wells uses another proverbial expression in relation to this momentous event as she recalls it later in her life, and her use of a well-known proverbial expression may be indicative of the extent that she cared about the outcome. For instance, she says in her autobiography: "I had already secured my appointment as a teacher in Memphis before the railroad case was finally settled; so I had my salary to fall back on to help pay the cost against me. None of my people had ever seemed to feel that it was a race matter and that they should help me with the fight. So I trod the winepress alone" (Duster 1970: 21; McMurry 1998: 30). The proverbial expression "to trod the winepress alone" is an allusion to the Bible (KJV 63:3). The full verse reads: "I have trodden the winepress alone; and of the people there was none with me: for I will tread them in mine anger, and trample them in my fury; and their blood shall be sprinkled upon my garments, and I will stain all my raiment" (KJV 63:3). In using the expression, Wells is showing several emotions. On the one hand, she feels betrayed and abandoned because Black people did not express any interest in her legal battles. On the other hand, Wells is expressing intense anger because many Blacks believed that it was not a racial issue despite the prevalence of Jim Crow laws, and the fact that white presses continually portrayed her in a racist manner, referring to her as the "Darky Damsel" in headlines (Fradin 2000: 23; Davidson 2007: 73–75). In retrospect, Wells feels that the outcome would have been different if more Black people had cared.

Proverbs and proverbial language are scattered throughout Wells's many writings, but no Wells biographer ever really says that she was known for this feature. However, the proverbs and sayings that she incorporates in her work are significant because much like her diary, they may provide us with a view of Wells from a different perspective. They may offer a glimpse into the way that she thought, and they may also illustrate some of the many moral lessons that she has internalized and communicated throughout her lifetime. This chapter is not a chronology of her life and writings, nor is it an attempt to document every single saying that Wells has ever spoken or written. It is instead a look at some of the most important and recurring sayings and expressions that exist in her corpus of work and in the relatively small amount of scholarship that has been written about her life.

Proverbs and proverbial sayings that Wells uses come from several different places. On the one hand, Wells uses proverbs from the Bible, from all kinds of literature, and from famous political figures of her day, among them Frederick Douglass, Thomas Jefferson, and Abraham Lincoln. On the other hand, some of the proverbs and proverbial expressions that she employs are cultural. They may illustrate some inherent or widely accepted "truth" without being attached to any one figure, and there may be a reason for this. In her later years, Wells traveled widely, both nationally and internationally, and while she may not have ever created her list of "Sayings and Doings" of the people that she met, incorporating proverbs into her work may have been her primary way of documenting these sayings without having to do so explicitly. She devoted nearly all her time and energy to the antilynching crusade, African American and women's suffrage, and other related causes. The untiring pace at which she worked more than likely did not leave much time or energy for much else. Nevertheless, this may be viewed as a positive because, instead of static lists, readers see her using proverbs and proverbial expressions through her writings and correspondences for specific purposes, and these purposes tend to be invariable and dynamic to convince her readers to think in particular ways that are associated with her causes and to express certain aspects of her worldview.

One of the first proverbs that she uses in support of her cause appears in the publication that launched her antilynching crusade, *Southern Horrors* (1892). Wells wrote this pamphlet to denounce the murders of her best friends and the practice of lynching in general. Additionally, she sought to expose the widespread myth of violent Black brutes who go around raping white women as an insidious form of propaganda that was generated to justify murdering and stealing from African Americans and to cover up consensual relationships between Black men and white women. Furthermore, since the racial climate in Memphis was becoming increasingly hostile towards Blacks, in *Southern Horrors* (1892) she also urges Black Memphians to discontinue all patronage of white-owned businesses and to migrate to northern towns and cities and to newly established territories in the West such as Oklahoma, which many Black homesteaders were already taking advantage of (Taylor 1999; Wilson-Moore and Taylor 2008). The proverb that she uses appears at the conclusion of the very last paragraph of the pamphlet, which reads, "Nothing is more definitely settled than he must act for himself. I have shown how he may employ the boycott, emigration and the press, and I feel that by a combination of all these agencies can be effectually stamped out lynch law, that last relic of barbarism and slavery. 'The gods help those who help themselves'" (reprinted in Harris 1991: 45). The proverb "God helps those who help themselves" dates to the early fifteenth-century writings of Dutch Renaissance scholar Erasmus (Mieder et al. 1991: 255; Speake 2015: 128) and is used by Wells here to convince a community of terrified African Americans in Memphis to be proactive and to engage in activism. After the publication of *Southern Horrors*, six thousand African Americans heeded Wells's warning and left Memphis within two months, and those who stayed followed her suggestion to boycott so closely that many white-owned businesses were forced to close (Sterling 1988: 81). In fact, the owners of a newly established electric trolley system in Memphis assumed that Blacks were simply afraid of the new form of transportation and pleaded with Wells to write an article stating that electric trolleys were not dangerous. In response, Wells told them that Blacks did not fear electric trains, they only feared discrimination and racial violence, and she refused to redact her message. Wells was out of town traveling with friends when white papers began to reprint some of the explicit messages from her pamphlet. As a result, an angry mob destroyed her newspaper office, which was the office of *Free Speech*, where she was writer, part-owner, and chief editor. They also published an explicit threat to lynch her and her colleague, J. L. Fleming, if they ever returned to Memphis. Despite her brush with death, she moved to New York where she immediately began working in the same capacities for another popular Black paper, the *New York Age*, which was owned and edited by T. Thomas Fortune (1856–1928).

Some other proverbs used by Wells appear in *Mob Rule in New Orleans* (1900). Wells wrote this pamphlet in response to the lynching of Robert Charles, a thirty-four-year-old African American man, who was killed protecting his own life from police officers who brutally assaulted him. Wells writes that "Charles had his first encounter with the police Monday night, in which he was shot in the street duel which was begun by the police officer after Officer Mora had beaten Charles three or four times over the head with his billy in an attempt to make an illegal arrest. In defending himself against the combined attack of two officers with a billy and their guns upon him, Charles shot officer Mora and escaped" (reprinted in Harris 1991: 302). Charles's troubles do not end here. In fact, the scenario only worsens as Wells continues: "Early Tuesday morning Charles was traced to Dryades street by officers who were instructed to kill him on sight. There again defending himself, he shot and killed two officers. This, of course, in the eyes of the American press, made him a desperado, make statements which will be interesting to examine" (reprinted in Harris 1991: 302). Wells's report does a lot to counteract the salacious claim that Charles was a bloodthirsty and racist criminal who was simply looking to take his anger out on white officers. Calling him things such as "desperado," "daredevil," and "ravisher," a white newspaper even employs a proverb to make it seem as if Charles was motivated to kill white officers by reading racist propaganda. Wells even includes an excerpt from the article in *Mob Rule*. It says that "an examination of his personal effects revealed the mental state of the murderer and the rancor in his heart toward the Caucasian race. Never was the adage: 'A little learning is a dangerous thing,' better exemplified than in the case of the negro who shot to death the two officers'" (reprinted in Harris 1991: 303). The article then goes on to describe an individual who "burnt the midnight oil" reading "back to Africa" propaganda with hopes to "conquer the hated white race" (reprinted in Harris 1991: 303). Generally viewed as a positive statement, the proverb "a little learning is a dangerous thing" (Mieder, Kingsbury, and Harder 1991: 367; Speake 2015: 186) is instead used here by the white press in a negative way, to imply that it is unsafe or risky for Charles to read certain material. This is a notion that hearkens back to the antebellum era when it was illegal to teach Blacks to read. In the same pamphlet, in a section entitled *Died in Self-Defense*, Wells tries to counteract the dangerous public image of Robert Charles created by white presses. Wells instead portrays a hard-working student that was not bent on racial hatred, but on bettering himself and conditions for Black people. She writes: "He knew that he was a student of a problem which required all the intelligence that a man could command, and he was burning his midnight oil gathering knowledge that he might better be able to come to an intelligent solution. To his aid and his study of this problem he sought the aid of a Christian newspaper, *The Voice of Missions*, the organ of the African Methodist Episcopal Church" (reprinted in Harris

1991: 310). Here Wells clarifies the misconception that Charles's reading materials indoctrinated racial hatred. Contrarily, she asserts that he only "burnt the proverbial midnight oil" reading Christian materials with the intent of gaining more knowledge about problems faced by Black people and how to address these issues in moral ways. Three paragraphs later, Wells employs a proverb and some proverbial language to reemphasize this point: "If it is true that the workman is known by his tools, certainly no harm could ever come from the doctrines which were preached by Charles or the papers and pamphlets distributed by him" (reprinted in Harris 1991: 311). The proverb "the workman is known by his tools" is well-known, although it is not attributed to any single individual. Wells uses the proverb here to make the point that there is no evidence that Charles had any violent intentions based simply on the Christian reading materials that were found in his room. Wells continues: "Nothing ever written in the 'Voice of Missions,' and nothing ever published in the pamphlets above alluded to in the remotest way suggest that a peaceable man should turn lawbreaker, or that any man should dye his hands in his brother's blood" (reprinted in Harris 1991: 311). The proverbial language that appears at the end of this statement may be a subtle allusion to Shakespeare's seventeenth-century tragedy *Macbeth* (1603). As a young child, Wells read all the works of Shakespeare and later, as a young woman in Memphis, she often participated in plays and public readings of his work. Wells's statement "to dye his hands in his brother's blood" is more than likely a reference to act II, scene 2, in which Lady Macbeth, in a delusional state, repeatedly washes her hands imagining that her hands are stained with Duncan's blood. She says: "Will all the water in the ocean wash this blood from my hands?" If Wells's statement is a reference to *Macbeth*, she more than likely uses it to imply that Robert Charles, the criminal-minded murderer, is as equally imagined as the blood that stained Lady Macbeth's hands. Another important point that Wells makes in *Mob Rule* is that the false negative portrayals of Charles in white presses dehumanizes him to the point that it ultimately leads to his lynching. Wells attempts to bring some form of justice to Robert Charles, posthumously, while also revealing some of the aspects of racism that contributes to his downfall. Her work demonstrates that false characterizations are a common denominator in most lynchings and mob violence.

Other examples of proverbs and proverbial language used by Wells appear in her autobiography *Crusade for Justice* (1970), which was edited by Wells's youngest daughter, Alfreda M. Duster (1904–83), and published forty years after her mother's death. In her autobiography, Wells discusses what it was like knowing and working with the world-famous abolitionist and self-freed ex-slave Frederick Douglass (1818–95). Wells became good friends with Frederick Douglass during her lifetime, and she regarded him as a father figure and a mentor. They worked together on a pamphlet that she created in response to the lack of African American representation at the World's Fair held in Chicago in 1893. The World's Fair was held annually in different places around the globe to display and celebrate scientific and cultural achievements of different nations. The Chicago fair took place over six months, represented nearly fifty nations, and attracted nearly thirty million visitors from around the world, and it was considered special for at least two other reasons. Firstly, it marked the four hundredth anniversary of Christopher Columbus's inadvertent arrival in North America. Secondly, it also marked a time in history when African Americans, thirty years after gaining freedom, had made substantial contributions to American culture. Wells and Douglass attempted to convince the fair organizers to showcase some of the achievements of African Americans—the only American ethnic group that was not adequately represented. Unsatisfied with their results, they decided that they would distribute a pamphlet to expose the fair's racism. The pamphlet is entitled *The Reason Why: The Colored American Is Not in the World's Columbian Exposition, the Afro-American's Contribution to Columbian Literature* (1893). The pamphlet is compiled, published, and distributed by Wells and includes contributions from Frederick Douglass, who wrote the introduction, T. Thomas Fortune, and Wells's future husband, the lawyer and highly esteemed editor F. L. Barnett. In the pamphlet, they discuss Jim Crow laws and America's history of racism. Wells also provides detailed accounts of lynchings that have taken place in the South, including the lynchings of her best friend, Thomas Moss. She includes vital statistics regarding thousands of lynching victims, including the years that the crimes take place, the general locations, and the specified reasons. The overall purpose of producing the pamphlet was to help their international audience to realize that the lack of African American representation at the fair was due to America's inherent racism and not a lack of innovation or intelligence on the part of the Black race. Wells was able to distribute over three thousand copies of the pamphlet (Giddings 2008: 268–81).

 There were two exhibits at the fair that included Black people, but they were considered insults as opposed to a celebration of accomplishments. One was an exhibition featuring a French-speaking indigenous African tribe. The Africans were asked to look and act as primitive as possible. The other was in a section for new products, and featured Nancy Green, "a dark-skinned domestic worker with a wide, flashing smile. She was advertising a premade pancake mix for increasingly time-limited housewives. Trademark for the product was Aunt Jemima" (Giddings 2008: 273). One thing that quickly became apparent to both Wells and Douglass is that "white Americans wanted nothing to detract from their shrine to Anglo-Saxon superiority" (McMurry 1998: 200). The African tribal exhibit took place in the Haitian Building, which was managed by Frederick Douglass due to his service as United States Minister to Haiti. Douglass and Wells did experience a minor victory despite their obvious setbacks. The organizers agreed to designate one day on the fair's program as Negro Day, also referred to as Colored People's Jubilee Day, and Douglass was given the freedom to organize all the events. Wells and other African Americans felt that it would be even more demeaning and exploitative than the indigenous tribe exhibit—a sentiment that was only exacerbated by the horticultural department's promise to provide plenty of free watermelons (promoting another pernicious Black stereotype). However, Douglass expressed satisfaction with the plan, using a proverb to do so. He told Wells that "it was better to accept half a loaf than to have no bread at all" (Duster 1970: 118; Bay 2009: 168). Douglass believed that it was important to do the best that they could with the limited time and resources they had, while Wells felt that Negro Day could only result in more degradation. The proverb "it is better to accept half a loaf than to have no bread at all" is first documented in the sixteenth century and has several variations which all convey the same meaning (Mieder et al. 1991: 274; Speake 2015: 141). Douglass did well in orchestrating the event and "Colored American Day," as they agreed to rename it, turned out to be a success (McMurry 1998: 204). As Wells would recount in her autobiography: "Mr. Douglass's oration was a masterpiece of wit, humor, and actual statement of conditions under which the Negro race of this country labored. Paul Dunbar read from his poems, and the Negro music presented was of high order. The thousands of people gathered at the fair who heard the story were given the opportunity they would otherwise have been denied of hearing our foremost orator at his best" (Duster 1970: 119). Wells also communicates that she regretted her previous stance: "I was among those that did not even go to the meeting—I was so swelled with pride over his masterly presentation of our case that I went straight out to the fair and begged his pardon for presuming in my youth and inexperience to criticize him for an effort which had done more to bring our cause to the attention of the American people than anything else which had happened during the fair" (Duster 1970: 119). All in all, Douglass's attitude towards the planning of Colored American Day, and the proverb that he uses to point out the brighter side of their predicament, taught Wells an important life lesson that she would never forget: "it is better to accept half a loaf than to have no bread at all."

It is common for bread as a universal symbol of life-sustaining elements to be used in sayings and expressions to express fundamental necessities that one may not be able to survive without. In addition to the aforementioned saying from Douglass, Wells would use expressions involving bread on least three separate occasions. In a diary entry dated for Saturday, July 16, 1887, her twenty-fifth birthday, Wells reflects on life and the lessons that she has learned from all the trials and tribulations that she has endured. Disappointed in herself, Wells vows to be a better person and ultimately regrets any missed learning opportunities that may have come her way. Wells writes:

> When I turn to sum up my own accomplishments I am not so well pleased. I have not used the opportunities I had to the best advantage and find myself intellectually lacking. And excepting my regret that I am not so good a Christian as the goodness of my Father demands, there is nothing for which I lament the wasted opportunities as I do my neglect to pick up the crumbs of knowledge that were within my reach. Consequently I find myself at this age as deficient in a comprehensive knowledge as the veriest school-girl just entering the higher course. I heartily deplore the neglect. . . . Thou knowest I hunger and thirst after righteousness & knowledge. (DeCosta-Willis 1995: 151)

Most would agree that at that point in her life Wells had already more than made up for any proverbial crumbs of knowledge that she may have overlooked in the past.

In an article entitled "The Negro's Case in Equity" (1900), Wells again uses bread symbolically to make a serious point. "The Negro's Case in Equity" is written in response to an *Independent* article urging Black leaders to stop other Black people from taking the law into their own hands (Thompson 1990: 112; McMurry 1998: 260; Schechter 2001: 126; Bay and Gates 2014: 256). In response, Wells admonishes the author of *The Independent* article for ignoring the fact that most African Americans obey the law even as they are frequently the targets of most lynching attacks. Wells writes:

> The *Independent* publishes an earnest appeal to negro editors, preachers and teachers "to tell their people to defend the laws and their own rights even to blood, but never, never to take guilty participation in lynching white man or black." This advice is given by way of comment on the double lynching in Virginia the other day. Theoretically the advice is all right, but viewed in the light of circumstances and

conditions it seems like giving a stone when we ask for bread. (Bay and Gates 2014: 256)

Wells's proverbial expression "like giving a stone when asked for bread" effectively summarizes her opinion of the advice presented to Black leaders. She feels that it is an absurd statement to make, especially at a time when Blacks were being lynched in the South at alarming rates.

In another article written early in her career entitled "The Model Woman: A Pen Picture of the Typical Southern Girl" (1888), Wells writes about the significance of Victorian ideology to late nineteenth-century life. In accordance with Victorianism, Wells believed that all women should strive to steer clear of sin and to take it upon themselves to enlighten the uneducated and lower classes of the race. Additionally, Black women should exhibit diligence and industriousness. To illustrate this mentality, Wells proclaims in her autobiography to be a "southern girl, born and bred, who tried to keep herself spotless and morally clean as my slave mother had taught me" (Duster 1970: 44; DeCosta-Willis 1995: 188). To further emphasize this point in "The Model Woman," Wells writes:

> She is far above mean, petty acts and venomous, slanderous gossip of her own sex as the moon—which sails serenely in the heavens—is above the earth. Her bearing toward the opposite sex, while cordial and free, is of such nature as increases their respect for and admiration of her sex, and her influence is wholly for good. She strives to encourage in them all things honest, noble and manly. She regards all honest toil as noble, because it is ordained of God that man should earn his bread by the sweat of his brow. She does not think a girl has anything of which to be proud in not knowing how to work, and esteems it among her best accomplishments that she can cook, wash, iron, sew and "keep house" thoroughly and well. This type of Negro girl may not be found so often as she might, but she is the pattern after which all others copy. (DeCosta-Willis 1995: 189; Bay and Gates 2014: 32–33)

The saying "man should earn his bread by the sweat of his brow" is derived from biblical text. The original verse from the Bible reads: "In the sweat of thy face shalt thou eat bread, till thou return unto the ground; for out of it wast thou taken: for dust thou art, and unto dust shalt thy return" (KJV Genesis 3:19). The saying used by Wells equates bread with the valuable and essential trait of having a work ethic. It illustrates that even in 1888, at the young age of twenty-six, Wells did not only make the decision to be a leader of her people in all matters regarding social justice, but she also wanted to lead her people in matters of moral character.

Wells also had a propensity for using proverbial expressions that incorporated animals when discussing matters of great importance. Perhaps she acquired this rhetorical strategy from her mentor, Douglass. Other scholars such as Wolfgang Mieder also cite Douglass's propensity for using animal proverbs and expressions. Mieder contends: "It should not be surprising that Douglass often cites proverbs and proverbial expressions which contrast innocent lambs or sheep with rapacious wolves where the docile animals represent the victimized slaves while the wild beasts are interpreted as perpetrating slaveholders" (Mieder 2001: 43). One of the most widely cited instances of Wells's use of expressions involving animals appears in her autobiography, and it is written in response to the 1892 lynching of her best friend, Thomas Moss. The following passage illustrates that Wells had expected to be lynched herself in return for urging Black Memphians to migrate. She uses the popular proverbial expression "to die like a dog" in the process (Whiting 1989: 178). Wells writes:

> I had been warned repeatedly by my own people that something would happen if I did not cease harping on the lynching of three months before, I had expected that happening to come when I was at home. I had bought a pistol the first thing after Tom Moss was lynched because I expected some cowardly retaliation from the lynchers. I felt that one had better die fighting against injustice than die like a dog or a rat in a trap. I had already determined to sell my life as dearly as possible if attacked. I felt if I could take one lyncher with me, this would even up the score a little bit. (Duster 1970: 62; McMurry 1998: 149; Davidson 2007: 148)

Furthermore, in her autobiography Wells incorporates a proverb involving animals to describe the social and political climate of Memphis immediately following the Moss lynching. Describing the Black migration that ensued, she says: "Besides, no class of people like Negroes spent their money like water, riding on streetcars and railroad trains, especially on Sundays and excursions. No other class bought clothes and food with such little haggling as they or were so easily satisfied. The whites had killed the goose that laid the golden egg of Memphis prosperity and Negro contentment; yet they were amazed that colored people continued to leave the city by scores and hundreds" (Duster 1970: 63–64). Wells's statement that "whites had killed the goose that laid the golden egg" is a variation of the proverb "don't kill the goose that lays the golden egg" (Mieder et al. 1991: 262), which may have not been formally documented until 1908. Wells's use of it here describes the sudden and unexpected economic downturn that the city took as Black people began to leave.

Wells utilizes the same proverbial rhetorical strategy of incorporating animals in another instance in her autobiography when she expresses a growing sense of urgency felt by Black people in Illinois to protect a prominent African American dentist, Dr. LeRoy C. Bundy, who, immediately following the East St. Louis Riot of 1917, unjustly faced life imprisonment for urging Black people to protect their own neighborhoods. Authorities believed that Dr. Bundy's writings were the primary cause of the deaths of two plainclothed officers who were shot as they rode through a Black neighborhood. If authorities did not believe that Bundy caused the officer's deaths, they were still willing to use Dr. Bundy as their scapegoat. Of course, the tragic events that unfolded in East St. Louis were the result of mounting racial tensions and not the work of any one individual. Immediately following the officer's shootings, 150 Blacks were murdered, and millions of dollars of property damage to Black communities were recorded. No whites were charged with crimes, but fifteen African Americans would serve over ten years in prison for simply returning fire after whites had shot into their homes (Duster 1970: 391). Dr. Bundy's case was the worst because he was the only person who faced life imprisonment even though he was never directly involved in the killings. Wells writes: "A meeting was held in Brooklyn, the Negro town, that night at which time all these facts were given and the people urged to take the bull by the horns, open a subscription list, and start at once to employ a lawyer" (Duster 1970: 394–95). Dr. Bundy was eventually released and absolved of all wrongdoing, and Wells's use of the proverbial expression "to take the bull by the horns" (Taylor and Whiting 1958: 46–47); Whiting 1989: 79–80) illustrates that it took a concerted effort to free Dr. Bundy. Ultimately the effort would involve the Negro Fellowship League (NFL), the National Association for the Advancement of Colored People (NAACP), and the popular Black periodical the *Chicago Defender*, in which Wells and other Black writers were able to convince thousands of people to donate in support of Dr. Bundy's legal defense.

In a letter to Herbert Hoover (1874–1964), who was campaigning for the presidency which he eventually won, Wells expresses her disappointment with Hoover's lack of regard for the many African Americans who ultimately decided to put their faith in the Democratic Party as opposed to facing continual disappointment caused by the failed promises of Hoover and the

Republican Party. In her letter to Hoover, Wells uses the expression "to spend money like water" which she also uses when writing about Blacks migrating from Memphis (Taylor and Whiting 1958: 395; Whiting 1989: 419), and she also incorporates the saying "to be a wolf in sheep's clothing" (Taylor and Whiting 1958: 407–8; Whiting 1989: 691–92). Wells, who clearly wants Hoover to pay more attention to the needs of Black voters, writes: "This time the wolf in sheep's clothing is spending money like water to hire our folks in the Democratic camp, but very few of them are going to betray our race for 30 pieces of silver or for the prospect of a drink of liquor" (Thompson 1990: 124; McMurry 1998: 335). The use of the saying "to be a wolf in sheep's clothing" depicts the growing sense of alienation that Wells experiences at the hands of Republicans and it also shows the extreme sense of distrust that she felt because of propaganda and unethical campaign tactics employed by white Democrats. The shifting tide of the Black vote from the Republican Party to the Democratic Party described in the Hoover letter becomes a major catalyst for Wells seeking political office as an independent in 1930.

This would not be the first time that Wells would use her proverbial wisdom in support of abandoning partisanship. In an article entitled "Freedom of Political Action" (1885), writing in agreement with an editorial written by T. Thomas Fortune of the *New York Freeman*, Wells voices her support of Fortune's notion that Black people should remain politically independent. Wells says:

> To the Editor of the New York Freeman: There is an old saying that advises to "give the devil his due," and after reading your editorial on "Mr. Cleveland and the Colored People," I was forcibly struck with the thought, that so few people are willing to admit that he has any "due." Evidently there is very little reasoning powers among those who need such a plain rehearsal of historical facts. According to their logic the side they espouse is all good, the opposite—all bad; the Republican party, can do no wrong—however often they use the colored men for tools; the other, the Democratic side, can do no good—whatever the profession—because of past history. (Bay and Gates 2014: 22)

The proverb "to give the devil his due" (Whiting 1989: 166; Mieder et al. 1991: 146) in this case is appropriate because the imagery evoked by the devil helps to illustrate Wells's point that the Black voter can only attempt to choose the lesser of two evils. Furthermore, this passage is a prime example of how at just twenty-three years of age, Wells was already developing a sarcastic and sharp style. She was becoming known for her brazen choice of political targets and her cutting sense of wit (Bay and Gates 2014: 20).

Wells also used the proverb "you shall reap what you sow" (Mieder et al. 1991: 554–55). On at least two different occasions she either alludes to this saying or creates a variation. In her autobiography, she describes the rash of racial riots that seemed to plague the nation in the early twentieth century as "simply a reaping of the harvest which has been sown by those who administer justice" (Duster 1970: 391). On another occasion, Wells alludes to the proverb "you shall reap what you sow" in writing about exiled leader Marcus Garvey, whom her husband, Ferdinand Barnett, represented in an unsuccessful civil suit against the *Chicago Defender* for libel (McMurry 1998: 323). Wells, being very supportive of Garvey and his efforts to uplift the race, writes: "It may be that even though he has been banished to Jamaica the seed planted here will yet spring up and bring forth fruit which will mean the deliverance of the Black race—the cause which was so dear to his heart" (McMurry 1998: 323).

When Wells was presented with an opportunity to go on a lecture tour in England to talk about American lynch law, she expressed serious doubt over whether it was a good idea to go or not. The invitation was extended to her by English philanthropist Catherine Impey (1847–1923) and Scottish novelist Isabelle Fyvie Mayo (1843–1914), who were both organizers of a humanitarian organization called the Society for the Recognition of the Brotherhood of Man (SRBM), which was devoted to ending the British caste system in India. The organization also published a newsletter called *Anti-Caste*. They wanted both Wells and Douglass to travel to Europe to speak about lynching, but Wells wanted to decline the invitation because Douglass felt that he was too old to travel. She writes: "Thus it was that I received the invitation to go to England. I was a guest in Mr. Douglass's home when the letter came, forwarded from New York. It said that they knew Mr. Douglass was too old to come, and that if for that reason I could not come, to ask him to name someone else. I gave him the letter to read and when he finished he said, 'You go, my child; you are the one to go, for you have the story to tell'" (Duster 1970: 85–86). Wells then states that the invitation, "seemed like an open door in a stone wall" (Duster 1970: 86). She had already spent almost an entire year in the North trying to gain more support, only to no avail, and she uses the proverbial expression, "like an open door in a stone wall" to communicate that the rare opportunity to travel to Europe, at the time, felt like a much-needed blessing. Once news about Wells's plans spread, many Black presses were divided on the issue. Some of the presses that were against the idea of Wells representing African American people in Europe felt that

Wells's speeches may only serve to fuel British snobbery towards Americans. Others felt that speeches in general would do no good at all. Likewise, many political leaders felt that the lynching problem would disappear on its own. In fact, Wells uses a couple of proverbs in a *New York Age* article in response to these notions. She says: "They forget . . . that no wrong ever rights itself and that whom the gods would destroy they first make mad" (Giddings 2008: 327; Speake 2015: 131). While the first proverb may be taken literally, the second proverb has a somewhat figurative meaning. "Whom the gods would destroy, they first make mad" is a seventeenth-century saying meaning that sometimes evil will appear as good to those who are being led to their own destruction (Mieder et al. 1991: 256; Speake 2015: 131). Wells issues a similar statement regarding right and wrong on a leaflet advertising one of her many antilynching speeches. The leaflet reads: "The way to right wrongs is to turn the light of truth upon them" (Bay and Gates 2014: 7). In another *New York Age* article entitled "The Lynchers Wince," Wells targets an aphorism used by a white paper in order to reveal the hypocrisy or double standard that exists in regard to lynch law. She says: "the *Commercial Appeal* drops into philosophy and declares that two wrongs do not make one right; and that while white people should stick to the law, if they do not do so, the blacks can hope for nothing but extermination if they attempt to defend themselves" (Bay and Gates 2014: 38). All the Wells sayings regarding right and wrong illustrate that Wells is certain that her journalistic efforts and public-speaking engagements could possibly help.

In addition to the groups that supported her European efforts, there were still some that believed that Wells was only interested in traveling to Europe to make money for herself, which was a misconception. She received very little pay for her efforts. Nonetheless, some Black presses supported the move. For instance, the *Parsons Weekly Blade* uses a popular proverb to summarize Wells's predicament. The paper replies to the suggestion that Wells will be more effective on American soil by saying that "it would be another case of casting pearls before swine" (McMurry 1998: 218). The proverb "don't cast your pearls before swine" is from the Bible (KJV Matthew 7:6; Mieder et al. 1991: 577; Prahlad 1996: 241; Speake 2015: 245) and it means "do not give valuable things to people who cannot appreciate them" (Speake 2015: 245). The proverb is fitting because many people thought that Wells's pleas for help would fall on deaf ears. It was no secret that many negative sentiments that Wells faced were also attributed to sexism. In fact, Wells's colleague and friend T. Thomas Fortune used the very same proverb to conceptualize the dilemma faced by all women writers. Fortune comments: "I think our women are going to stretch our men in the variety of their information, the purity of their expression and in having the courage of their convictions, without which these are but pearls cast before swine" (McMurry 1998: 89). Fortune uses the proverb to illustrate that the men had some growing to do before they could fully appreciate Black female journalists. Fortune is also making the point that Black female journalism would play a critical role in eradicating sexism.

While touring Europe, Wells gave hundreds of speeches to highly receptive audiences. Overall, Wells was left with the impression that people of color were accepted more in Europe than they were in the US. In a section of her autobiography entitled "What Liverpool Has Learned," she states: "And the city, with its population of six hundred thousand souls, is one of the most prosperous in the United Kingdom. Her freedom loving citizens not only subscribe to the doctrine that human beings regardless of color or condition are equal before the law, but they practice what they preach" (Duster 1970: 135). Variations of the proverb "practice what you preach" are documented as early as 1377, and it is one of Wells's favorites (Mieder et al. 1991: 479; Speake 2015: 254). She uses this proverb several times in the diary that she kept as a young woman living in Memphis (DeCosta-Willis 1995: 44, 134). The diary entries that include this proverb also reveal the extent that European Victorianism permeated American culture and dictated interactions between men and women during the nineteenth century. Wells aimed to be a prototype of Victorian womanhood. She always dressed well and spoke properly, but nevertheless many Victorian ideals still conflicted with her own sense of identity. Women were not supposed to show anger, be outspoken, or even flirtatious, but Wells's use of the proverb "practice what you preach" seems to illustrate an ongoing inherent struggle with these expectations. In one entry written on February 14, 1885, Wells seems to denounce the idea of flirting with a potential male suitor. She says: "Right here comes my temptation to flirt with him; to make him declare himself and forget all others, but I cannot—I *will* not consider it. I have preached and I must practice under *all* circumstances" (DeCosta-Willis 1995: 44). In another diary entry marked February 20, 1887, Wells writes about being criticized by male colleagues who feel that it is unladylike for a female teacher to be seen in theatres. She accepts this criticism with grace, fearing that she may be setting a bad precedent for her students. Wells writes: "Mr. Dardis Jr. walked home with me & read me a severe lecture on going to the theatre; he showed me how his father Prof. Thompson, Mr. Greenlee, Mr. Selectman, Dr. Burchett etc regarded it, & that he now considered that I was one who failed to practice as I preached. I regretted it more than I can say all along, but not so keenly did I see the wrong, or think of the influence my example would exert until then" (DeCosta-Willis 1995: 134). The proverb "practice what you preach" means that "if you tell other people how to act you should follow your own instructions" (Speake 2015: 254). Her frequent use of the adage illustrates that she has always valued being a good example to others. Wells uses the proverb in reference to Europe because she feels that Europe is a much better example of this proverbial wisdom than America—a place in which democracy and equality are celebrated but not extended to all citizens. In contrast, Wells says that Liverpool is a place where "a colored person can ride in any sort of conveyance in any part of the country without being insulted; stop in any hotel or be accommodated at any restaurant one wishes without being refused with contempt; wander into any picture gallery, lecture room, concert hall, theater or church and receive only the most courteous treatment from officials and fellow sightseers" (Duster 1970: 135). At this point in Wells's narrative, she uses a popular proverbial expression to emphasize the point even further: "The privilege of being once in a country where 'a man's a man for a' that,' is one which can best be appreciated by those Americans whose black skins are a bar to their receiving genuine kindness and courtesy at home" (Duster 1970: 135). Wells may have acquired this particular expression as she traveled throughout Scotland or other parts of Europe. She may have also heard it being sang. The expression "a man's a man for a' that" was popularized by the song "For a' That and a' That," written by Scottish poet Robert Burns in 1795. Throughout the song, the speaker rejects the notion of placing value on a person's appearance or material wealth and instead preaches that a man's character is his most valuable possession. As opposed to royal titles, money, or high social status, the speaker of the song values honesty, integrity, and independent thinking. Furthermore, Burns wrote the song to convey the message that people of all social classes should be valued equally, and that all should have voting rights and be afforded with opportunities to own their own land. Wells's use of the expression "a man's a man for a' that," in reference to her experience in Liverpool, illustrates that she was pleased to witness universal value being placed on equality.

While in Europe, Wells also visits the city of Bristol in England, where she speaks to several prominent people and describes the shock and disbelief that her audiences express to her upon hearing the facts about lynching in America. She comments, "There were two drawing-room meetings in the homes of wealthy and influential persons. In these drawing rooms, in which there were one hundred persons each, were gathered the wealthiest and most cultured classes of society who do not attend public meetings. One was presided over by Dr. Miller Nicholson, the pastor of the largest and most influential Presbyterian church in the city, and the other by

Mrs. Coote, president of the Women's Liberal Association of Bristol. Their shock on being told the actual conditions of things regarding lynching was painful to behold" (Duster 1970: 154). Many members of the group were under the impression that African Americans had been relishing in complete freedom since emancipation while other members of the group believe that lynching only happens to Black men that rape white women. After realizing that her audience had internalized a number of popular misconceptions, Wells states: "I read the account of that poor woman who was boxed up in a barrel into which nails had been driven and rolled down hill in Texas, and asked if that lynching could be excused on the same ground" (Duster 1970: 154). In addition to the shock of hearing about American atrocities committed against Blacks, the Bristol audience also cannot believe that the American government does nothing to prevent such carnages from taking place. Wells writes: "Again the question was asked where were all the legal and civil authorities of the country, to say nothing of the Christian churches, that they permitted such things to be?" (Duster 1970: 154). In response to this question, Wells explains to her audience that the problem of lynching is largely ignored by all of the institutions that have any power to help, and she uses a proverb that is very similar to the one that she employs to criticize the inactivity of Black leaders in America: "I could only say that despite the axiom that there is a remedy for every wrong, everybody in authority from the president of the United States down, had declared their inability to do anything; and that the Christian bodies and moral associations do not touch the question" (Duster 1970: 154). Wells's use of a variation of the proverb "no wrong without a remedy" (Wilson 1970: 924) seems fitting when one takes into account the imagery that she conveys after employing it: "American Christians are too busy saving the souls of white Christians from burning in hell-fire to save the lives of black ones from present burning in fires kindled by white Christians" (Duster 1970: 154–55). The irony invoked by her statement helps to reveal the paradox that is created by the simultaneous acceptance of both Christianity and lynch law in American culture. Overall, Wells employs proverbs strategically to convince her Christian audience that it is their moral duty to help right the wrong of lynch law in America.

Upon returning to New York from her successful European campaign, Wells was eager to try to gain more support in the US, so she sought to improve race relations by reaching out to the white clergy in America and the white presses. She wanted them both to take more interest in her antilynching crusade, and she used her newly established European ties as leverage. "I brought back to this country an appeal to the Christian ministers of the United States to give me the same opportunity for speaking from their pulpits as had been given me by the English clergymen. This appeal had been signed by the leading ministers of all denominations in Great Britain, that when I sought an interview with an American minister he was presented with this appeal. Rarely was it unsuccessful, because our American ministers knew that this powerful committee in London would receive reports as to their attitude on this burning question" (Duster 1970: 220).

Before meeting for an interview with the *New York Sun*, Wells is surprised when a group of African American men waiting for her ask her to "put the soft pedal on charges against white women and their relations with black men" (Duster 1970: 220). Wells adamantly refuses to do so and then tells the men how difficult it had been for her in Europe to reverse the awful stereotype that "black men were wild beasts after white women" (Duster 1970: 220). Furthermore, she explains to them that if she abandons her stance after returning home from overseas it will only give her audiences the impression that the outrageous stereotypes are accurate. Wells is then forced to defend her standpoint in the interview. She explains to the reporter that ever since her findings were published overseas and, in the US, she has had to defend her views. She then employs an important proverb from classical literature to make her case:

> The subject was mentioned on the floor of Congress, and passionate letters in protest were written. Mr. Richard Henry Dana himself sent for me and questioned me on the subject. I asked him if he ever read Burton's *Arabian Nights*? When he said that he had, my reply was "then you know that I tell of nothing new under the sun." Not only this, but he let me make that same statement in reply to a letter published in his columns which attacked me for "defaming the honor of the white women of the country." In that letter I said, just as I had told Mr. Dana, "those who have read Burton's *Arabian Nights* know that I tell of no new thing under the sun when I say white women have been known to fall in love with black men, and only after that relationship is discovered has an assault charge been made." (Duster 1970: 221)

Wells employs this proverb "there is nothing new under the sun" for a number of reasons (Speake 2015: 230). The first and most obvious reason that she uses it is because she knows that many people are familiar with *The Arabian Nights* (1885), a collection of ancient Middle Eastern tales that have been retranslated and published by Sir Richard Francis Burton (1821–90). Since the work is very popular, she hopes to punctuate her argument if her listeners can recall the proverb in Burton's text which reads: "'What hath been shall be, and there is nothing new under the sun,' is one of the many wise sayings of him whose words, to adopt his own language, are 'like apples of gold in settings of silver'" (Burton 2011: 270). Wells hopes that being reminded of the extravagant imagery from the scene in *The Arabian Nights* will help to convey to her audience the seriousness of her words.

Another reason she employs the proverb is because it is also found in the Bible. The verse reads: "The thing that hath been, it is that which shall be; and that which is done is that which shall be done: and there is no new thing under the sun" (KJV Ecclesiastes 1:9). Both *The Arabian Nights* and the Bible verse contain identical messages. However, while the Bible verse may lack the imagery and popularity of *The Arabian Nights*, it does provide Wells with an air of sagacity. Furthermore, the Bible is not considered fiction by most people, especially clergy and others involved in the church. Thus, Wells is able to "kill two birds with one stone" in using a proverb that will appeal simultaneously to two different audiences, the younger crowd, which may enjoy popular fiction, and also the more conservative groups, who may only regard the Bible as being the ultimate "truth."

Wells was always very keen in pointing out unfair practices and racial double standards in the American legal system, and sometimes proverbs played instrumental roles in voicing this discontent. In response to the case of an African American man who was imprisoned for breaking Indiana miscegenation laws while his white wife was set free Wells writes: "If justice is blind in America it is blind in only one eye" (McMurry 1998: 266). This sharp refutation, incorporating the seventeenth-century proverb "justice is blind," illustrates Wells's humorous side (Mieder et al. 1991: 342). It also comes very close to being an antiproverb. It certainly incorporates the characteristic humor of most antiproverbs. According to Litovkina and Mieder: "We laugh at some anti-proverbs because they skew our expectations about traditional values, order, and rules. We are, however, sometimes struck by the absurdity of some situations portrayed in parodies, especially when they rely purely upon linguistic tricks employed for the sole purpose of making punning possible" (Litovkina and Mieder 2006: 44). On a more serious note, in the same address Wells also called out Black male leaders who seemed to be unable to unify themselves and who were too afraid to speak out against racial injustice. According to historian Linda McMurry, Wells labeled this group of Black men that she spoke to as "a small body of men who are anxious to pose as white men's n-----s" and she incorporates a saying to exemplify the message. Wells says: "No man builds well whose foundation is laid upon another's ruin" (McMurry 1998: 266). This is more than likely a variation of another American proverb, which reads: "When a man lays the foundation of his own ruin, others will build on it (Mieder et al. 1991: 518). Wells's use of this proverb shows the immense value that she placed on unity among Black community leaders. It also demonstrates the extent that Wells was committed to reversing what historians Catherine Meeks and Nibs Stroupe describe as the *plantation mentality*, or an inherent sense of inferiority and learned helplessness which became internalized by many African Americans during Reconstruction as a direct result of southern "neo slavery" which included indiscriminate violence and unjust economic and legal systems (Blackmon 2008: 8; Meeks and Stroupe 2019: 217).

In addition to lynching, Wells also used proverbs to advocate for the temperance movement. While on her first European tour, Wells met temperance reformer and women's suffragist Frances E. Willard (1839–98). Willard served as the president of the Woman's Christian Temperance Union (WCTU), the most powerful women's organization in America at the time, from 1879 until her death. Shortly after meeting her, Wells learns quickly that Willard was racist. Racism among club women was not at all uncommon during the nineteenth and twentieth centuries. According to historian Rosalyn Terborg-Penn, "The experiences of many leaders indicated the pervasiveness of white female prejudice and discrimination against Black females in women's groups, even among those who were part of the woman suffrage coalition" (Terborg-Penn 1998: 119). Willard's racist sentiments were made clear in an interview that was published in 1890 in the *New York Voice*. In the interview, Willard expresses pity for Americans in the South for having to tolerate Blacks who "multiply like the locusts of Egypt. The grog-shop is its center of power" (McMurry 1998: 210). After voicing the opinion that she considers "grog-shops" or illegal liquor stores to be pseudo-cultural centers for Black people, Willard continues by saying that "'better whiskey and more of it' has been the rallying cry of great dark-faced mobs in the southern localities where local option was snowed under by the colored vote" (McMurry 1998: 210). In this interview, Willard, who is more than likely afraid of losing the support of southern white women, wholeheartedly denies the idea that temperance is important for Blacks, and she also suggests that Black people are even subhuman. Additionally, Willard expresses feeling threatened by what she describes as an increasing Black population. She says: "The safety of women, of children, of the home is menaced in a thousand localities at this moment, so men dare not go beyond the sight of their own roof-tree" (McMurry 1998: 210). Willards words quickly became the center of attention for Black presses. Wells denounced Willard's racist views in an article for the *A.M.E. Church Review*, saying: "In his wildest moments he seldom molests others than his own . . . and this article is a protest against such wholesale self-injury" (McMurry 1998: 210). Wells uses the term "self-injury" because unlike Willard, she sees Black intemperance as a serious issue that will ultimately have a negative impact on the Black community in two ways. Firstly, it slowly divests the community of valuable resources that could be used in service of education and community outreach. Secondly, intemperance contributes to exorbitant Black incarceration rates in the South. To better emphasize these points, Wells invokes a well-known proverbial expression: "It is like playing with fire to take that in the mouth which steals away the brains" (McMurry 1998: 210). The expression "to play with fire" is first cited in 1655 and means "to tinker with something potentially dangerous" (Whiting 1989: 226; Speake 2015: 250). For Wells, Black intemperance really was "like playing with fire." She goes on to write that intemperance provided "judges and juries the excuse for filling the convict lease camps of Georgia alone with fifteen hundred Negroes," and furthermore, the money that Black men wasted on alcohol only contributed to "enormous profits flowing into Anglo-Saxon coffers" (McMurry 1998: 210).

Wells also wrote a short story that focuses on the issue of intemperance in the Black community. At one point in her career, she had plans to become a novelist, but soon after she stopped teaching, her antilynching efforts took precedence in her life. Nevertheless, Wells published one short story entitled "Two Christmas Days: A Holiday Story" (1894), and it is a romance that many believe is based loosely on Wells's own life. The protagonist, Emily Minton, is a young well-educated teacher who is being courted by George Harris, a fledgling but talented lawyer who is just starting out in the legal business. George expresses interest in marrying Emily, but Emily is reluctant to do so due to George's intemperance. At one point in the story, Emily tells George that his intemperance is to blame for his lack of ambition. She says, "The race needs the best service our young manhood can give it, my friend, and it seems so wrong to divert any part of it to the practice of a habit which can bring you no credit and gratify no noble ambition" (Thompson 1990: 231). This is a major turning point in the story, and Wells punctuates the tense moment with a bit of proverbial wisdom. Wells writes:

> George's mind was in a conflicting whirl of emotions. He knew she spoke the truth; and yet with all his feelings of anger and mortification, he seemed to feel that this peerless girl was slipping away from him. He wanted her to think well of him and forgetful of the French proverb: "He who excuses, accuses," he said eagerly: "But this habit of mine never interferes with my business, Miss Emily. Indeed it rather helps me. I am the only Afro-American at this bar, and I must have

some stimulus to help me through the difficulties the wall of prejudice throws my way." (reprinted in Thompson 1990: 231)

The French proverb "he who excuses himself, accuses himself" basically means that if a person creates excuses in response to some accusation, then they are by default also admitting guilt or wrongdoing (Whiting 1989: 207). The proverb contributes to the omniscience of the narrator, and it also adds to the story's didactic feel. In addition to the proverb, Wells's use of the proverbial expression "wall of prejudice" helps to emphasize the fact that the American legal system, from a historical perspective, was rooted in racism. Wells also uses the proverb and proverbial expression to help to emphasize the strong moral message which is that Black men from all classes and levels of society should not treat prejudice as an excuse for intemperance. Black men should resist the urge to drink away pain, anger, or stress that may be caused by bigotry and racial injustice. This point becomes that much more poignant at the end of the tale when George and Emily marry after he finally realizes the errors of his ways.

Wells also concludes her autobiography with an important political proverb. She writes: "Eternal vigilance is the price of liberty, and it does seem to me that notwithstanding all these social agencies and activities there is not that vigilance which should be exercised in the preservation of our rights" (Duster 1970: 415). According to paremiologist Wolfgang Mieder, the first recorded instance of the proverb "eternal vigilance is the price of liberty" being used is by Philpot Curran who wrote a speech entitled "Speech upon the Right of Election," which he delivered on July 10, 1790 (Mieder 2001: 70). The speech reads: "The condition upon which God has given liberty to man is eternal vigilance; which condition if he break, servitude is at once the consequence of his crime, and the punishment of his guilt" (Mieder 2001: 70). Another recorded instance of the proverb "eternal vigilance is the price of liberty" being used in public discourse is by President Andrew Jackson (1767–1854). On March 4, 1837, during his farewell address, Jackson says: "But you must remember, my fellow-citizens, that eternal vigilance by the people is the price of liberty, and that you must pay the price if you wish to secure the blessing. It behooves you, therefore, to be watchful in your States as well as in the Federal Government" (Jackson 1837; Mieder 2019: 16). Wells's close friend and mentor Frederick Douglass also used it on March 17, 1848, in an article that he wrote for his journal, *North Star*, which was devoted to abolitionism. Douglass says: "It is strict accordance with all philosophical, as well as all experimental knowledge, that those who unite with tyrants to oppress the weak and helpless, will sooner or later find the groundwork of their own rights and liberties giving way. 'The price of liberty is eternal vigilance.' It can only be maintained by a sacred regard for the rights of all men" (Mieder 2001: 70). Additionally, abolitionist Wendell Phillips (1811–84) used the proverb in a speech in 1852. Later, Charles W. Chesnutt would also use it. Both are addressed in chapter two. In each instance, the proverb is being used to advance one's own view of democracy and justice. There is no doubting that Wells's use of it in her autobiography has done a lot to popularize it. Nearly every Wells biographer has mentioned her use of this saying (McMurry 1998: 26, 321; Fradin 2000: 161; Giddings 2008: 659; Bay 2009: 315). It seems fitting that she should use it in the forty-sixth and final chapter of her autobiography because it effectively summarizes her life's work. Wells displayed vigilance as a young woman battling Jim Crow laws in Memphis, and the vigilance that she shows in the latter part of her life helped her to initiate countless numbers of clubs and organizations that were devoted to the advancement of African Americans. Furthermore, Wells's investigative journalism and public speaking tours played a major role in reducing the frequency of lynchings around the nation, but despite all her milestone achievements, she still feels that complacency is the ultimate enemy of Black people. It may be the same sense of vigilance expressed in this saying that compelled Wells to run for Congress in Illinois the year before her death. There is plenty of evidence in her writings and actions that illustrate that Wells believed that her struggle for civil rights would never end, and her use of the proverb "eternal vigilance is the price of liberty" may be proof that she also believed that it never should end.

Chapter two addresses the proverb use of another famous writer and Wells contemporary, Charles W. Chesnutt (1858–1932), the first African American novelist. There is evidence that Chesnutt and Wells influenced one another in positive ways, despite having no known surviving recorded correspondences. They both cared greatly about social justice issues before such efforts evolved into the global movements that are now generally recognized by scholars, and they both sought to utilize the presses to convince others to do the same during a time when Black writing was largely discouraged. Chesnutt's early work may have motivated Wells's early attempts at writing moralizing fiction. Likewise, Wells's investigative journalism could have influenced Chesnutt to leave the comfort of his home for two weeks to personally investigate the Wilmington Massacre of November 10, 1898—the only major racial massacre that Wells did not investigate personally or write about. Perhaps Wells and Chesnutt exchanged important ideas on occasion as founding members of the National Association for the Advancement of Colored People (NAACP). One would think that they would have had to have crossed paths and exchanged ideas at some point, if not often. Regardless of how frequently they may or may not have corresponded, chapter two demonstrates that some of the obvious influences that their respective writings had on one another is something to be grateful for, in and of itself. *The Marrow of Tradition* (1901), based on the Wilmington Massacre, is arguably Chesnutt's most powerful work of fiction, and as chapter two emphasizes, *Marrow* and some of Chesnutt's other writings are also filled with much proverbial insight.

Chapter Two

"LITERATURE IS THE EXPRESSION OF LIFE"

Sayings, Proverbs, and Proverbial Expressions of Charles W. Chesnutt

Charles Waddell Chesnutt (June 20, 1858–November 17, 1932) was born to Andrew Jackson Chesnutt and Ann Maria Sampson in Cleveland, Ohio. Although his paternal grandfather was a slave owner, his parents were both free born African Americans of mixed heritage who met one another as they fled the war-torn South by wagon train in search of better opportunities. They returned to their original home in Fayetteville, North Carolina shortly after the Civil War (1861–65). Chesnutt's parents were educated and civic-minded people, even though where they were taught and whom they were taught by remains unclear to scholars. Despite an apparent lack of formal education, Chesnutt's father was a farmer, businessman, and held several public offices during his lifetime. He once was arrested for helping a group of men return a captured fugitive slave to freedom—a clear violation of the Fugitive Slave Law, a federal crime for which the senior Chesnutt barely escaped sentencing. It later became widely known as the Oberlin and Wellington Rescue Case of 1858 (Pickens 1994: 2). In an ironic turn of events, the senior Chesnutt was freed on account of a misspelling in his name on court documents: "the writ of arrest read 'Andrew Chestnut' and not 'Andrew Chesnutt'" (Ashton and Hardwig 2017: 1). His wife, Ann Maria, is known to have clandestinely taught enslaved African Americans to read (which was deemed an offense punishable by up to thirty-nine lashes in the state of North Carolina). They both valued hard work and education, and they instilled these values in all their children. Their youngest son, Charles, was educated at the Howard School in Fayetteville, North Carolina, which was named for Major General Oliver Otis Howard (1830–1909) of Union Forces. The school was established in 1867 with funds procured by the Howard-led Freedman's Bureau of which

Andrew Jackson Chesnutt was also a founding member. It would be the state's second school for educating African Americans.

Charles Chesnutt was one of the Howard School's best and brightest students, and at the age of fourteen he would become a teacher there. Later, he would also serve as principal, and after it became the State Colored Normal School (1877) for educating teachers, Chesnutt would briefly serve as the school's second president. During the latter part of the twentieth century, it became known as Fayetteville State University (1969). One unique aspect of Charles Chesnutt's formal education is that it would be so short-lived. After his teenage years, Chesnutt was largely a self-taught individual. He was an avid reader who managed to learn French, German, and Latin, primarily on his own. He also took up fiction writing, stenography, and law. He learned stenography (or shorthand) in his teenage years, at a time when stenography was still a new and emerging field. Nevertheless, it was a move that would yield dividends for him later in life. After earning the highest score on the Ohio state bar examination in 1887, he went on to establish a successful stenography and court reporting business in Cleveland, Ohio. Although Chesnutt wanted to write fiction for a living, he felt that practicing law and stenography would provide him with enough financial stability to one day be able to write full-time while still being able to fully support his wife and three children. Chesnutt's goal was to become the first celebrated African American writer of fiction, and he lived to see his goal come to fruition. He became well-known for writing short stories throughout much of the 1880s by submitting his stories to various newspapers and journals. He later published two volumes of short stories, *The Conjure Woman* (1899) and *The Wife of His Youth* (1899), and a biography on one of his heroes, Frederick Douglass (1899). Three novels quickly followed, all exploring issues surrounding racial prejudice: *The House Behind the Cedars* (1900), *The Marrow of Tradition* (1901), and *The Colonel's Dream* (1905).

Chesnutt became a public figure and spokesman for African Americans amid the Progressive Era (1890–1920) in American history. During the Progressive Era, the nation saw many of the concessions made during Reconstruction (1865–77) on behalf of the first generation of free African Americans completely abolished. As a result, things became increasingly worse for Black people. The forty acres and a mule or subsistence farmstead, the only specific request made of newly freed slaves and granted by the Lincoln Administration (1861–65), became a forgotten memory, the Freedman's Bureau went bankrupt, and the government enacted a series of stringent laws that severely restricted the movements and activities of African Americans. Across the South, peonage, sharecropping, and convict lease systems replaced chattel slavery. The government also implemented Black Codes and vagrancy laws that made it much easier to legally incarcerate scores of African Americans. Additionally, the Grandfather Clause, land ownership conditions, and literacy requirements all prevented Black people from voting and participating in other aspects of politics. To make matters even worse, campaigns of terror plagued the South as lynching, race riots, and mob violence were frequently implemented to scare African Americans, kill them in large numbers, and eradicate any and all hopes of ever attaining social, economic, and political equality. According to historian Ernestine Williams Pickens, white southern Progressive racism was driven by fear. Pickens contends: "White supremacy campaigns and disfranchisement of blacks were measures instituted by white Progressives to perpetuate a racial caste system which was immoral because it deprived blacks of their basic rights. The Progressives took action in order to maintain their traditional way of life in the face of a changing society" (Pickens 1994: 52). White southern Progressives practiced racism to eliminate competition for resources by creating a widespread sense of cohesion and purpose among the multitudes of white ethnic groups that originally migrated to the US from other parts of the world. Many foreign ethnicities chose to become invisible under the cloak of whiteness. Likewise, many light-skinned Blacks who could pass as white oftentimes chose to do so out of desperation. Some of Chesnutt's relatives chose this route, wanting to avoid racist treatment at all costs, even if it meant ostracizing themselves from other Black relatives. Nevertheless, Chesnutt was a light-skinned Black man of mixed heritage who refused to pass himself off as being white, but by all accounts, Chesnutt appeared to be white. Both of his grandfathers were white men, but Chesnutt, despite being invited to pass on multiple occasions by potential employers, refused to pass solely on grounds that he felt racism was immoral. From Chesnutt's perspective: "tradition and change were in serious conflict in the South, and, as a result, southern economic, social, and political progress were divorced from morality" (Pickens 1994: 52). In fact, Chesnutt would spend much of his life trying to eradicate the racist aspects of white southern Progressivism in American society, and he did so by concentrating on Black Progressive ideals. Some scholars consider Chesnutt to be the ideal Progressive reformer because of his middle-class upbringing and the enormous value that he placed on economic upward mobility. According to Pickens, Chesnutt's principles were very much in line with what scholars call the Mugwump Progressive ideal. Pickens asserts that it was "Chesnutt's belief in the Protestant ethic and the egalitarian aspect of the American dream, his desire for economic comfort, and his affinity for organizations reveal his inclination toward the values of the Progressive Mugwump and the new middle-class. For Chesnutt, as for the Mugwumps, one's purpose in life was to find a place in the community, work hard, make a decent living for one's family, fight for principles, serve God, and instill these values into the next generation" (Pickens 1994: 8). Chesnutt became a champion of the Black middle-class, and like white Progressives, Chesnutt never lost faith in the American political process, fighting tirelessly for Black suffrage. Additionally, "social reform, legal redress, judicial equity, political egalitarianism, truthful public representation of blacks, women's rights, establishment of institutions of public service—all became elements of Chesnutt's Progressive commitment and hallmarks of his private and public impact" (Pickens 1994: 31). There were several Black Progressive leaders who shared Chesnutt's values, and they all demanded to be heard. Some of the most notable voices included W. E. B. Du Bois (1868–1963), Booker T. Washington (1856–1915), William Monroe Trotter (1872–1934), and T. Thomas Fortune (1856–1928). Chesnutt was among this group of outspoken Black Progressives who took a decisive stance against the vehement forms of racism advocated by white southern Progressives. Chesnutt "was active in many groups whose special interest was to help African Americans fight racial injustice and become assimilated into American Society. The National Negro Committee, the Niagara Movement, and the National Association for the Advancement of Colored People are among the organizations of this type in which Chesnutt was most involved" (Pickens 1994: 8). What sets Chesnutt apart from other Black Progressives is primarily his unique attitude concerning racial issues and the mediums by which he chose to express antiracist sentiments. Chesnutt viewed racial prejudice as being primarily a moral issue which simultaneously connected him to and set him apart from contemporaries such as Booker T. Washington and W. E. B. Du Bois, who championed the attainment of vocational education and political power for Black people, respectively. While Chesnutt agreed with many of their ideas, he felt that an absence of moral values on the part of white people was at the heart of southern Progressive racism. In his own words, Chesnutt felt that southern bigotry ultimately "warps all judgement, darkens all counsel and confuses standards of right and wrong" (Pickens 1994: 41). Consequently, he sought to affect the moral conscious of white America through his writing. Chesnutt, while still young, would expound on this lofty goal in his journals, exclaiming that his writing would be "for a purpose, a high and holy purpose . . . not so much the elevation of the colored people as the elevation of whites . . . for I consider the unjust spirit of caste which is so insidious as to pervade a whole race and all connected with it to scorn and social ostracism—I consider this a barrier to the moral progress of the American people" (Keller 1978: 77; Andrews 1980: 13). Chesnutt wanted to prove four things regarding racism through his work. Firstly, he wanted to illustrate the superficial quality of race as a scientific category. Secondly, he wanted to convince white people that racism was unethical. Thirdly, he sought to persuade white people that racism benefited no one. Fourth and lastly, he wanted to convince white people that racism was detrimental to themselves and to all Americans.

One key aspect of Chesnutt's work that has largely gone unnoticed by scholars is the important role that proverbs and proverbial language play in his communication of moral values and Black Progressive ideals. According to folklorist and paremiologist Wolfgang Mieder, "A proverb is a short, generally known sentence of the folk which contains wisdom, truth, morals, and traditional views in a metaphorical, fixed and memorable form and which is handed down from generation to generation" (Mieder 2004: 3). Throughout Chesnutt's career he used proverbs and proverbial language for the purpose of denouncing racism and communicating middle-class values. Like other Black Progressives, he consistently preached that racism is the one barrier preventing the nation's Black people from obtaining the proverbial "American dream," and since Chesnutt primarily viewed racism as an ethical matter, it is no surprise that much of the proverbial language that he used was done so with didactic intentions, that is with moral lessons implied.

Some good examples of Chesnutt perpetuating Protestant middle-class values with didactic sayings occur early on in his career during his years as a teacher and administrator in Fayetteville, North Carolina. Chesnutt was a teacher for a short amount of time, but his lessons were not just limited to the classroom. He wrote essays and speeches that were filled with good advice and moralizing sayings and aphorisms to help uplift his race. In one speech entitled "Etiquette (Good Manners)" (1881), which Chesnutt gave to the Normal School Literary Society in Fayetteville, North Carolina, Chesnutt "frames proper etiquette, polite conduct, fastidious personal appearance and hygiene, and temperance as matters essential to the maintenance of young men's character" (Sussman 2017: 88). In the speech there are several instances of proverb and proverbial language use. Chesnutt is speaking to an audience of young students, and he wants to impart on them as many life lessons as he can, so that they may be successful in their studies. Early in the speech, he says: "We should try in our intercourse with others to remember the Golden Rule, 'Do unto others as you would have them do unto you'" (McElrath et al. 1999: 2; Bryan and Mieder 2005: 322). Most would agree on the appropriateness of beginning a speech on etiquette with one of the most well-known didactic proverbs from Matthew 7:12 (KJV). Chesnutt follows up his advice with another proverb regarding etiquette that is from collective folk memory, as opposed to being attributed to any single individual or source. He says: "It is good policy to be well behaved. You know the old proverb, 'Manners will carry you where money will not'" (Whiting 1989: 402); McElrath et al. 1999: 2). Chesnutt then reinforces this proverbial lesson with an explanation, saying: "The power of money is very great; but however much wealth you may have, there are others as rich as you, and all of your money will not bring you into their society unless you can render yourself agreeable to them" (McElrath et al. 1999: 2). Chesnutt does not end the lesson there. He relates to his audience a story about how Sir Walter Raleigh (1552–1618), as an unknown lad, earned a place in Queen Elizabeth's (1533–1603) court through his display of courtly manners saying: "As the dainty lady hesitated to place her foot on a muddy place in the path, the gallant young cavalier sprang forward, threw his rich cloak across the wet place, and stood by with a polite obeisance while the Queen stepped safely across" (McElrath et al. 1999: 2). This brief tale is no doubt a reflection of Chesnutt's Progressive values and he wants his young audience to share this bourgeoisie aspiration of rising to a much higher station in life.

In addition to the lessons on manners, Chesnutt also advises his audience on the many benefits of having good hygiene, and he uses a well-known proverb to help make his point. He says: "'Cleanliness is next to godliness,' and I can hardly see how a clean heart can exist in a dirty body for any great length of time" (McElrath et al. 1999: 3; Bryan and Mieder 2005: 156). Another saying which has been attributed to Greek philosopher Aristotle helps to make Chesnutt's point even clearer. He says:

> A man who has made his toilet in the manner I have described above is prepared to begin the day feeling like a gentleman. "Well begun is half done"; and he can work better and enjoy life more than the dirty fellow who crawls out of bed, throws on his dirty clothes, wets his face and hands, makes a rake at his hair, and slouches off to his business feeling worse than when he went to bed. (McElrath et al. 1999: 4–5)

Chesnutt's effort at helping to shape the character and habits of the young people at the State Colored Normal School become increasingly evident as he digs deeper into his proverbial repertoire. After he warns his audience of the dangers of talking too much about other people in public, he repeats the Golden rule saying: "Do not talk slightly of the absent. You do not know who will carry your remarks to their ears. Do as you would be done by" (McElrath et al. 1999: 10; Bryan and Mieder 2005: 322). He even admonishes his audience on the dangers of announcing one's own affairs in public, incorporating a folk saying in the process. He says: "*Don't talk shop*: i.e., don't talk about yourself or your own affairs. It may be very interesting to you, but very stupid to other people. A preacher should not preach, nor a lawyer plead in the parlor. Talk about things that will interest the whole company" (McElrath et al. 1999: 10). The proverb "a preacher should not preach, nor a lawyer plead in the parlor" is another example of Chesnutt's folk wisdom more than likely derived from his day-to-day interactions with common folk in Fayetteville, North Carolina.

To further expound on his lesson on the risk of being too garrulous, he relies on another well-known proverb from the Bible saying: "Whispering, talking, laughing, etc. it is not necessary for me to mention. No one who wishes to be considered decent will indulge in these things at church; and it would be throwing pearls before swine to attempt to instruct those who do not wish to learn" (McElrath et al. 1999: 11). The proverb from Matthew 7:6 (KJV), "do not throw pearls before swine" (Bryan and Mieder 2005: 578), is Chesnutt's warning to his audience to avoid wasting their time, energy, or words on people who are not like-minded.

Near the end of Chesnutt's speech, he uses a well-known proverbial expression from Aesop's *Fables* (620–560 BC) to make a sincere point concerning authenticity. He says: "Finally, dear students, remember that it is only by being a gentleman or a lady that you can act like one. Otherwise, like the ass in the lion's skin, you will betray yourself as soon as you begin to bray. You cannot put on politeness with your Sunday clothes, for it will not keep like they" (McElrath et al. 1999: 12). The proverbial expression "like the ass in the lion's skin" is certainly evidence that he was well-read in Greek literature, and it also demonstrates his sense of humor.

Chesnutt concludes his speech by further emphasizing the all-important Golden Rule and its many benefits. He says:

> It is only by being a lady or a gentleman at all times that you can be a lady or gentleman at any time. And remember the golden rule "Do unto others as you", etc., and you will render yourself agreeable to all with whom you associate; your company will be sought after, your influence enlarged, and your success in life materially promoted. Any, and if you will take this Golden Rule, and carry it beyond the mere surface to the heart, and make it and all the words of Him who first uttered it the law of your life it will lead you beyond mere material success. (McElrath et al. 1999 12; Bryan and Mieder 2005: 322)

Being well-versed in scripture, Chesnutt would sometimes revert to the Bible for moral reinforcement, and at times, this practice could be very effective.

In another speech given at the Normal School, entitled "The Advantages of a Well-Conducted Literary Society" (1881), Chesnutt again uses a plethora of proverbs and proverbial expressions, some of which have biblical origins. Throughout the speech Chesnutt maintains that the overall purpose of a literary society is to provide its members with three things: recreation, instruction, and discipline, and he spells out each of these important principles very carefully for his audience. Near the beginning of the speech, drawing from Genesis 3:19 (KJV) and II Thessalonians 3:10 (KJV), he says:

> We have seen that amusement or recreation is useful and even necessary. But only a short portion of our time can be devoted to it. Man was made to work. The dictum went forth from Deity, "In the sweat of thy face shalt thou eat bread," and labor has since been the lot of mankind. It is true there are some drones in the hive; but of the great mass of mankind it is true, that "he who will not work shall not eat." (McElrath et al. 1999: 15)

The two proverbs "in the sweat of thy face shalt thou eat bread," and "he who will not work shall not eat" (Bryan and Mieder 2005: 863) are taken verbatim from the Bible. The second of these proverbs was also the motto of Captain John Smith (1580–1631) while he was the governor of the Jamestown Colony in 1608 (McElrath et al. 1999: 23). These proverbs are perfect examples of the Protestant sense of work ethic and the Progressive ideals that became second nature to Chesnutt. Additionally, in the following paragraph of the speech, Chesnutt alludes to another biblical proverb against indolence saying: "God did not make man to be idle, nor did he make him with mere instincts of self-preservation like the beasts of the field. He gave him a destiny to work out" (McElrath et al. 1999: 15). The first part of this statement, "God did not make man to be idle," is a subtle allusion to Proverbs 19:15 (KJV), which reads: "Slothfulness casteth into a deep sleep; and an idle soul shall suffer hunger."

Another saying that Chesnutt uses in this speech comes from German playwright Johann Christoph Friedrich von Schiller (1759–1805). Chesnutt says: "'*Ernst ist das Leben*'—life is a serious thing" (McElrath et al. 1999: 18), which is from Schiller's dramatic trilogy *Wallenstein* (1799). This saying from Schiller appears at a point in the speech when Chesnutt is urging his audience at the Normal School to take their literary society seriously and to not use it for amusement and recreation only. Instead, Chesnutt wants them to use their literary society as a tool for honing their rhetorical skills, and he uses two British orators and historians as examples. He says that Thomas Babington Macaulay (1800–59) perfected his speeches "with the skill of an artist" (McElrath et al. 1999: 18). Chesnutt then talks about the amount of emphasis that Louis Adolphe Thiers (1797–1877) placed on the preparation and delivery of his public speeches:

> A story is now going the rounds of the press about M. Thiers, late president of France. A gentleman was expressing surprise that M. Thiers could deliver such brilliant speeches without preparation. (M. Thiers uses no notes.) "Sir," responded the ex-president, "it is no compliment to me to have it thought that I speak without preparation. I hold it criminal in a man to discuss great public measures without careful thought and study. *My* speeches are the result of long and painful preparation." (McElrath et al. 1999: 18)

Chesnutt then adds: "This man has a proper idea of the vocation of an orator. 'If the blind lead the blind, shall they not both fall into the ditch'" (McElrath et al. 1999: 18; Bryan and Mieder 2005: 75). This biblical proverb from Luke 6:39 (KJV) sums up former French president Thiers's rationale for long and arduous preparation before addressing the public on political matters.

Chesnutt intends for the Normal School Literary Society to be a place for training hard-working, self-disciplined leaders, and this becomes even more evident by the next proverb that he incorporates into his speech. Chesnutt says: "Self-possession as we have learned, is the ability to control the intellect before an audience; but *self-control* is the ability to govern the temper under like circumstances. 'He that ruleth his own spirit is stronger than him that taketh a city'" (McElrath et al. 1999: 19). The biblical proverb "he that ruleth his own spirit is stronger than him that taketh a city" (Bryan and Mieder 2005: 717) is originally from Proverbs 16:32 (KJV). Chesnutt employs it here to convince his audience of the importance of discipline and self-control. He feels that from a mental standpoint these attributes are necessary if one is to become an effective speaker and leader.

Chesnutt also uses another biblical proverb in this speech. He says: "Seest thou a man wise in his own conceit? There is more hope of a fool than of him" (McElrath et al. 1999: 19). This bit of instruction against vanity from Proverbs 26:12 (KJV) is a warning to his young audience to never place too much importance on themselves or to value themselves more than the important organization that they have become a part of, which is good advice for all leaders and followers alike.

In another speech to the Normal Literary Society, entitled "Self-Made Men" (1882), Chesnutt begins his speech with a proverb, saying: "Mind is superior to matter" (McElrath et al. 1999: 33; Bryan and Mieder 2005: 509). He also speaks to his audience about the benefits of hard work and determination, borrowing another proverb from the Bible in the process. In a message of encouragement, Chesnutt urges his audience to be mindful of the Scripture injunction: "Whatsoever thy hand findeth to do, do it with all thy might" (McElrath et al. 1999: 38).

Throughout the Progressive Era, Chesnutt wrote profusely about the dangers of racism in the form of anti-Black legislation. In an article entitled "A Multitude of Counselors" (1891), Chesnutt explains what historian George Fredrickson calls "racial prognostication," or the "tendency of white writers, activists, and politicians to forecast the 'ultimate destiny of blacks'" (Sussman 2017: 87). Chesnutt talks about all the conflicting advice given to Black people from influential white leaders. In summing up some of the conflicting ideas, he uses another well-known proverb:

> A writer prominently identified with the cause of the colored people advises them to forget the fact that they are Negroes, and to endeavor to feel that they are simply men and citizens. One counselor advises them to emigrate largely from the South, and thus relieve that section of the strain caused by the fear of Negro majorities. Another advises them to stay in the South, and retain their majorities, on the theory that a bird in hand (even if the hand is shackled) is worth two in the bush. (McElrath et al. 1999: 79)

The folk proverb "a bird in hand is worth two in the bush" (Bryan and Mieder 2005: 60) is used as a way of saying that the situation in the South could possibly change for the better in the near or distant future. Therefore, if racist laws are eventually abolished, Black people will automatically have a much stronger political voice because they may have greater voting numbers by choosing to stay.

Additionally, Chesnutt also uses a saying from Frederick Douglass, whom he admired greatly, so much so that he published one of the first Douglass biographies early in his writing career. Chesnutt continues:

> One friend finds a specific for every race troubled in the division of the colored vote; another, many others in fact, see no hope for the Negro except in the supremacy of the Republican Party; they believe, in the language of Frederick Douglass, that to the Negro "the Republican Party is the ship; all else is the ocean." Judge Tourgeé openly predicts a guerilla warfare of races, and can only advise the colored people to

defend themselves in an uneven and hopeless conflict." (McElrath et al. 1999: 79)

The saying "the Republican Party is the ship; all else is the ocean" expresses Douglass's belief that Black people could attain equal rights if they placed all their trust in the Republican Party. The main point of Chesnutt's article is to illustrate the conflicting nature of advice, to point out the absurdity of some of the ideas proposed by others, and to urge Black people to speak up for themselves whenever such opportunities arise.

In an article entitled "The Disfranchisement of the Negro" (1903), Chesnutt talks about the importance of Black suffrage, and he employs a few proverbs in the process. In speaking about the dangers of the government waiting too long to abolish racist legislation preventing scores of African Americans from voting and having equal rights, Chesnutt derives some strength of meaning from an age-old proverb. He says:

> Time we are told, heals all diseases, rights all wrongs, and is the only cure for this one. It is a cowardly argument. These people are entitled to their rights-to-day, while they are yet alive to enjoy them; and it is poor statesmanship and worse morals to nurse a present evil and thrust it forward upon a future generation for correction. The nation can no more honestly do this than it could thrust back upon a past generation the responsibility for slavery. It had to meet that responsibility; it ought to meet this one. (McElrath et al. 1999: 186)

Chesnutt's variation of the proverb "time heals all wounds" (Bryan and Mieder 2005: 775) is a perfect way to emphasize the urgency of the situation and it is also a good way to emphasize that the issue would not be resolved on its own. In using traditional language in the form of the proverb to make a strong case against the southern tradition of racism, the proverb functions much as an antiproverb would, in the sense that his overall point is that time will not heal all wounds, regarding Black suffrage.

At another point in the speech, Chesnutt argues that among the differing opinions that exist, there are many white people in the South who are in support of equal rights. He feels that these voices often go unnoticed, saying:

> The South itself seems bent upon forcing the question to an issue, as, by its arrogant assumptions, it brought on the Civil War. From that section, too, there come now and then, side by side with tales of Southern outrage, excusing voices, which at the same time are

accusing voices; which admit that the white South is dealing with the Negro unjustly and unwisely; that the Golden Rule has been forgotten; that the interests of white men alone have been taken into account, and that their true interests as well are being sacrificed. (McElrath et al. 1999: 190-91)

In reminding his audience of the Golden Rule (Bryan and Mieder 2005: 322), Chesnutt is also emphasizing the central premise behind his rhetoric, mainly that morality has been a long-forgotten element in southern politics. Additionally, there are many whites who recognize this tragic flaw, but they are afraid to speak out. Chesnutt says: "There is a silent white South, uneasy in conscience, darkened in counsel, groping for the light, and willing to do the right. They are as yet a feeble folk, their voices scarcely audible above the clamor of the mob. May their convictions ripen into wisdom, and may their numbers and their courage increase!" (McElrath et al. 1999: 190-91). Chesnutt, playing off the contrasting imagery of darkness and light, urges his silent white audience to find the proverbial light of truth for themselves, and to also be brave enough to speak out against those in favor of denying equal rights to Black people.

Chesnutt then urges his northern brethren who have obtained the right of free speech to not ever take that right for granted. He says: "In the meantime the Northern colored men have the right of free speech, and they should never cease to demand their rights, to clamor for them, to guard them jealously, and insistently to invoke law and public sentiment to maintain them. He who would be free must learn to protect his freedom. Eternal vigilance is the price of liberty" (McElrath et al. 1999: 191).

The political proverb "Eternal vigilance is the price of liberty" is often attributed to several political figures, but Chesnutt more than likely first encountered it in the works of abolitionist heroes like Wendell Phillips (1811-84) and Frederick Douglass (1817-95). Phillips helped to popularize the proverb in an 1852 address to the Massachusetts Antislavery Society (McElrath et al. 1999: 195). It was also used at times by Frederick Douglass (Mieder 2001: 70) and, as discussed in the previous chapter, antilynching crusader Ida B. Wells (1862-1931). Chesnutt continues with a saying that was more than likely derived from the writings of Henry Wadsworth Longfellow (1807-82). Chesnutt says: "He who would be respected must respect himself" (McElrath et al. 1999: 191). Chesnutt was an avid reader of literature, and so there is no doubting his familiarity with the work of the famous American transcendentalist Longfellow, who famously wrote: "He that respects himself is safe from others. He wears a coat of mail that none can pierce." When

Chesnutt was still a teenager, he used a similar proverb in his journal as he contemplated the amount of work ethic that it would take to accomplish his goal of surviving in the North as a stenographer. He made a personal resolve to "work, work, work! . . . Trust in God and work" (Keller 1978: 64). Additionally, he says: "He who would master others should first learn to master himself" (Chesnutt 1952: 16–17; Keller 1978: 64; Bryan and Mieder 2005: 501). The proverb "he who would master others should first learn to master himself" illustrates that Chesnutt, even at a young age, had confidence that good work ethic and discipline would help him to overcome any form of discrimination that he might face in life.

In a speech entitled "Race Prejudice: Its Causes and Cures" (1905), which was presented to the Boston Literary and Historical Association, Chesnutt identifies ignorance as a leading cause of race prejudice, and he criticizes the government for not doing enough to educate people in the South, citing an extremely high illiteracy rate as evidence. He says:

> The percentage of illiteracy in the Southern States is so high, and those states so poor, relatively, and their system of separate schools so expensive, that it is yet an open question whether the nation ought not to take up the matter of Southern education for whites and blacks alike. We might well ask whether we have not a duty to perform at home before we spend the nation's money in carrying the blessings of civilization to distant and alien peoples. (McElrath et al. 1999: 228)

Chesnutt then poses an important question before employing a well-known proverb to help make his point, saying: "By what color of reason do we spend our own money in teaching science to the Filipinos when a great portion of our own population, white and colored, cannot read or write? Duty, to say nothing of charity, at least *begins* at home" (emphasis in original) (McElrath et al. 1999: 228). Chesnutt uses the proverb "charity begins at home" (Bryan and Mieder 2005: 145) for several reasons. Firstly, the proverb implies that one should take care of business in their own home before trying to help people in other countries. Secondly, there is the underlying message implied by the source, English scholar Sir Thomas Browne (1605–82), who is known for being well-educated on a variety of subjects, including religion, science, and medicine. Browne uses the proverb in his *Religio Medici* (1643) (McElrath et al. 1999: 237). Even though he may not have been the very first person to use the proverb, his work more than likely helped to popularize it. Chesnutt, in citing a well-known scholar, gets to play off the contrast between scholarship and age-old folk wisdom.

The last topic concerning racial prejudice that Chesnutt addresses in this speech is the issue of differences in human phenotype which Chesnutt, reflecting on his knowledge of evolutionary and biological science, understand to be caused by differences of geographical origin as opposed to any significant molecular difference in the human species. He says: "And now, in closing . . . I reach the last and most difficult of these differences which hold us apart from our fellow-citizens and give rise to that antagonism of hostile feeling which we call race prejudice. I refer to the still strongly marked difference, in physical characteristics—in other words, the difference in color, or in 'race,' as we use the term" (McElrath et al. 1999: 231). Being of mixed heritage himself, Chesnutt strongly believed that amalgamation or the mixing of the races through intermarriage would ultimately become the norm in American society, despite nearly every southern state having strict laws against miscegenation. He felt that the amalgamation of the races would ultimately provide a natural and permanent solution to racial prejudice in the United States. Citing his own audience as a prime example of this phenomenon, he says: "I have shown how this difference has been modified. I can look down into this audience and see how, in three or four generations, it has, with certain individuals and groups, almost entirely disappeared. Should it disappear entirely, race prejudice, and the race problem, would no longer exist. The question is, do we wish this difference to disappear, or do we wish to perpetuate it?" (McElrath et al. 1999: 231). In exploring this question further, Chesnutt incorporates a well-known proverbial expression that was most often used for the malevolent purpose of promoting racial bias in American society. He says: "And in discussing this question, we must dismiss the personal point of view, for so far as we are individually concerned, the leopard cannot change his spots, or the Ethiopian his skin, nor can a man by thinking add one cubit to his stature" (McElrath et al. 1999: 231). The statement "the leopard cannot change his spots," based on Jeremiah 13:23 (KJV) in its biblical form, is a metaphor, and as a derivative, the statement became proverbial over time through frequent usage. The meaning of the original passage has nothing to do with race. In the Bible, it is a metaphor regarding human nature. The passage reads: "Can the Ethiopian change his skin, or the leopard his spots? Then may ye also do good, that are accustomed to do evil." The passage means that an individual's human nature cannot change, but the proverbial expression, "the leopard cannot change his spots," was often used in support of racist philosophy throughout the nineteenth century. It is even used in the title of Thomas Dixon's very popular and influential racist novel *The Leopard's Spots*, which was first published in 1902. In the case of Chesnutt's speech, it is combined with a biblical saying from Matthew 6:27

(KJV), which reads: "Which of you by taking thought can add one cubit to his stature?" While this biblical passage is meant to be a cautionary statement that warns against the pointless act of worrying about one's problems, it makes the statement concerning the leopard's spots appear to be an absolute truth. Chesnutt more than likely saw this combination used often which may be why he uses it in the speech. The primary difference is that Chesnutt is speaking in favor of different races mixing and he is simultaneously denouncing the pernicious and widespread notion that one's race can be intrinsically connected to one's character.

In "Address Before the Ohio State Night School" (1928), Chesnutt uses a common proverbial expression to describe the antimiscegenation laws that were being implemented across northern and southern states during the twentieth century, saying: "Every winter in some one or more Northern States' legislature somebody introduces such a bill which so far, in spite of the KKK which always sponsors it they have all been defeated. But this seems to me is merely locking the stable door after the horse is stolen. These frantic efforts to preserve the purity of the white race are a little late" (McElrath et al. 1999: 500). In characterizing such laws against miscegenation as locking the proverbial stable door after the horse is already stolen (Bryan and Mieder 2005: 722), Chesnutt is emphasizing the absurdity of antimiscegenation legislation because it had already been a widespread phenomenon in American culture for centuries.

In "Age of Problems" (1906), Chesnutt expresses some hope that racial problems are only temporary. He speaks about what he considers to be a recent moral lapse on the part of the Roosevelt Administration (1901–09), and at one point in the speech, he incorporates a telling folk proverb which is followed by a biblical proverb. He says:

> Even the President of the United States, the apostle of the Square Deal, wishing to make an example, discharged, without honor, a whole battalion of colored troops, under circumstances which the press of the country unanimously, so far as I have followed comment, condemn as unjust and unfair. Everyone who wishes to can make an example of the man who has no friends. . . . And even when the Negro gets justice, it is rarely tempered with mercy. (McElrath et al. 1999: 239–40)

Here Chesnutt is referring to what became known as the Brownsville Affair (1906), when President Theodore Roosevelt (1858–1919) dismissed an entire battalion of colored soldiers in Brownsville, Texas, who were accused of murdering a bartender and wounding a white police officer. All 167 soldiers of the 25th Infantry Regiment received dishonorable discharge, which forfeited their pensions and barred them from ever obtaining federal civil service jobs. Roosevelt disciplined the men even though the evidence that was used against them, a few spent shell casings, was planted at the scene of the crime by someone apparently wanting to frame the men. Across the nation, there were both Blacks and whites who were outraged by the outcome of the case. After a new investigation, Roosevelt's decision would be overturned in 1972, by which time only one of the accused was still alive to see justice finally served.

In speaking about the Brownsville Affair, Chesnutt uses the proverb "everyone who wishes to can make an example of the man with no friends." Here Chesnutt is talking about Black people as a race, and the fact that during Reconstruction it was common for the justice system to use Black people as scapegoats when the real perpetrators of crimes were white or if the case could not be determined. Chesnutt follows the folk proverb up with a proverb that expresses optimism that this period in American history is only a temporary one. He says: "But enough of this phase of the subject—which is not a hopeful phase, unless one go upon the theory that the darkest hour is just before dawn" (McElrath et al. 1999: 240). "The darkest hour is just before dawn" is a well-documented aphorism (Bryan and Mieder 2005: 196) that also reflects Isaiah 26–27 (KJV).

It is no coincidence that Charles N. Hunter, editor of the *Progressive Educator*, uses the same proverb in a personal letter to Chesnutt. The *Progressive Educator* was a monthly journal published in Raleigh, North Carolina, that was devoted to "The Elevation and Culture of the Colored Race in America" (Keller 1978: 113). Hunter, writing from his office in Durham in 1889, expresses remorse that the state of North Carolina recently adopted stricter voting laws that would bar most Black people from being able to register to vote. With the new laws in place, Blacks would now be required to provide date and place of birth to cast a ballot which was virtually impossible for most African Americans who were born into slavery because such biological data was rarely recorded. Hunter says: "White republicans are showing a bitter proscription of Negro citizens. Thinking colored citizens now have under adjustment plans by which the race may be placed in an attitude that will command the just judgement of just men and women everywhere regardless of party. . . . I am not hopeless. This may be that dark hour just before the break of day" (Keller 1978: 112–13). Although Hunter's use of the variation of the proverb "the darkest hour is just before dawn" (Bryan and Mieder 2005: 196) illustrates some optimism that the worst has passed, such correspondences taught Chesnutt (in his own words) that in the state of

North Carolina, "the chapter of southern outrages is not yet complete, but the work of intimidating voters and killing prominent Negroes on trumped-up charges . . . still goes merrily on" (Keller 1978: 113).

In "Rights and Duties" (1908), a speech presented to the Bethel Literary and Historical Association, Chesnutt argues that society would be much better off if our civic leaders would be chosen on merit as opposed to race. He says: "Take the government of the Southern States. Would Negroes dominate? With no prejudices to push them aside and solidify them into antagonism against the whites, they would no longer vote as a class, but as individuals. They would be subject to the same influences which move other voters" (McElrath et al. 1999: 254). Chesnutt then incorporates a well-known proverb to help make his point. He says:

> The pen is mightier than the sword; the brain is stronger than the bludgeon. Under such a condition, those best qualified ought to rule, it is better for the interest of all concerned that they should rule; but they should rule with the consent of the governed, they should depend upon them for their power, and in that event the governed would see to it that their rights and their interests were respected. (McElrath et al. 1999: 254)

"The pen is mightier than the sword" (Bryan and Mieder 2005: 580) is a proverb which was also used by English writer and politician Edward Bulwer-Lytton (1803–73), who used it in *Richelieu* (1839) (McElrath et al. 1999: 261). Chesnutt strengthens his point on the power of intellect and reason by combining it with a saying of his own: "the brain is stronger than the bludgeon" (McElrath et al. 1999: 254). Chesnutt makes a profound statement against racism and political violence by simply mirroring the structure of the initial proverb.

Chesnutt also creates a saying which plays off the title of the speech "Rights and Duties." Near the end of the speech, he says:

> And now, what are his duties? I should say that duties are dependent upon rights, without rights there can be no duties. What were the duties of the slave? He was not a citizen and therefore he had no civic duties. He was denied the institution of marriage and the control of his family; hence he had no domestic duties. For a long time there were those who denied him a soul; one of these fossils was dug up. Like the skeleton of a plesiosaurus out in Missouri a year or two ago and published a book entitled, *Is the Negro A Beast*? Without a soul of

course he could have no duty to God. The only duty taught him was to obey his master.

Chesnutt believes that voting rights and equality are two entities that go hand in hand, and as he demonstrates, from a historical standpoint, one has never existed without the other. Chesnutt's influential speech may have popularized the saying "without rights there can be no duties." Some evidence of the saying's popularity comes in the form of a New Orleans-based newspaper, *The Lumberjack* (1913), which uses a variation of the saying in one of its headlines. It reads: "No Rights Without Duties; No Duties Without Rights."

Chesnutt spoke about the significance of Black literature on numerous occasions. He always encouraged Black authors to write, and he tried to persuade the reading public to buy Black books. Chesnutt felt that Black literature was important because there was so much reading material that offered only negative portrayals of African Americans, and such negative portrayals are a primary characteristic of the plantation tradition that Chesnutt chose to write against. The plantation tradition is represented by "southern writers who sought to romanticize the Antebellum South and to re-write the legacy of this slaveholding culture in an era (the 1880s and 1890s) that was losing citizens with strong personal memories of the region before the Civil War" (Ashton and Hardwig 2017: 4). In keeping with the plantation style of writing, many nineteenth-century writers avoided writing about race and politics at all. If they included any Black characters, they chose from a common stock of stereotypes which included: buffoons, minstrels, harmless children of nature, irresponsible beasts of devilish cunning, the soulless and depraved, the contented slave, the wretched freedman, the tragic mulatto, and the comic negro (Andrews 1980: 47). Chesnutt knew that "romanticized views of blacks ... could ... serve the need of political and social conservatives who wished to discredit or roll back civil rights gains" (Ashton and Hardwig 2017: 5). Chesnutt also understood that if there were more Black writers who were willing to portray Black people in a positive light, the general reading public would realize that the stereotypes regarding Black people that they encountered so frequently in periodicals and books were false. Chesnutt often complained vehemently about unrealistic and demeaning portrayals of Black people in literature. For instance, in a letter to editor and close friend George Cable in 1890, Chesnutt says:

> Thomas Nelson Page and Harry S. Edwards depict the sentimental and devoted Negro, who prefers kicks to half-pence. Judge Tourgée's cultivated white Negroes are always bewailing their fate and cursing

the drop of black blood which "taints"—I hate the word, it implies corruption—their otherwise pure race. An English writer would not hesitate to call a spade a spade, to say that race prejudice was mean and narrow and unchristian. (Chesnutt 1952: 58)

Paremiologist Wolfgang Mieder provides some insight into the double entendre implied by Chesnutt's use of the proverbial expression, "to call a spade a spade" (Bryan and Mieder 2005: 714). According to Mieder, dating back to Greek antiquity: "the proverbial expression 'to call a spade a spade' has been used for hundreds of years as a harmless metaphor for direct and plain communication instead of using indirect and convoluted euphemisms. Once the noun 'spade' took on the derogatory slang meaning of a Black person in the first quarter of the twentieth century, the 'spade' phrase could in certain contexts be understood as a racial slur" (Mieder 2002: 213). In using the phrase, Chesnutt is invoking language that could be deemed racist to make a serious point regarding racism. Chesnutt feels that by showcasing Black characters who are helpless or who exhibit self-hate, white authors are simply avoiding the issue that racism is inherently wrong.

In a speech entitled "The Negro in Books" (1916), Chesnutt expounds on his criticism of negative portrayals of Black people in literature, and he employs an interesting proverb in the process. Chesnutt says:

> When the Negro as a man and a social unit is referred to, we do not want him referred to *en masse* as lazy, shiftless and inefficient. Many Negroes are, but many more are not. We do not want it assumed that because he is of humble origin, that he is necessarily a low person—for, as I heard it wittily put the other day, it does not necessarily follow that because a man was born in a stable he is therefore a horse. (McElrath et al. 1999: 435)

It was Daniel O'Connell (1775–1847), the first Duke of Wellington, who famously said: "Being born in a stable does not make a man a horse." O'Connell coined this aphorism in a speech that he gave in defense of his Irish roots, so it is only fitting that Chesnutt uses it here in defense of his African American roots.

In "The Negro in Books" (1916), a speech that Chesnutt makes in support of "The National Buy-a-Book Campaign in the Interest of Negro Literature," Chesnutt makes it known again that he is fully aware of the way that Black people of mixed heritage are portrayed in literature. He says: "We would like to read a novel in which the man of mixed blood is not always a traitor and a sneak, a degenerate or a pervert. We would like to read about a colored politician who is not a grafter, willing to sell his vote, himself and his people for a very mess of pottage" (McElrath et al. 1999: 436).

The proverbial expression "a mess of pottage" is a reference to Genesis 25:29–34 (KJV), in which Esau sells his birthright to Jacob for a single meal, thus denouncing his own heritage while receiving only a small meal in recompense. The use of the expression by Chesnutt is fitting because Chesnutt was often mistakenly thought to be white by people who did not know him personally, and he was offered to pass as white by several prospective employers in his lifetime, and he always refused such offers, choosing instead to embrace his Black heritage. Chesnutt also includes a direct reference to the same biblical passage in his novel *The Marrow of Tradition* (1901), which is addressed again later in this chapter. One character, Aunt Polly, exclaims, "Esau sold his birthright for a mess of pottage," in response to hearing about her family's land being sold to Black people (Andrews and Gates 2008: 301). Additionally, Chesnutt makes a reference to the very same Bible verse in a letter that he wrote to the Outlook Publishing Company. Chesnutt, in voicing his discontent with southern legislature's negative stance towards Black suffrage, says that although southern lawmakers "may be alright on paper, as the *Outlook* laboriously explains—the voice is the voice of Jacob, but the hand is the hand of Esau" (McElrath and Leitz 1997: 185). In other words, Chesnutt had very little trust for politicians in the South despite their efforts to appear to be in support of equal rights.

In "Negro Authors" (1918), a speech presented to the Association of Colored Men in Cleveland, Chesnutt opens his address with an interesting proverbial expression during a moment of levity as he talks about the experience of being Black and how it may have affected his life as a writer. He says:

> I am neither proud nor ashamed of the colored blood in my veins. If it has brought me any good, as I think it has—it gave me the impulse to write, the material for, and a hearing for the books to which I owe such a little reputation as I have, and the invitation to address you today—I am duly thankful for it. If it has subjected me to any disabilities, as I am sure it has, as it has all of us who share it, I have tried to bear them with patience and to look upon the bright side of the shield. (McElrath et al. 1999: 459)

The proverbial expression "to look upon the bright side of the shield" is an allusion to a folk tale that Chesnutt was familiar with. In the tale, two knights are approaching one another from opposite sides of a road when they begin to argue about the color of a shield which is suspended above the road. One knight insists that the shield is gold while the other knight contends that the shield is silver. They stage a jousting duel to settle the matter. It is only after they have both fallen off their horses that they realize they are both correct because the shield is gold on one side and silver on the other. Thus, the expression "to look upon the bright side of the shield" means that one is willing to acknowledge the fact that there may be positive aspects of any seemingly negative situation. Chesnutt is known to have first related this tale and expression in reference to the Washington/Du Bois political debate of his era. Washington believed that Blacks fared much better if they focused on obtaining financial independence by way of vocational education while Du Bois was in favor of Black people obtaining liberal education and fighting for equal rights in the process. Chesnutt, being close friends of both Washington and Du Bois, relates the tale of the two knights in his letter as a way of saying that they are both correct. In relating the tale and expression, he simultaneously articulates the uselessness of choosing a side when both positions may yield positive outcomes for Black people.

In addition to his refusal to take any one side on the Washington/Du Bois debate, Chesnutt also had his own unique stance which he articulates clearly in "Address Before the Ohio State Night School" (1928). In the speech, Chesnutt uses some common proverbial expressions that add emphasis to his message, while also giving his audience more insight into the distinctiveness of his position. Chesnutt says:

> Now, what is this equality that the colored people demand and cannot do without? Of course it does not imply and is not dependent upon parity of mental endowment, nor upon equal attainment. These things, other things being equal, cannot be conferred by law or by social custom. It means simply equality of opportunity—or as we phrase it, a white man's chance—in politics, in industry, in education, in the public service, in the social and professional activities of the community—in fact an equal opportunity everywhere, not in the dim and distant and uncertain future when the race has performed the impossible feat of lifting itself up by its boot-straps to the highest level of the white race, but now, while they are living and can make some use of that freedom of opportunity. (McElrath et al. 1999: 495–96)

Chesnutt makes it clear that he is not a proponent of conditional equality; instead, he demands a proverbial "white man's chance" for all African Americans in all areas of life, and not on the impossible condition that they pull themselves up by their own proverbial "bootstraps" (Whiting 1989: 67) to the levels of white people. For Chesnutt, equality was an urgent moral issue that needed to be addressed immediately and not an issue of a political nature.

Chesnutt returns to the issue of African American literature in "The Negro in Present Day Fiction" (1929). In this speech, he expresses his philosophy on good writing, saying: "Literature, like the fine arts and the best music, is, as I have said, the fruits of culture. 'You cannot gather grapes of thorns or figs of thistles'" (McElrath et al. 1999: 519). Chesnutt describes literature as the proverbial fruit of culture, and then follows with the proverb "you cannot gather grapes of thorns or figs of thistles," which is gleaned from scripture. It is also used by English writer Sir John William Watson (1858–1935), who uses it in his *Epigrams of Art, Life and Nature* (1847), (McElrath et al. 1999: 528) but one can clearly see how closely the proverb reflects the actual biblical passage, which reads: "Ye shall know them by their fruits. Do men gather grapes of thorns, or figs of thistles? Even so every good tree bringeth forth good fruit; but a corrupt tree bringeth forth evil fruit. A good tree cannot bring forth evil fruit, neither can a corrupt tree bring forth good fruit" (Matthew 7:16–18 KJV). The proverb expresses Chesnutt's belief that Black literature accurately reflects the African American experience. Chesnutt ingeniously reflects on the same biblical passage as he coins another famous saying regarding Black literature. In a speech entitled "The Literary Outlook" (1905), he says: "For literature after all is but an expression of life. Men write books as the trees put forth leaves, in obedience to the creative instinct" (McElrath et al. 1999: 212). Chesnutt closes his speech by returning to the very same metaphor, saying: "And as the life of our people grows broader and deeper and higher, so its literature will expand and become riper and finer and more enduring. And in due time, and that trust not long hence, works of men of Negro blood shall by common consent be ranked among those books which represent the finest fruit of American civilization" (McElrath et al. 1999: 213). Chesnutt's saying used in combination with his extended metaphor illustrates that he was very hopeful about the future of African American literature. Chesnutt also employs the saying during a speech to the Literary Historical Society in 1899. He says:

> Literature may be viewed in two aspects—as an expression of life, past and present, and as a force directly affecting the conduct of life, present and future. I might call these the subjective and objective sides of literature—or, more lucidly, the historical; and the dynamic, the forceful, the impelling. History is instructive, and may warn or admonish; but to this quality literature adds the faculty of persuasion,

by which men's hearts are reached, the springs of action touched, and the currents of life directed. (McElrath et al. 1999: 212; Izzo and Orban: 2009: 82)

Likewise, Chesnutt closes the speech "Literature in Its Relation to Life" (1899) by saying: "Literature is an expression of life. As another has tersely said, 'The literature of any age is but the mirror of its prevalent tendencies.' Would you know a nation, read its books" (McElrath et al. 1999: 114).

A prime example of the philosophy which is embodied by the saying "literature is an expression of life" is Chesnutt's realist novel, *The Marrow of Tradition*, which depicts the Wilmington Massacre of 1898. *Marrow* is a realist novel in the sense that it is written "in opposition to 'escapism,' calling on its readers to shift perspective so that they acknowledge, understand, and respond to the world's realities rather than averting their eyes" (Simmons 2006: 5). Chesnutt chose the title for the metaphor that it implies: that the tradition of racism is as deeply entrenched in American culture as the marrow that is engrained in human bones. *Marrow* is based solely on factual events which Chesnutt spent two weeks in Wilmington, North Carolina, researching, although he alters the names of people and places to protect the identities of those involved. Chesnutt even had several family members who lived there at the time provide him with their own personal accounts of what took place as well. Overall, the Wilmington Massacre involved the killing and displacement of hundreds of Black residents and the destruction of countless Black homes and thriving Black businesses. According to historian Ernestine Williams Pickens: "the rising black middle class, caused the white aristocrats and poor whites alike to feel insecure about their economic, social, and political positions" (Pickens 1994: 56). Consequently, the white aristocrats and poor whites joined forces against the Black bourgeoisie ultimately leading to the annihilation of the flourishing Black seaport community of Wilmington, North Carolina. Throughout his novel about the event, Chesnutt illustrates his belief that racism that pervaded the South was a moral issue and not one to be confused with convoluted politics. There are several instances in the novel in which Chesnutt uses proverbs to make his point regarding the unethical nature of racism. At one point in the novel, Chesnutt uses a proverb to describe the irreversible harm done after racist politicians stage a coup d'état to rest political control from the racially mixed party who gained control lawfully through local elections. The omniscient narrator says: "The great steal was made, but the thieves did not turn honest, — the scheme still shows the mark of the burglar's tools. Sins, like chickens, come home to roost. The South paid a fearful price for the wrong of negro slavery; in some form or other it will doubtless reap the fruits of this later iniquity" (Andrews and Gates 2008: 384). The proverb "sins, like chickens, come home to roost" is a variation of the proverb "chickens come home to roost" (Bryan and Mieder 2005: 149), and the narrator's use of it expresses the belief that the insurrectionists ultimately hurt themselves and the entire South. The premonition that the South will someday reap the proverbial fruits of this grave injustice to mankind alludes to the biblical proverb: "Be not deceived; God is not mocked: for whatsoever a man soweth, that shall he also reap" (Galatians 6:7 KJV). In *The Marrow of Tradition*, Chesnutt refers to the proverb "as you sow, so shall you reap" (Mieder 2001: 444) on several instances. At one point in the novel the proverb is used to characterize one of the racist antagonists, Captain McBane. The narrator says: "McBane had lived a life of violence and cruelty. As a man sows, so shall he reap. In works of fiction, such men are sometimes converted. More often, in real life, they do not change their natures until they are converted into dust. One does well to distrust a tamed tiger" (Andrews and Gates 2008: 429). McBane is ultimately killed by Black militant vigilante Josh Green in an act of retribution for killing Green's father years earlier.

At another point in the novel, during the midst of the town massacre, the wife of a white aristocrat, Olivia Carteret, begs the husband of her estranged Black half-sister, Janet, to save her infant son who lies dying of an ailment that is preventing him from breathing. Olivia is quickly running out of time to save her child, and Janet's Black husband, Dr. Miller, is the only one who can save him, but he adamantly refuses to help her. In a final act of desperation, Olivia convinces her husband, Major Carteret, who is also one of the white supremacists behind the riot, to beg of Dr. Miller's services, but since Dr. Miller is Black, helping the Carteret's would mean breaking the color line. Another caveat is that saving Olivia's child would also require him to abandon his own grieving wife, who sits by the bedside of their toddler son who has just been killed after being struck by a bullet from town rioters. Dr. Miller uses the proverb as he explains his calamity to Major Carteret. Dr. Miller says:

> There he lies . . . an innocent child . . . dead, his little life snuffed out like a candle, because you and a handful of your friends thought you must override the laws and run this town at any cost!—and there kneels his mother, overcome by grief. We are alone in the house. It is not safe to leave her unattended. My duty calls me here, by the side of my dead child and my suffering wife! I cannot go with you. There is a just God in heaven! —as you have sown, so may you reap! (Andrews and Gates: 441)

The narrator emphasizes the proverb's meaning in explaining that Major Carteret fully understands Dr. Miller's rationale for not wanting to save his dying child: "Miller's refusal to go with him was pure elemental justice, to avenge his own wrongs. In Dr. Miller's place he would have done the same thing. Miller had spoken the truth, —as he had sown, so must he reap! He could not expect, could not ask, this father to leave his own household at such a moment" (Andrews and Gates 2008: 441). The novel ends abruptly as Dr. Miller finally agrees to save the Carteret's dying infant. The novel's resolution is only reached after underscoring the importance of the proverbial message several times. The biblical proverb "as you sow, so shall you reap" (Mieder 2001: 444) provides the novel with a seamless reflection of Chesnutt's belief that the Wilmington Massacre, like all acts of racism, are the result of flawed morals—a problem for which Chesnutt saw dire consequences for the nation if left unresolved. Nevertheless, Chesnutt did not want to anger his audience with *Marrow*; he instead wanted to "clarify that the work of ending racism is work for both whites and nonwhites" (Simmons 2006: 102).

Chesnutt ends *The Marrow of Tradition* on a positive note, but a letter to his close friend and editor George Cable reveals Chesnutt alluding to the proverb without expressing the same kind of optimism that he does in *Marrow*. Chesnutt, responding to a national outbreak of lynchings, writes:

> The shootings in Mississippi and Louisiana, the whippings in Georgia, and the burning at the stake in Kentucky, not to mention such trifles as burning postmasters in effigy—, would seem to be rather a bad way. If things keep on at this rate much longer, I shall be compelled to believe, with Judge Tourgée, that serious and widespread race troubles in the South are not improbable in the near future. Such conflicts would probably result to the injury of the negroes, but as sure as there is heaven and an earth the white people of the South are sowing a crop from which they will reap an abundant harvest of hatred; the plant has already attained a vigorous growth, and what its fruit will be none can tell. (McElrath and Leitz 1997: 42)

Chesnutt, while still in his youth, decided that he would use literature as a way of convincing prejudice people of the immoral nature of racism. However, Chesnutt knew that many Americans were still ambivalent about the issue, and that some would even be quick to resist his antiracist messages. In turn, Chesnutt decided that he would entertain people with his work as opposed to the more direct approach that he would take in his public speeches. His fiction, in his own words, would provide him with a way to "accustom the public mind to the idea; and while amusing people, lead them on, imperceptibly, unconsciously step-by-step to the desired state of feeling" (Keller: 1978: 77; Simmons 2006: 99). The feelings that Chesnutt wanted to achieve in his audience would be compassion and understanding as opposed to the cold indifference toward the issue of racism, which had become the norm. Chesnutt, expressing great enthusiasm for his decision wrote in his journal, "I would gladly devote my life to the work" (Keller: 1978: 77). While this chapter is not a survey of every single saying, proverb, or proverbial expression that Chesnutt ever used, it does demonstrate that proverbs and proverbial expressions were an important part of Chesnutt's verbal repertoire as he sought to affect the emotional sentimentalities of wide-ranging and diverse American audiences. Chapter three explores the life and proverbial language use of civil rights activist A. Philip Randolph (1889–1979). There is no doubting the fact that Randolph was positively influenced by the work of his predecessors, Wells and Chesnutt. Randolph holds an interesting place in civil rights history due to the fact that his social justice efforts transcends nearly an entire century—connecting what scholars recognize as the long civil rights movement (Hall 2005) to contemporary civil rights struggles which are still ongoing.

Chapter Three

"WINNING FREEDOM AND EXACTING JUSTICE"

A. Philip Randolph's Use of Proverbs and Proverbial Language

A. Philip Randolph (April 15, 1889–May 16, 1979), considered by many to be the father of the modern civil rights era, is one of the most important and dynamic political figures in America for several reasons. Randolph was the driving force behind the biggest watershed moment in American civil rights history. The March on Washington for Jobs and Freedom took place on August 28, 1963. At seventy-four years of age, Randolph, and his March on Washington Movement Committee would lead over 250,000 peaceful protesters to the steps of the Lincoln Memorial in what would be the largest display of nonviolent direct action ever recorded. For many, this event represents the pinnacle of Randolph's political influence, and it is the event that would propel Martin Luther King Jr. to international prominence. From a historical perspective, the 1963 March on Washington for Jobs and Freedom became known as a figurative passing of the torch, from Randolph to King, or from the old guard to the new, but in addition to the march, Randolph should be remembered for a lot of different reasons. Firstly, Randolph is one of the first Black leaders of the early twentieth century to demand economic, social, and political freedom for African Americans, at a time when most of Black America was divided on such issues. The Booker T. Washington, W. E. B. Du Bois, and Marcus Garvey debates had reached their height during the mid-twentieth century, and many felt that Blacks should focus on either economic gain, which Washington advocated for, social and political advancement, which was supported largely by Du Bois with his "talented tenth" ideology, or complete separatism, which Garvey promoted with the Back to Africa movement. Randolph instead insisted on total equality for all people and regarded the philosophies of his contemporaries as being separatist and undemocratic. Secondly, Randolph's success in implementing nonviolent direct action as a sustainable form of protest helped to make peaceful mass demonstrations common place in American society.[1] Lastly, Randolph initiated the African American labor movement. The Socialist Party was a valuable political platform for Randolph during his early years because they claimed to advocate for the rights of all workers, but they were not very concerned with achieving better wages and working conditions for Blacks. Randolph was concerned specifically with African American worker's rights, and after fighting for over a decade, he was able to establish the nation's first predominantly Black labor union, the Brotherhood of Sleeping Car Porters (BSCP) on August 25, 1925. This huge accomplishment would serve as a natural segue from the labor movement to the civil rights era. The first labor union of its kind, this milestone achievement helped to pave the way for a succession of monumental events that would soon follow. For instance, he established the Fair Employment Practices Committee (FEPC), which sought to end wage discrimination and prejudice in hiring practices, and aimed for the eventual desegregation of all areas of American society. Over the years, several presidents would issue executive orders that would help to alleviate the problems of racism, segregation, and unfair wages largely paid to African Americans and poor whites. Yet, the most important detail about this era in history is that the many changes in legislation that took place during the twentieth century, including President Roosevelt's 1941 executive order that ended racial prejudice in American defense industries and President Truman's 1948 executive order to abolish segregation in the military, would more than likely have simply amounted to nothing more than empty promises if Randolph did not apply constant political pressure to acting commanders in chief and their governing bodies. Randolph "talked personally with every President since Calvin Coolidge. To all he had pleaded for justice for black people. Sometimes he met with failure, sometimes with success. But every President for . . . forty years knew that sooner or later, Phil Randolph would be on his doorstep asking him to take political risks on behalf of black citizens" (Davis 1972: 149–50).

Randolph had several personal traits that made him an effective political leader. He was largely a self-taught and independent thinker. He was always smart, graduating at the top of his class from the Cookman Institute (now Bethune-Cookman College) and serving as the valedictorian of his class in 1907. When he moved to Harlem in 1911, he took advantage of the many free courses offered at the City College of New York. He valued knowledge greatly throughout his entire life. Randolph also possessed the unwavering values of honesty, integrity, and fearlessness. These important values would be exemplified repeatedly throughout his lifetime through his use of proverbs and proverbial language. This chapter argues that it is, in fact, Randolph's proverbial proficiency that allowed his strong values to be transformed into political weapons. Although Randolph did not use proverbs frequently, when he did employ them, it was done to move people emotionally and for the purpose of persuasion—either to persuade political adversaries or to persuade political constituents.

Proverbs have and always will play important roles in uniting multitudes of people in America for the cause of social justice, and it is important to realize were Randolph falls on this continuum. According to Mieder, proverbs may be defined as "concise traditional statements of apparent truths with currency among the folk. More elaborately stated, proverbs are short, generally known sentences of the folk that contain wisdom, truths, morals, and traditional views in a metaphorical, fixed and memorizable form and that are handed down from generation to generation" (Mieder 2004: 4). Additionally, from a stylistic perspective, there are several poetic devices such as alliteration, parallelism, hyperbole, paradox, personification, and metaphor which may serve as internal and external markers (Mieder 2004). The transmission of important ideas and values are a very significant function of proverbs. In this sense they may also be viewed as "well-established ideology" configured to a "certain form" (Fabian 1990: 29). Understanding the significant amount of moral authority that people place in proverbs helps political figures such as Randolph to employ them strategically. He often used a number of different kinds of proverbs, and surprisingly enough, the proverbs that Randolph used are not shown to have African origins. According to folklorist and peremiologist Anand Prahlad: "Based on the printed collections, we can safely say that very few proverbs in currency among African Americans are of African origin. A primary reason for this is that proverb texts exist as preformed linguistic units, making the retention of items difficult in an extreme situation such as slavery, where language groups were stripped of their native tongues and given new ones to replace them" (1996: 28). This explains why among all the many different sources for proverbs that Randolph uses, none of them seem to be African.

As opposed to a chronological organization, this chapter is organized according to the different sources for proverbs that Randolph employed. The first major source of proverbs for Randolph is the Bible. Biblical proverbs appear most frequently in Randolph's writings. The second source of proverbs to be discussed here are the sayings that Randolph employs that come from important political figures. The third source for proverbs that are addressed are the proverbs that Randolph uses that may be attributed to famous literary figures. In mapping out a discussion of Randolph's proverb use, it is important to note that Randolph used all the proverbs recorded here with one purpose in mind, to advance the causes of social justice, and it is in this sense that they may also be viewed as political weapons. According to Mieder, proverbs frequently materialize through economic circumstances, and in his fight for social, political, and economic freedom for African Americans, Randolph was able to coin several memorable sayings of his own, so lastly, there will be discussion of some of the proverbs that Randolph created himself.

Randolph's biblical adages comprise the majority of the extensive repertoire of sayings that he would use frequently. Many of these sayings were more than likely acquired as a young child in Florida. Randolph was born in Crescent City, Florida, on April 15, 1889, to James and Elizabeth Randolph, who were both a part of the very first generation of newly emancipated slaves. Throughout his early years, James Sr., an African Methodist Episcopal minister, would instill in Randolph a love for learning. Randolph and his older brother, James Jr., read daily with their parent's insistence. The Reverend James Randolph spent a lot of time searching the shelves of old bookstores to find texts that he felt his sons should read. He wanted his sons to be familiar with the history of the AME church as well as about every Black leader in America, including "Hannibal, Crispus Attucks, Nat Turner, Denmark Vesey, Toussaint L' Ouverture, Frederick Douglass, and Richard Allen" (Taylor 2006: 11). They would also often spend countless hours reading the Bible, arguing about the meaning of scripture, and, against their parent's wishes, debating the existence of God. In addition to reading literature, they would also spend time listening to their father's sermons and the sermons of other southern Black ministers which were, no doubt, filled with proverbial folk wisdom. Although Randolph became an atheist in adulthood, southern African Methodist Episcopal values would be ingrained in him for the rest of his life.

The values that Randolph acquired in the AME church and the values that his parents instilled in him were always on full display because of his proverb proficiency. Proverbs never dominated Randolph's oratory, but he did use them at times in very strategic and calculated ways such as to emphasize important points, or to end his speeches or letters. Many of the proverbs that Randolph used were from the Bible—a book that is filled with well-known proverbs that can easily be used to contextualize the plight of Black people in America, which is more than likely one reason they suited Randolph's purposes so well. Furthermore, Randolph knew from personal experience as a preacher's son that biblical proverbs generally resonate well with large audiences.

During his commencement address at Morgan State College in 1959, Randolph works hard to communicate some of his values to the graduating student body, and he uses important well-known proverbs from scripture in the process. Throughout the speech he urges students to read often, to register to vote, and to invest in Black communities. Randolph ends his commencement address by employing a biblical proverb. He says, "The night, however dark, is never endless. The star of the break of dawn is not far. The hour of decision and action is now. In the words of the Psalmist, 'I will lift mine eyes unto the hills from whence cometh my strength'" (Kersten and Lucander 2014: 256). The first statement is an allusion to the proverb "the darkest hour is that before the dawn" first recorded in the biblical writings of English author Thomas Fuller, in 1650 (*A Pisgah- Sight of Palestine*) (Wilson 1970: 168). It is also used on at least a few occasions by Martin Luther King Jr. (Mieder 2010: 348); the second part of Randolph's closing statement, "I will lift mine eyes . . ." (KJV Psalms 121), is also biblical. The complete idea in this passage is best captured in reading the first two lines of Psalms 121 together, which reads, "I will lift mine eyes unto the hills from whence cometh my help, My help cometh from the LORD which made heaven and earth" (KJV Psalms 121). The first line having become proverbial through frequent usage, is used by Randolph on several different occasions to instill a sense of faith in his audiences and to encourage them to stay strong in the face of adversity. It takes hearing only a very small portion of the first line of this very powerful passage to remind Randolph's audience that in difficult times, help will only come from God. Furthermore, Randolph wants his audience to realize that the fight for justice will be long and difficult, and that they will be able to continue the fight by keeping faith.

In "African Methodism and the Negro in the Western World" (1962), a speech made in commemoration of the Diamond Jubilee of the Bermuda African Methodist Episcopal Conference, Randolph celebrates the history of the AME church. In the speech, he also emphasizes the significance of the church's role in American and African American history, and he praises the AME founder, ex-slave Richard Allen, by characterizing him as a revolutionary thinker along the same lines as European Protestant reformist Martin Luther (Kersten and Lucander 2014). Randolph says:

> And in reaffirming his deep concern about the people, Jesus said: "I have compassion on the multitude because they have now been with me three days and have nothing to eat. And if I sent them away fasting to their own houses they will faint by the way, for divers of them came from far." And he blessed a few loaves of bread and fishes and

fed them. This strange witness of the will of God startled his followers, when he observed: "For whosoever will save his life shall lose it, but whosoever shall lose his life for my sake and the gospel's, the same shall save it." He shocked the Pharisees, Sadducees and scribes, as well as his own disciples, when he declared: "It is easier for a camel to go through the eye of a needle than for a rich man to enter the kingdom of God." (Kersten and Lucander 2014: 148–49)

The biblical proverb "it is easier for a camel to go through the eye of a needle than for a rich man to enter the kingdom of God" (KJV Mark 10:25) is used here to stress the important values of: leadership, selflessness, compassion, devotion, and generosity. In the biblical passage recited by Randolph, Jesus places the needs of his followers above his own needs and Jesus is employing the proverb to further emphasize to his followers, the importance of self-sacrifice. His followers have suffered to travel with him and Jesus ultimately, rewards his disciples for their devotion. He also wants to emphasize the importance of helping others while denouncing earthly materialism. These are all values that have been fundamental to the AME church since its inception. Randolph lived his life according to these same principles which is why, in his later years, those that were still around him largely viewed him as a Christ-like figure. Many knew that his dream of Black liberation started in his youth during Reconstruction. According to historian Cynthia Taylor, "As a young man, he dreamed about 'carrying on some program for the abolition of racial discrimination' because his generation had an obligation to engage in pursuits that would benefit all people regardless of color. 'I got this from my father,' Randolph observed, 'that you must not be concerned about yourself alone in this world'" (2006: 8). Randolph is trying to convince his audience to stay true to themselves and to not place value on material items. He is also imparting on them one of his greatest strengths as a political leader, that is, his selflessness. It is well documented in history texts that Randolph would not sell out, and he could not be bought. Randolph would often shun material wealth for the cause of gaining economic and political freedom for African Americans. For instance, Randolph always refused to be overpaid as the leader of any organization that he was a part of including the Brotherhood of Sleeping Car Porters (BSCP), preferring instead to pay his staff and to use excess funds to maintain daily operations. When political rivals sent him a check for an exorbitant amount money to try to convince him to abandon the cause, Randolph returned the check with a simple message attached that read, "Negro principle, not for sale" (Santino 1983: 407). During the height of economic depression, when Randolph and most of his

BSCP affiliates were literally struggling to survive, Randolph would refuse a high-ranking position from the then-mayor of New York City, Fiorello H. LaGuardia, even though the position came with an annual salary of $7,000 per year (roughly $130,000 in today's currency). Based on these events from Randolph's life, one can easily see that Randolph always shunned worldly riches to advance the movement.

According to Mieder, proverbs of all kinds, even biblical ones, when used politically, may be used with positive or negative intentions. As Mieder asserts in *The Politics of Proverbs: From Traditional Wisdom to Proverbial Stereotypes*: "As can be imagined, proverbs as a powerful verbal tool in the hands of politicians become a two-edged sword, employed both as a positive and negative device to influence, if not manipulate, citizens" (1997: 4). Randolph primarily used proverbs in positive ways, but there does exist at least one instance, in which biblical proverbs are used to characterize political opponents negatively. "A New Crowd—A New Negro" (1919) was first published in Randolph's *Messenger* magazine. Randolph edited *The Messenger* with Chandler Owen from 1917 to 1928. The magazine was used to denounce prejudice, racial violence, and to promote Socialism as an answer to global capitalism and racial oppression. Inspired by the Russian Revolution (1917–23) and similar political uprisings that opposed traditional European hierarchies during the late nineteenth and early twentieth centuries, Randolph felt that these movements were a clear sign of a global paradigm shift in political thought (Kersten and Lucander: 2014). In "A New Crowd—A New Negro," Randolph argues that the ineptitude of the Republican Party to address lynching and increasing racial violence in America has become apparent enough for Blacks to finally abandon them for the Socialist Party. In doing so, he characterizes this new generation of politics as representing both a "New Crowd" and "New Negro" while Blacks who still place their faith in the Republican Party represent the "Old Crowd" of Black leadership. In addition to representing Black Republicans, it becomes evident, in part, through Randolph's use of biblical proverbs that the "Old Crowd" also represents the Black church and their failure to engage in social and political issues. Randolph says:

> In the church the old crowd still preaches that "the meek will inherit the earth," "if the enemy strikes you on one side of the face, turn the other," and "you may take all this world but give me Jesus." "Dry Bones," "The Three Hebrew Children in the Fiery Furnace" and "Jonah in the Belly of the Whale," constitute the subjects of the Old Crowd, for black men and women who are overworked and underpaid, lynched, Jim Crowed and disfranchised—a people who are yet

languishing in the dungeons of ignorance and superstition. Such then is the Old Crowd. And this is not strange to the student of history, economics, and sociology. (Kersten and Lucander 2014: 123)

The proverbs "the meek will inherit the earth" (KJV Psalm 37:11; KJV Matthew 5:5) and "if the enemy strikes you on one side of the face, turn the other cheek" (KJV Matthew 5:39)[2] are both used negatively in this instance by Randolph to represent issues with the Black church that he felt would eventually be detrimental to all African Americans—namely, the Black church's complacency with pulpit politics, blind faith in the Republican Party, and their ineffectiveness in addressing racial violence. As Randolph asserts, the New Crowd "would not send notes after a Negro is lynched" (Kersten and Lucander 2014: 124).

The "A New Crowd—A New Negro" issue was published immediately following the "Red Summer" of 1919 when at least twenty-five bloody race riots erupted across several states and nearly forty cities. Nearly three hundred African Americans were murdered and at least five whites were killed. According to Taylor, "Randolph and Owen judged the Negro Church's apolitical, antiracial position as a contributing factor in the riots" (2006: 49). Randolph and Owen knew that racial prejudice was the primary cause of the riots, and according to them breeding grounds for race hatred were "American institutions like social clubs and groups, schools, newspapers, and the Christian Church ... [and] as part of the Christian Church, the Negro church was just as guilty" (Taylor 2006: 49).

In addition to publishing the article, Randolph and Owen printed a political cartoon alongside it using the proverb from Matthew 5:39 as a caption.[3] "Above the caption 'Following the Advice of the Old Crowd Negro' are three figures: Booker T. Washington saying, 'Be modest and unassuming'; W. E. B. Du Bois saying, 'Close ranks. Let us forget our grievances'; and a third figure in clerical collar and garb saying, 'When they smite thee on one cheek—Turn the other.' The second cartoon above the caption 'The New Crowd Negro Making America Safe for Himself' depicts a young Negro driving an armored car while shooting at soldiers, saying, 'Since the government won't stop mob violence, I'll take a hand'" (Taylor 2006: 49). Although they are political cartoons, Randolph seriously believes that the Black church should play a much larger role in putting an end to lynchings and mob violence. As a young child, Randolph witnessed his father, Reverend James Randolph Sr., preventing the lynching of a Black man who had been accused of molesting a white woman. After hearing that a lynch mob was on its way to the county jail, Randolph's father tucked a handgun underneath his jacket and gathered as many church members as he could to go and meet the angry mob. His wife, Elizabeth, with young Asa and James Jr. would keep watch at home on the front porch with a shotgun resting comfortably across her lap. Randolph Sr. successfully averted the mob, and no one was hurt or injured, but the notion that the church should play an active role in preventing lynching stayed with Randolph all of his life, and he fought to instill this notion in others. At no point would Randolph ever advocate "turning the other cheek" (Anderson 1972: 42; Taylor 2006: 7).

Randolph would publish another article the same year entitled "The Failure of the Negro Church" (1919) in which he would criticize the Black church for rejecting labor unionization and for placing too much emphasis on increasing its own profits. In the article, Randolph asserts that "collections occupy three-fourths of the time of most services. Sermons are selected with a view to impressing the members with the importance of the injunction that 'it is more blessed to give than to receive'" (Kersten and Lucander 2014: 125). Randolph exemplifies his criticism of the church with the popular biblical proverb "it is more blessed to give than to receive" (KJV Acts 20:35). While this proverb is generally viewed as containing a positive message, it is used in this instance negatively, to illustrate ways that the wealthy Black church, as an institution, is effectively stifling the social, political, and economic progress of African Americans. Many felt that Randolph's frequent attacks on the Black church signaled his conversion to atheism which Randolph, at the time, would neither confirm nor deny to prevent the loss of supporters.

Regardless of Randolph's position on the existence of God, Randolph still felt that the Black church offered a spiritual model for what he had hoped to achieve for African Americans in the labor movement, and many agree that his use of biblical proverbs illustrate this fact. As Kersten and Lang assert: "To have the porters build a union as they had helped members of their racial group build powerful churches was the motive behind Randolph's use of religious appeal and terminology . . . 'Ye shall know the truth, and the truth shall set you free' was the heading for most of the bulletins sent out by national headquarters of the Brotherhood and [was also] used on the cover page of the Brotherhood's publication *The Black Worker*" (2015: 24–25). In general, Randolph felt that religion would always be a major source of spiritual strength for most African Americans, and he also knew that he could easily tap into this force whenever he wanted to by using biblical proverbs as powerful forms of political rhetoric.

In addition to biblical proverbs, Randolph also employed the well-known proverbs of famous political figures such as Karl Marx, Alexander Hamilton,

Booker T. Washington, Henry Highland Garnet, and Frederick Douglass. The sayings that Randolph chose are as equally significant as the political figures that he borrowed them from. In a *Messenger* article entitled "Lynching; Capitalism Its Cause; Socialism Its Cure" (1919), Randolph, in an appeal for socialism, says: "Black and white workers unite. You have nothing to lose but your chains; you have the world to gain" (Kersten and Lucander 2014: 122). The proverb is taken from chapter four of Marx's *Communist Manifesto* (1888). The original passage reads: "The proletarians have nothing to lose but their chains. They have a world to win." Randolph's spin on these famous lines illustrates the faith that he placed in Marx, and it also illustrates the extent that he was familiar with Marx's writings. It is well documented that in his early years, Randolph read Marx like most children would read fairy tales. Throughout Randolph's early adulthood, he remained highly engrossed in Marx, and there is no doubt that Marx provided Randolph with a model for fighting for the rights of the working class in the United States.

From Hamilton, one of the founding fathers of the United States, Randolph acquires the proverb "the power over a man's subsistence is the power over his will." The proverb is written into the Constitution of Massachusetts by Hamilton in 1780 and the proverb seems to encapsulate the foundational tenet of chapter 2, section I, article 13. The opening of this section reads:

> NEXT to permanency in office, nothing can contribute more to the independence of the judges than a fixed provision for their support. The remark made in relation to the President is equally applicable here. In the general course of human nature, A POWER OVER A MAN'S SUBSISTENCE AMOUNTS TO A POWER OVER HIS WILL. And we can never hope to see realized in practice, the complete separation of the judicial from the legislative power, in any system which leaves the former dependent on pecuniary resources on the occasional grants of the latter. (emphasis in original) (*The Avalon Project, Yale*)

This section of the Constitution establishes the separation of the judicial and legislative branches of government, and the proverb in this case is employed to emphasize the fact that this stark division of powers is imposed to prevent any degree of interdependence among the various branches of government. Randolph's use of the proverb is evidence that he was well-versed in political science. He would employ this proverb on at least three notable occasions, in *The Messenger* article entitled "The Negro in Politics" (1919), at another time while speaking before the US Senate Committee on Interstate Commerce

(1934), and in an article entitled "March on Washington Movement Presents Program for the Negro" (1944).

In "The Negro in Politics," Randolph is basically advocating for the Socialist Party as a solution to many problems that African Americans faced during Reconstruction, which included racial violence, disenfranchisement, joblessness, and industrial capitalism. Randolph feels that if African Americans continue to put their moral and financial support in either the Democratic or Republican Party, they will only continue to see the same results. Randolph says, "Negro leaders, generally, have been creatures of the Republican or Democratic Parties, which hold them in leash and prevent them from initiating consideration of the appointment policy. Aptly, and truly too, has it been said that the 'power over a man's subsistence is the power over his will' or expressed more popularly 'he who pays the fiddler will call the tune'" (169). Randolph often liked to stack these two proverbs together. The second proverb, "he who pays the fiddler will call the tune," has been documented as early as 1895 and is much more common; not being attributed to any single individual (Speake 2015: 244; Wilson 1970: 615). In some ways, Randolph's use of the proverb "the power over a man's subsistence is the power over his will" is a direct reflection of Hamilton's reason for employing it in the Constitution. Hamilton wants to emphasize the dangers of granting too much power to any single branch of government, while Randolph employs it to emphasize that African Americans are granting too much power to the Republicans and Democrats who have been largely unsuccessful in fighting on their behalf. In other words, if African Americans continue to financially support the same political factions, then they would continue to be pigeonholed.

The scenario is slightly different, but the message is the same when Randolph speaks before the US Senate Committee on Interstate Commerce in 1934. Randolph is advocating for a bill to amend the 1934 Railway Labor Act, because the bill would greatly help the chances of the Brotherhood of Sleeping Car Porters (BSCP) gaining union recognition and collective bargaining rights. Randolph must convince the committee that if the bill is not passed, then the Railway Labor Act will be in danger of being severely weakened. In an authentic display of true diplomacy, Randolph would employ the two proverbs at the most opportune moment. Randolph says, "If you eliminate that phase of the bill, permitting the companies to pay the representatives of the company unions, then you really destroy the power of the bill, because if the companies are able to pay the representatives of the company union, then they will be able to intimidate the employees and practically prevent them from joining legitimate and bona-fide unions. So, that I think is basic, because the power over a man's subsistence is the power over his will, and usually the man who pays the fiddler calls the tunes, so the Pullman Company by paying these representatives of the company union, they make them do just what they want done" (Kersten and Lucander 2014: 62–63). According to anthropologist Ruth Finnegan, in some African societies proverbs are often used for the purpose of deliberation. She says, "In court and elsewhere there are also frequent occasions for using a proverb to smooth over a disagreement or bring a dispute to a close. According to the Yoruba proverb, 'A counsellor who understands proverbs soon sets matters right,'[4] and a difficult law case is often ended by the public citation of an apt proverb which performs much the same generalizing function as citing legal precedents in other societies" (Finnegan 1970: 28).[5] The proverbs that Randolph employs are not African in origin, but this information is evidence that there is a universal element to the way that they function. Finnegan also explains that proverbs may also help one to maintain composure during times of social conflict. She says: "Though proverbs can occur in very many different kinds of contexts, they seem to be particularly important in situations where there is both conflict and, at the same time, some obligation that this conflict should not take on too open and personal a form" (1970: 30). It is well documented that Randolph never used profanity or "lost his cool" during intense battles in courtrooms or during White House visits. Therefore, one may assert that proverbs may have helped Randolph to maintain his poise.

A decade later, Randolph would use the same two proverbs again in "March on Washington Movement Presents Program for the Negro" (1944). According to historians Andrew E. Kersten and David Lucander, this represents Randolph's clearest articulation of the aims of the March on Washington Movement (MOWM) because Randolph's philosophy is so thoroughly explained, and his political goals are so intricately mapped out. In this article, he argues for a number of things, including unity among the Black race, Black unionization, equal employment, the widespread use of nonviolent direct action, mass social pressure in the form of marches, and a nonpartisan Negro political block. In a subsection entitled *Political*, Randolph articulates what he sees as a need for a Black nonpartisan political bloc. Randolph says:

> It is common knowledge that Negroes as Democrats do not amount to much. They can get but little done for Negroes. Similarly, Negroes as Republicans are not very strong and their voice is seldom heeded. Negroes as Socialists or Communist are helpless, but when Negro Republicans, and Democrats step forward in a united front expressed in a powerful non-partisan political bloc, they will be heard and

heeded by political boss or mayor, governor, president, Senate or House Committees. (Kersten and Lucander 2014: 219)

Randolph is still arguing for increased African American involvement in politics, only now he is abandoning the notion of partisanship all together. As Randolph continues, he reiterates his point by employing the same two proverbs, and they are as equally applicable. The concluding paragraph of this section reads:

> Therefore, upwards of 15 millions of Negroes need not forever play the role of political mendicants. They have power if they will mobilize by registering in mass for non-partisan political action. Such a political bloc should be financed by Negroes entirely. It is still true that the power over man's subsistence is the power of his will, and he who pays the fiddler calls the tune. Therefore, such a non-partisan political bloc should not accept any money from Republican, Democratic, Socialist or Communist Party. It should be entirely free. It cannot be free if it is subsidized by any politicians. (Kersten and Lucander 2014: 219–20)

Randolph envisions a Black voting body that is united and fully able to advocate for the needs of the African American community. Randolph employs the two proverbs to emphasize the notion that this Black political bloc would need to maintain its economic freedom to continue to be effective. "The power over a man's subsistence is the power over his will" rang true for Hamilton in the late eighteenth century, and it is remarkable that it would still be equally relevant for Randolph nearly two centuries later.

Earlier in his career, Randolph would use a proverb that was coined by former slave and abolitionist Frederick Douglass. Douglass's successful struggle for freedom would be used as a theme in a 1926 *Bulletins* leaflet for the Brotherhood of Sleeping Car Porters (BSCP). *Bulletins* were one-page publications that were created to supplement *The Messenger* because they were much less expensive to produce (Hawkins 2015: 105–6). This particular *Bulletins* edition features a sculpture entitled "The Chrysalis," which depicts a kneeling Black minstrel performer, hat in hand, begging for change. Emerging from the minstrel is a respectable, dignified, looking Black man wearing a suit. One caption reads: "Douglass fought for the abolition of chattel slavery and today we fight for economic freedom. The time has passed when a grown-up black man should beg a grown up white man for anything" (Hawkins 2015: 105). Another feature of this leaflet is a short letter written to BSCP members from Randolph which reads: "Ye Brotherhood men, hold high your banner of solidarity. Remember that a quitter never wins and a winner never quits. Remember that he who would be free must himself first strike the blow. Let us stand firm and be unafraid. Pay your dues and assessment. The Mediation Board will call us soon. If we fight and faint not, we shall reap our just reward in due season" (Kersten and Lang 2015: 105). Frederick Douglass and the abolitionist cause serve as the theme, while the adage embodies the primary message. The proverb "he who would be free must himself strike the first blow" is generally credited to Douglass, even though he was certainly not the first to use it. In fact, he was not even the first abolitionist to use it. Henry Highland Garnet employs this proverb in his "Address to the Slaves of the United States of America" (1843). Garnet's address would first appear as a preface to the second edition of abolitionist David Walker's *Appeal to the Coloured Citizens of the World* (1830). In the address, Garnet says, "It is an old and true saying, that 'if hereditary bondmen would be free, they must themselves strike the blow.'" More than likely, as an ode to his abolitionist predecessor, Douglass would employ the same proverb in a famous speech that he would deliver on the streets of Rochester, New York, on March 2, 1863, entitled "Men of Color, to Arms." In the speech, Douglass says: "Words are now useful only as they stimulate to blows. The office of speech now is only to point out when, where, and how to strike to the best advantage.... 'Now or never.' Liberty won by white men would lose half its luster. 'Who would be free themselves must strike the blow.'" In using Douglass as a theme and employing the same proverb, Randolph can effectively communicate to porters that the fight for union representation would be a herculean battle, but certainly no more difficult than the struggle for emancipation. Randolph is also emphasizing the fact that it is a battle that they must initiate and fight themselves.

There are also other proverbs included in this leaflet as well. For instance, there is "a quitter never wins, and a winner never quits" (Doyle, Mieder, and Shapiro 2012: 277) as well as several truncated proverbs. "Fight and faint not" and "we shall reap our just reward" are both biblical references to verses that appear in the book of Galatians. The actual Bible verse reads, "And let us not be weary in well doing: for in due season we shall reap, if we faint not" (KJV Galatians 6:9). It may also be a truncated version of the proverb "for whatever a man soweth, that shall he also reap" (KJV Galatians 6:7). When Randolph employs proverbs even in truncated forms, he does so very strategically, and they are always meaningful.

In "The March on Washington Movement and the War" (1943), Randolph is warning all involved in the March on Washington Movement (MOWM) that nonviolent direct action would not be an easy tactic to implement, especially in the face of extreme violence, but fear of retaliation would jeopardize the entire cause. In the process of communicating this message, Randolph alludes to an important passage from Garnet's "Address to the Slaves of the United States of America" (1843). Randolph says: "a people who have fear in their hearts are doomed to be slaves" (Taylor 2006: 163). Exactly, one hundred years before Randolph, Garnet would use nearly identical language in speaking about the abysmal emotional and psychological state of the newly arrived Africans to the new world. Garnet says: "But, they came with broken hearts, from their beloved native land, and were doomed to unrequited toil, and deep degradation." For Garnet, his address is a call to awaken the spirits of African Americans who remain in bondage in the South. Unlike the newly arrived Africans, Garnet wants them to forget their troubles and unite for the purpose of freeing themselves. Perhaps Randolph's variation of the passage is a centennial celebration of Garnet's famous address which was delivered exactly one hundred years prior. After all, it was near this time that Randolph would send King and other civil rights leaders to be trained in nonviolent direct action by the Highlander Folk School, which was built and dedicated to Garnet in 1932.

In 1964, Randolph would receive a humanitarian award presented to him by Histadrut, whose name translates as "General Federation of Laborers of the Land of Israel." According to Kersten and Lucander: "As a trade unionist and believer in independence for the colonial world, Randolph looked to Israel as an example in nation building. . . . Randolph saw great value in Israeli collective farming practices and the potential of consumer co-ops to empower the working class" (Kersten and Lucander 2014: 342). In Randolph's acceptance speech, he would employ a proverb that was popularized by Booker T. Washington, who used it in his "Atlanta Compromise" (1895): "cast down your bucket where you are" may not have been a proverb at the time, but after gaining international fame, for most it only takes this brief sentence to convey Washington's entire message. When Washington says, "Cast down your bucket where you are," it is a way of describing in metaphorical terms, to an all-white audience, the need for African Americans to abandon their fight for social and political freedom and to focus instead on improving their own economic circumstances by concentrating on learning agricultural and industrial trades. This was the overarching goal of Washington's Tuskegee Institute. Similarly, Randolph would employ the proverb because he recognizes in Histadrut, a global struggle for democracy, independence, freedom, and the universal struggle to overcome the colonial condition. For Randolph, Washingtonian philosophy represents a very important and necessary first step towards independence. Of this struggle, Randolph says:

"For the Afro-Asian students to watch the operation of the cooperative farms or consumer co-ops, or trade unions at work in factories and shops, to look at the projects for irrigation and the experiments in scientific agriculture, and to discuss how the same techniques may be used back home in Nigeria or Kenya or Ceylon, in fact, in practically all of the Afro-Asian countries where freedom is new and fragile and the problems are big, is a valuable lesson in self-help. Association by African and Asian leaders with the purpose and spirit, as well as the pragmatic life of Histadrut, is a basic lesson in creative experience. The heart of the lesson is the wisdom of one's 'letting his bucket down where he is'" (Kersten and Lucander 2014: 344). The proverb, in this case, more than likely resonated well with every audience member that had knowledge of Washington and what he was able to accomplish at Tuskegee.

Randolph also uses proverbs from famous literary figures. This is not surprising considering how widely read Randolph was. As a youth, he would read a great deal of American and English literature, including "Charles Dickens, John Keats, Jane Austen, Charles Darwin, and William Shakespeare" (Kersten 2007: 3). One quote from English poet John Donne that Randolph employs comes from Randolph's magazine, the *Black Worker*, which was used by Randolph to keep porters notified of all BSCP activities and to alert them to any Pullman Company litigation that he felt they should be aware of (Taylor 2006). In an article entitled "Brotherhood and Our Struggle Today" (1929), Randolph says: "no man can live unto himself alone. Workers must organize, fight and hang together or they will hang separately" (Taylor 2006: 114–15). The first part of this statement is a variation of a passage that was originally written by Donne in his *Devotion Upon Emergent Occasions* (1624) in a subsection entitled "Meditation XVII." The original statement reads: "No man is an island, entire of itself; every man is a piece of the continent, a part of the main" (Donne 574–75). The very same line of this section also contains another famous phrase that has also become a well-known proverb, "never send to know for whom the bell tolls; it tolls for thee" (Donne 574–75). One could easily make the inference that Donne's musings of life and death were on Randolph's mind when he employed the proverb. In fact, when Randolph combines the two statements, Donne's "no man is an island," and his own statement "hang together or hang separately," in a philosophical sense, Randolph's message begins to mirror Donne's. While Donne is explaining every man's responsibility to contribute to humanity, Randolph is explaining the role that every porter must play in contributing to Black labor unionization. Likewise, in the fight for unionization the proverbial death of one porter could very well mean the literal death of the entire union.[6]

Randolph also found proverbial wisdom in Shakespearean lore. In fact, he was well versed in it. When Randolph first moved to Harlem in 1911, he founded a Shakespearean society called Ye Friends of Shakespeare. According to historian Cornelius L. Bynum: "This acting troupe, which included Randolph's future wife [Lucille Green], performed scenes from *Hamlet, Julius Caesar, Othello, The Merchant of Venice,* and *Romeo and Juliet* in Harlem churches and community centers. These productions helped to draw Randolph into the social life of the community, but they also informed his evolving worldview" (2010: 58–59). Another Shakespearean proverb that Randolph uses comes from *Hamlet*: "above all to thine own self be true then canst be false to no man" (Bynum 2010: 59). It is a proverb that Randolph would perform countless times in front of audiences and is derived from a few lines in act I, scene III, when Lord Polonius says to Laertes: "This above all: to thine ownself be true, And it must follow, as the night the day, Thou canst not then be false to any man." Thinking about his life retrospectively years later in an interview Randolph says that "throughout his life and career he strove to abide by Polonius's admonition" (Bynum 2010: 59). Randolph's desire to stay true to himself was always made evident by his actions. From his early years of adulthood, Randolph was devoted to ending racial and economic disparity for African Americans even if it meant creating financial losses for himself. Randolph "lost his porter job at Consolidated Gas Company for trying to organize a union, then he got fired from a waiter position for doing the same thing. Randolph was content to tread water, promoting the cause while living hand to mouth" (Welky 2014: 20).

Randolph also uses several common sayings or proverbs that were already in circulation but not necessarily attached to any important figure. When people are already familiar with certain proverbs, they often require no build up, and little or no explanation. For instance, in *The Messenger* in an article entitled "The Issues—The Negro and the Parties" (1924), Randolph employed a variation of the well-known proverb "last hired, first fired" (Doyle et al. 2012: 121).[7] In the article, Randolph is urging new Black voters in Harlem to support the Progressive Party as opposed to Democrats or Republicans. He says, "The [Robert] La Follette Progressives are committed to a plan of social legislation which is calculated to meet the problems of unemployment. Negroes will benefit from any policy which will bring a solution of unemployment, for they are the first fired and the last hired" (Kersten and Lucander 2014: 176). The order here is reversed, but the message remains the same.

Randolph would employ the proverb again in a testimony given before the Committee on Labor and Public Welfare in 1963. In this testimony, Randolph argues for a permanent Fair Employment Practices Committee (FEPC).

Randolph says: "It was with the beginning of the defense industry, when 'No Help Wanted' signs changed to 'Help Wanted—White' that the indignant organization of Negroes to gain a fairer share in the nation's reviving economy spurted. It took the combination of a wartime manpower shortage and the threat of a march on Washington to secure Executive Order 8802 on June 25, 1941, and the establishment of the President's Committee on Fair Employment Practices. But as soon as the national war emergency was over—and Democracy safe—the old, national pattern of 'last hired, first fired' crept back" (Kersten and Lucander 2014: 104). Randolph established the National Council for a Permanent Fair Employment Practices Committee (FEPC) in 1943 and would continue to work to make the FEPC permanent for over two decades. Due to Randolph's continued efforts, the FEPC would finally become permanent with the Civil Rights Act of 1964, only under a different name. It would now be known as the Equal Employment Opportunity Commission (EEOC). Thus, Randolph did see his plan come to fruition. Nearly six decades after being established from blueprints that Randolph created, the EEOC is still actively working to make the "last hired, first fired" sentiment a thing of the past.[8]

Another common proverb that Randolph expresses is "familiarity breeds contempt" (Speake 2015: 105). Randolph employs the proverb in *The Messenger* in an article entitled "Segregation in the Public Schools" (1924). In this essay, Randolph is advocating for the desegregation of the public school system, and the proverb helps him to explain the psychology behind segregation. Randolph says:

> The plain people are permitted only periodically, on some august or state occasion, to view the person of the King. It is ever shrouded in the halo of mystery, thereby investing the ruler with the power, authority and aspect of the supernatural. In democracies and republics, too, those who own for a living struggle to be worshipped and obeyed as little uncrowned kings by those who work for a living. In order to be so regarded, they avoid contact with the despised common herd. True is the old adage: familiarity breeds contempt. It is a fact of common knowledge to all students of the history of the slave regime that the slave owners prevented, upon pain and severe punishment, the association of free Negroes with Negro slaves. (Kersten and Lucander 2014: 130)

In the very same essay, Randolph employs a variation of another well-known proverb: "A man is known by the company he keeps" (Speake 2015: 57). He employs the proverb to describe some of the drawbacks of maintaining segregated schools. The passage reads:

> Assuming, for the sake of argument, that there are persons in society better than they, criminals undoubtedly could improve themselves through contact with the so-called "best people." Imitation in society, according to [Gabriel] Tarde, is one of the greatest forces for modern progress. Certainly the association of criminals with their betters could not make them worse. The old saying "show me the company you keep and I will tell you who you are," carries with it the idea that if one associates with criminals, he is a criminal; if he associates with respectable people, he is respectable. It goes further, and implies that if one is respectable and associates with bad people, he will become bad. But the reverse should also be true, viz.: that if the "no-good" associate with the good, they will become good. (Kersten and Lucander 2014: 131)

All in all, Randolph uses the proverb "familiarity breeds contempt" to elucidate the psychology behind segregation while he uses the proverb "show me the company you keep, and I will tell you who you are" in order to explain an important reason why this kind of psychology and practice should be impermissible in the United States.

In 1944, Randolph was asked to run for Congress for the Twenty-Second Congressional District of New York, a district that included Harlem. Randolph's previous two attempts at public office had failed, so he declined this invitation and chose to endorse his friend Adam Clayton Powell Jr. instead (Kersten and Lucander 2014). In a speech entitled "Why I Did Not Elect to Run for Congress," he would explain his decision, citing his distaste for politics and his desire to continue the fight for social and political equality as primary reasons. Randolph uses a well-known proverb to capture some of these sentiments. He says: "I want to remain free and independent to pursue the course I think best in doing my humble bit in the interest of winning freedom, justice, and democracy for the Negro people in America and the world.... In politics, as in other things, there is no such thing as one getting something for nothing. The pay-off may involve compromises of various types that may strike at the basic convictions and ideals and principles that one has held dear all of his life" (Kersten and Lucander 2014: 189–90). Randolph's variant of the proverb "you don't get something for nothing" (Speake 2015: 190) effectively emphasizes the fact that a third political run would impose a number of trade-offs that Randolph was simply not willing to make.

In 1969, in an interview for *Ebony* magazine with journalist Phyl Garland, Randolph uses the common proverbial expression "to stand upon one's shoulders." This expression has been used by several Black political leaders over the years to describe the process by which political gains are achieved. Randolph feels that all the advances made by the leaders that lived before him paved the way for himself and others like him to continue the struggle for equality. In what would be one of Randolph's last recorded interviews, he says:

> We are creatures of history . . . for every historical epoch has its roots in a preceding epoch. The black militants of today are standing upon the shoulders of the "new Negro radicals" of my day—the '20s, '30s and '40s. We stood upon the shoulders of the civil rights fighters of the Reconstruction era and they stood upon the shoulders of the black abolitionist. These are the interconnections of history and they play their role in the course of development." (Garland 1969: 31)

The proverbial expression that Randolph uses certainly tells an interesting story. Other civil rights leaders have also used the proverbial expression "to stand upon one's shoulders," one of the most notable and earliest being Frederick Douglass. In one instance, Douglass employs a variation to describe what he sees as the sole task of a democracy, which is to be led by the people. Douglass says: "Keep no man from the ballot box or jury box or the cartridge box, because of his color—exclude no woman from the ballot box because of her sex. Let the government of the country rest securely down upon the shoulders of the whole nation; let there be no shoulder that does not bear up its proportion of the burdens of the government" (Mieder 2001: 91). In addition to Douglass, Georgia Congressman John Lewis (Mieder 2014: 387) and President Obama also used the expression from time to time. Obama proclaims that he "stands on the shoulders of giants" in reference to Lincoln, Douglass, and other influential political leaders that fought for social justice (Mieder 2009: 116). This expression speaks to the significance of being knowledgeable about history. It is impossible to realize whose proverbial shoulders one is standing on, if one is not cognizant of the past.

The most well-known and celebrated of Randolph's proverbs appear in a speech entitled "A Vision of Freedom" (1969). The address would be delivered at a gala at the Waldorf-Astoria hotel in New York in honor of him on his eightieth birthday. Bayard Rustin, a close friend, and key coordinator behind the March on Washington, organized the event. Randolph's speech would be delivered in front of important business leaders, labor leaders, government officials, and dozens of influential civil rights leaders, including Coretta

Scott King (Kersten and Lucander 2014). Randolph discusses many of his life accomplishments and urges all the leaders in attendance to continue the struggle for equality. The proverbs that Randolph uses may not have been proverbs at the time, but a half-century later, they appear in nearly every text written about his life. In the closing of the speech Randolph says:

> Salvation for the Negro masses must come from within. Freedom is never granted: it is won. Justice is never given: it is exacted. But in our struggle we must draw for strength upon something that far transcends the boundaries of race. We must draw for strength upon the capacity of human beings to act with humanity towards one another. (Kersten and Lucander 2014: 110)

Randolph was not the first civil rights leader to use the proverb "Freedom is never granted: it is won." As a proverbial quotation, it was first used by Martin Luther King Jr. in his book *Where Do We Go from Here: Chaos or Community?* (1967). In King's text, the saying is originally worded as: "Freedom is not given, it is won" (King 1967: 19; Mieder 2010: 313). Peremiologist Wolfgang Mieder devotes an entire chapter in his text on King to this very saying. The chapter is entitled: "'Freedom is not given, it is won': Martin Luther King's Proverbial Quotation" (2010: 143–45). This is a very important civil rights quote that has since become proverbial by Randolph's later use of the phrase. Likewise, Randolph's second saying, "justice is never given: it is exacted," is a variation of the "freedom" proverb.

A variation of Randolph's statement also appears in the epitaph of his first biography, *A. Philip Randolph: A Biographical Portrait* by Jervis Anderson (1972). It reads:

> Salvation for a race, nation or class must come from within. Freedom is never granted; it is won. Justice is never given; it is exacted. Freedom and justice must be struggled for by the oppressed of all lands and races, and the struggle must be continuous, for freedom is never a final fact, but a continuing evolving process to higher and higher levels of human, social, economic, political and religious relationships.

In both cases, the proverb stays the same while the wording of the messages is slightly different. Randolph uses the sayings to articulate a universal call for activism, which speaks to the very core of his philosophy. From the start of his career as an activist, Randolph did not only advocate for the rights African Americans, but he believed that he was improving America for people of all races. By improving conditions for Black people, he knew that the restraints imposed on society by capitalism would also slowly dissipate, and that the dehumanizing effects of industrialization would also gradually be abated. Above all, Randolph wanted the newly found empowerment of working-class African Americans to gradually permeate all facets of American culture. Randolph's statement—"Freedom is never granted: it is won. Justice is never given: it is exacted—is intended to serve as a rallying call for all people to unite in the name of freedom and justice to make the mirages created by prejudice and divisive politics much more transparent.

In conclusion, while this chapter is not a comprehensive collection of every proverb that Randolph ever used, it does offer a glimpse at some of the proverbs, and his methodology for employing them. Overall, evidence illustrates that Randolph used them in very calculated ways. He used them strategically and politically, to make people listen to him, and to convince others of the significance of his message. In this sense, Randolph's proverbs may be viewed as political weapons. If he felt strongly enough about any issue, he would use them. Another thing that is fascinating about Randolph's proverb use is that it clearly illustrates how well read he was and how well-versed he was in scripture, classic literature, and American and world history. He would often offer his audiences simple sayings that also contained a lot of historical significance. A huge part of the process of employing proverbs for Randolph was contextualization, meaning that he would oftentimes match proverbs to certain situations with dead-on precision. A. Philip Randolph was truly a proverb master.

Chapter four explores the life of another proverb master who was also not afraid to advocate on behalf of Black people during the civil rights movement: folk musician Bob Dylan (1941–). Dylan was largely self-taught. He dropped out of the University of Minnesota after only one semester to focus entirely on his music. However, like Randolph, Dylan was an avid reader throughout his youth, a connoisseur of books, which undoubtedly contributed to his proverb use. Dylan became affiliated with the civil rights movement primarily through his affinity for writing protest songs. Dylan wrote and performed many of them throughout the 1960s and 1970s. Dylan addressed issues such as capitalism, poverty, death caused by unnecessary wars such as Vietnam (1955–75), and different forms of racial injustice experienced by Black people in America. One overarching idea in chapter four is that the involvement of white people was necessary for the civil rights movement to be successful, of which Dylan is a good case in point. Dylan's physical presence and his music were both welcome by Student Nonviolent Coordinating Committee activists and also the students at Highlander Folk

School, two organizations who were known for making music a part of each meeting. As chapter four demonstrates, Dylan's contributions to the civil rights movement motivated others to pay attention to social justice issues and to even participate in mass protest demonstrations themselves, and this feat was accomplished in part due to the proverbial wisdom interspersed throughout his song lyrics.

Chapter Four

"WORDS ARE BUT WIND"

The Proverbs and Proverbial Sayings of Bob Dylan

Bob Dylan was an important voice throughout the civil rights movement even though his influence is often overlooked by some who would prefer to only think of him as a musician. Some people also view the civil rights movement only as a Black struggle; however, this could not be further from the truth. Political and social advances made during the civil rights movement could not have been accomplished without help from antiracist people of all ethnicities. There were white people who willingly sacrificed alongside Black people; and just like Black people, they were beaten by police, jailed, and expelled from universities for participating in protests. In some cases, they were even disowned by their families (Holsaert 2010). As historian Cedric Johnson asserts: "The political triumphs of the postwar civil rights movement were always interracial in composition, with Americans of diverse racial and ethnic backgrounds and classes contributing to the movement as donors, volunteers, legal counsel, activists, trainers, participants, lobbyists, legislators, and supporters" (Johnson 2022a: 29). Some argue that America still needs more white involvement in the twenty-first century to fully eliminate discriminatory legal policy, economic disparity, and racial violence. According to journalist and political analyst Roland S. Martin,

> We need modern-day white abolitionists. We need modern day John Browns. . . . We're doing ourselves and future generations a disservice if we only associate with the same kind of people that we've always known and don't venture outside of our comfort zone to eat with other people, worship with other people, or understand where other people are coming from. We are living a lie every day if we don't acknowledge the truth of how we're living in this country. (2022: 143–44)

Martin's powerful statement echoes the very same sentiments that Malcolm X shared in the 1960s regarding white radicals (addressed in chapter seven). It is also a concept that Dylan understood. Even as a teen, Dylan understood the power that his influence might have on people of all races. Dylan used the platform created by his musical talent and success to influence people who may have been unknowledgeable about or afraid to get involved in struggles for social justice. Any fear or apprehension on the part of white activists was certainly understandable. Crossing the color line and "stirring up trouble" made white activist frequent targets of vicious racial violence. Several white student activists were murdered in the 1960s, including Michael Henry Schwerner, and Andrew Goodman, who were shot while riding with a Black activist, James Earl Chaney. The authorities found their bullet-riddled bodies on a secluded farm in Neshoba, Mississippi, buried underneath tons of dirt after receiving tips from a KKK informant. Additionally, activist and Detroit native Viola Fauver Liuzzo was killed by blasts from a shotgun as she rode in a car with several Black activist returning from King-led civil rights demonstrations in Montgomery, Alabama (Johnson 2022a: 29; Whitaker 2023: 1). Other white activists were murdered during the 1960s,[1] and Dylan could have easily been killed for associating with Black civil rights activists.

Dylan and the Student Nonviolent Coordinating Committee (SNCC) members knew well the dangers involved in riding around together in the Deep South.[2] To get around this dilemma, they would sometimes hide Dylan underneath a sheet as he laid in the back seat scribbling down lyrics in his notebook (Marqusee 2003). Music was a very important part of the movement; in fact, every single SNCC meeting ended in song (Charron 2009). The significance activists placed on music helped to make socializing and interacting with SNCC a natural fit for Dylan. They fraternized, sang, exchanged views on social injustice, and worked on music together. Dylan's values converged in several ways with the values of Highlander Folk School (HFC). Dylan understood how capitalism fueled racism in the Deep South. He recognized the fact that Jim Crow laws were a safety net for white farm owners who felt that they would always be able to profit by paying Black farmers miniscule wages. Highlander Folk School was originally established by Myles Horton in 1932 to help overworked and underpaid coal miners. HFC gave a voice to coal miners who didn't have the political leverage of unionization. Likewise, Dylan grew up in the small coal-mining town of Duluth, Minnesota, where his father sold and repaired small appliances. As a teenager, he was sometimes given the task of repossessing appliances of those who could not pay. At times the unfortunate patrons were the poor coal-mining fathers of some of his own friends and classmates. It was a task that Dylan did not enjoy. Nevertheless, it was also an experience that opened his eyes to poverty and helped shape his views on capitalism. Dylan wrote "Ballad of Hollis Brown" (1963), based on a true story, depicting the effects of extreme poverty faced by a Midwestern farmer who eventually kills himself and his family to end the suffering. Dylan wrote "North Country Blues" (1963) to illustrate the widespread economic depravity created when the mining industry began turning to South American countries to avoid paying American coal miners livable wages. Dylan understood wholeheartedly how critical Highlander was to resisting both capitalism and racism. While visiting Highlander, Dylan often sat strumming tunes on his guitar for people as they sang, and he sometimes performed his music for sharecroppers as his way of alerting them to the importance of social justice issues (Marqusee 2003).

Dylan's interactions with SNCC, HFC, and other activists may have inspired one of his most famous songs, "Blowin' in the Wind" (1962), which is a protest song appearing on Dylan's second studio album, *The Freewheelin' Bob Dylan* (1962). A defining moment for Dylan from the civil rights era is when he and Joan Baez (1941–) performed "Blowin' in the Wind" on the steps of Lincoln Memorial in Washington, DC, on August 28, 1963, before King delivered his famous "I Have a Dream" speech. "Blowin' in the Wind" is widely interpreted as an outcry against racism, capitalism, and war, and Dylan has performed it frequently for seven decades. On election night, November 4, 2008, forty-five years after the March on Washington, Dylan would perform the song again before a crowd of five thousand at the University of Minnesota, the school that he attended in 1960, to celebrate the election of Barack Hussein Obama II, who would become the forty-fourth US president, and the nation's first and, to date, only African American president (Epstein 2011: 428–29). President Obama would later award Dylan the Presidential Medal of Freedom (2012), the nation's highest civilian honor, for the extraordinary amount of significance that he placed on social justice issues in his music. Dylan was also awarded the Nobel Prize for Literature (2016). The time span separating the March on Washington and Obama's inauguration is proof of the timelessness of "Blowin' in the Wind."

Mike Marqusee asserts that the music that Dylan wrote during the 1960s "still exudes the spirit and the pain of human liberation" and it also "still asks demanding questions of anyone who wants to change society" (Marqusee 2003: 282). "Blowin' in the Wind" carries the label protest music, although in some early interviews Dylan is quick to shun the term "protest," preferring instead to think of his music as an overt expression of individualism, or a way of conveying his own very strong personal convictions (Marqusee

2003: 56–57). In some early interviews, Dylan denies being a spokesman or leader for any social or political movement, but during the 1960s and 1970s many people had become disillusioned by Jim Crow Laws, the Red Scare, McCarthyism, and the Vietnam War. Dylan's music addresses all of these topics. The music that Dylan produced during the civil rights era primarily did three things. Firstly, his music filled a huge void for young people who did not want to align themselves with the Ku Klux Klan. Secondly, Dylan's music filled a void for those desperately wanting change, even if they did not fully understand how to go about obtaining it. Thirdly, Dylan's music provided hope for those needing something righteous to believe in. Consequently, Dylan gained a vast following in a very short span of time, and he maintains an even larger following today.

Dylan wrote a plethora of popular "protest" songs during the 1960s and 1970s. One important aspect of Dylan's protest music is that it inspired others to write protest music too. For instance, "We Shall Overcome," a Black spiritual and important anthem of the civil rights era, shares the same melody as Dylan's "No More Auction Block" (1962) (Marqusee 2003: 44, 55). Dylan is also one of the inspirations behind Sam Cooke's (1931–64) "A Change Is Gonna Come" (1964) (Marqusee 2003). Cooke enjoyed Dylan's music and was equally angered by racism. Like Dylan, music became one of Cooke's ways of protesting American apartheid. Despite being a strong moral force during this turbulent era in American history, Dylan vehemently denies being a revolutionary or a prophet; he instead thinks of his songwriting talent as his way of speaking truth to power.

The inherent power in his music is derived, in part, through his use of proverbs and proverbial language. For decades, scholars, historians, and self-proclaimed Dylanologists (Kinney 2014) have worked tirelessly to reveal underlining sources of oratorical strength in Dylan's music. This process has often involved making connections between Dylan's music and other literary and musical art forms. Dylan has said in some interviews that it is impossible to find any one source for any of his songs, but due to scholarly archeological evidence, strong correlations have been established between his music and other sources (Gilmour 2004; Ricks 2005; Rogovoy 2009; Thomas 2017). Among the many, these sources include the Bible (especially the Torah), the writings of Aristotle (and other classics), American and British poets (such as Jack Kerouac, Lord Tennyson, and William Blake), popular blues artists (such as Muddy Waters and Robert Johnson), and influential folk artists (such as Pete Seeger and his idol since childhood, Woody Guthrie). A diverse and seemingly unlimited range of influences in Dylan's music is a reason it is so resistive to labeling and categorization. In addition to social justice, Dylan has also written songs on a wide range of subjects, among them love, life, personal relationships, and more. Many of them incorporate proverbs, although this chapter focuses specifically on songs addressing the civil rights era. Dylan's music is simultaneously folk, blues, and rock 'n' roll. He is the first artist to be labeled folk-rock, and over the years he has also gained experience with other musical art forms including gospel and rap, recording music with gospel great Shirley Caesar (1938–) and hip-hop pioneer Kurtis Blow (1959–). It is difficult to say what allows him to be so effective at transcending genres or why his music resonates with so many diverse audiences worldwide. Perhaps the proverbs and proverbial expressions help him to connect with so many people; one may even argue that proverbs and proverbial language are a driving force.[3]

According to folklorist Barbara Kirshenblatt-Gimblett, proverbs are a very important aspect of folkloristics because they "sound authoritative. The truths they proclaim feel absolute. This impression is created by the proverb's traditionality and the weight of impersonal community consensus it invokes" (Kirshenblatt-Gimblett 1981: 111). Therefore, historically, proverbs have always been a vital part of folk music. Like early folk music, proverbs are created through slow communal processes over time. They must be shared from person to person, oftentimes by word of mouth. Likewise, when people recognize proverbs, it is because they have heard and used them at some point in their lives. There is no doubting that this has been the case with Dylan. Some Dylan scholars have ignored this quality in his work while others have addressed proverbs while completely ignoring the meaning behind them. This is a mistake because a proverb's meaning is often decided by the context in which it is used (Kirshenblatt-Gimblett 1981; Mieder 1989; Prahlad 1996), and Dylan's music holds a plethora of noteworthy examples.

According to paremiologist Wolfgang Mieder: "proverbs in modern songs of all genres are more often than not cited in truncated and altered ways, i.e., the proverbs are intentionally changed to fit the needs and thoughts of modern people" (Mieder 1989: 195). Over the years, Dylan has popularized a lot of proverbs and proverbial expressions. One example of Dylan's knowledge of proverbs appears in the protest song "Blowin' in the Wind." Many people may know that the song speaks to many of the social and political issues of the 1960s, but they may not know that the song is also reflective of the well-known proverb "words are but wind," which first appears in thirteenth-century England (Wilson 1970: 915). An expanded version of the proverb "'words are but wind, but blows unkind (dunts are the devil)' is first documented as early as the 17th century" (Wilson 1970: 915). This proverb means that the words of men oftentimes lack substance, rendering them meaningless like the wind. By contrast, since words are harmless like the wind, physical blows or dunts are the only thing to be feared. Thus, they are equated with the devil. The seventeenth-century English proverb embodies much of the same meaning as the popular Frederick Douglass saying: "Words are meaningless unless they precipitate to blows" (Mieder 2009). In Dylan's case, words are meaningless unless they translate to social and political action. Dylan's use of the proverb expresses a strong distrust of politics and the seemingly endless amounts of political jargon and red tape that it is often associated with. The philanthropic message implied in the song's title and refrain is reiterated through rhetorical questioning: "Yes, 'n' how many years can some people exist / Before they're allowed to be free? / Yes, 'n' how many times can a man turn his head / Pretending he just doesn't see?" (Dylan 2016: 53). Lines such as these openly denounce racism and Jim Crow while establishing a strong connection between politics and human suffering. The song "Blowin' in the Wind" incorporates the proverb "words are but wind, in a multitude of ways"; thus, it may rightly be called a proverb song. As Mieder asserts: "In those cases where one proverb is used as a title and as a recurrent statement of a basic truth within a song we feel justified in calling such a poem a 'proverb song'" (Mieder 1989: 196). In the case of "Blowin' in the Wind," the proverb is used in the title, as an overall theme, and as a significant refrain that contributes to the song's overall structure. This song and others like it may rightfully be labelled proverb songs. Surprisingly, due to the lyrics, one does not have to be familiar with the original proverb to understand the music.

Lyrics Dylan wrote during the civil rights era reverberated to the extent that they even helped President Jimmy Carter (1924–) communicate his vision for a better America. President Jimmy Carter used some of Dylan's lyrics in his acceptance speech for the Democratic Party nomination on July 15, 1976. The governor of Georgia at the time, Carter quotes a line from Dylan's "It's Alright, Ma (I'm Only Bleeding)" (1964). Carter says, "My vision of this nation and its future has been deepened and matured during the nineteen months that I have campaigned among you for president. I have never had more faith than I do today. We have an America that, in Bob Dylan's phrase, is busy being born, and not busy dying" (*The American Presidency Project*). The original song lyrics which appear in the second verse read: "Plays wasted words, proves to warn / That he not busy being born is busy dying" (1964). Some may argue that Dylan's words contain a Shakespearean essence; after all, he does mention plays and he is also known for having a penchant for quoting Shakespeare. However, it is Dylan, not William Shakespeare, who coined the proverb: "He not busy being born, is busy dying." According to historian Donald Brown, Carter's variation of the proverb "stressed the degree to which American politics needed to resurrect itself after the debacle of Nixon" (Brown 2014: 132). "It's Alright Ma, (I'm Only Bleeding)" was written during the civil rights era and released nearly a decade before the Watergate Scandal (1972–74). The scandal ultimately forced Nixon's resignation. The song is evidence that the tumultuous and racist political climate of the civil rights era was teaching Dylan all he needed to know about American politics. He warns of the dangers involved in following leaders, a sentiment often expressed by Dylan in his lyrics. He says in the seventh verse: "But even the president of the United States / Sometimes must have to stand naked" (1964). It is no coincidence that Carter would use Dylan's words in his speech. There is also evidence that Dylan's words also taught Carter to view capitalism differently. According to journalist Ron Rosenbaum: "Jimmy Carter has said that listening to [Dylan's] songs [taught him] to see in a new way the relationship between landlord and tenant, farmer and sharecropper" (Rosenbaum 1978: 150). There is no doubting the fact that Dylan's music contains many life lessons concerning race, class, and leadership in American society.

Within Dylan's extensive catalogue of music exists a vast treasure trove of proverbs and proverbial language. Dylan's most memorable sayings are powerful one-line proverbs that can seem to define a song. Some of these sayings he creates himself while others are derived from different sources. As evidenced in speaking patterns displayed in his interviews, Dylan does not usually begin conversations with proverbs, and his songs are no different. Instead, Dylan often builds up to the proverb, using his characteristic penchant for rhyme and sublime literary imagery. The proverbs that Dylan incorporates usually stand out dramatically from other lyrics. This is due to his remarkable accuracy in assigning proverbs to appropriate rhetorical situations. After the buildup, the proverb helps to emphasize the song's theme. A song that displays this feature and which also reflects the civil rights era is "Subterranean Homesick Blues" (1965).

"Subterranean Homesick Blues" may be described as a fast-paced "talking blues" containing a series of melancholy images portraying the struggles of city life during the civil rights era. As the title suggests, the chaos, confusion, and remorse that many may have felt during that time was simply not visible on a surface level. As Dylan's song illustrates, everyone coped with the 1960s in different ways. The imagery evoked in the song demonstrates the same sense of desolation or gloom exhibited in traditional blues music. Talking blues as a genre is considered to be one of several precursors to rap. The fast-paced delivery of "Subterranean Homesick Blues" slightly resembles rap's stream-of-consciousness style. The first four lines read: "Johnny's in the basement / Mixing up the medicine / I'm on the pavement / thinking about the government" (Dylan 2016: 141). Each of the four stanzas begins with an uninviting, forbidding image that may characterize 1960s city life in America during a time when many people were simply trying to survive. The song displays the 1960s drug craze, the feeling of being trapped in a dead end nine to five, and an overall distrust of the government, brought about, in part, by government organizations (such as the FBI and COUNTELPRO) that were known for closely watching individuals thought to be communist and for infiltrating civil rights groups such as Highlander, SNCC, the Nation of Islam (NOI), and the Black Panthers for the sole purpose of creating internal discord and building false criminal charges against them. The second stanza marks the height of the inherent feeling of paranoia that seems to drive much of the narrative: "Maggie comes fleet foot / Face full of black soot / Talkin' that the heat put/ Plants in the bed but" (141). Maggie's paranoia seems to be fueled by conspiracy theories involving government plots to arrest anyone deemed suspicious: "The phone's tapped anyway / Maggie says that many say / They must bust in early May / Orders from the D.A." (141). The speaker of the song advises listeners to use indiscriminate caution: "Look out kid / Don't matter what you did / Walk on your tiptoes / Don't try "No-Doz" (141). The last four lines of the second stanza— "Keep a clean nose / watch the plain clothes / you don't need a weatherman / to know which way the wind blows"—convey the image of a speaker looking over their shoulder, both literally and figuratively (Dylan 2016: 141). The proverb-like formulation "You don't need a weatherman / to know which way the wind blows" became a very popular proverb because of this song. Of course, it was not a proverb when Dylan released the song, but it became a proverb over the course of time, as many people used it and easily recognized it as a reference to the song. According to Seth Rogovoy, the song "contains the seeds of an entire revolution" (Rogovoy 2009: 77). In fact, "the underground terrorist group Weatherman (1969–77) (a.k.a. the Weathermen and the Weather Underground Organization)," a more radicalized faction of the Students for a Democratic Society (SDS), derived its name from this song (Rogovoy 2009: 77). It would also become the banner slogan for a special issue of *New Left Notes*, an SDS circular devoted to issues such as racism, imperialism, and the Vietnam War. The paper circulated at a Student Democratic Society (SDS) convention held in June of 1969 in Chicago. The paper's headline reads: "YOU DON'T NEED A WEATHERMAN TO KNOW WHICH WAY THE WIND BLOWS" (emphasis in original) (Marqusee 2003: 257). Unlike most weather proverbs that may predict the direction of wind, the "weather proverb" in this song predicts ensuing trouble for America. If the proverb foreshadows the problem, then another famous Dylanism appearing at the end of the third verse embodies the solution: "Don't follow leaders / Watch the parkin' meters" (Dylan 2016: 141). This proverb-like statement serves as a warning against the blind acceptance of bogus political agendas, and as folklorist Betsy Bowden contends, "Don't follow leaders / Watch the parking meters" is very much significant because it conveys the message that "a listener must depend not on precedents, but on her own perceptions of what's wrong with authority figures and with the symbols of power they erect along every street" (Bowden 1982: 140).

In interviews Dylan has often expressed disdain for explicating his own lyrics, preferring instead to leave this task to others. One reason he may feel this way is because there is always the possibility that his own interpretation could limit the scope of his music. As Dylan scholar Michael Gilmour reminds us, "readers of literature themselves bring a bundle of (con) texts to the objects of their study. This introduces further subjectivity; it is not only difficult to distinguish what an author has created from what is borrowed; it is also true that what is heard or read by different listeners or readers will not always be the same" (Gilmour 2004: 15). The aim in this chapter is to illustrate ways that proverbs and proverbial expressions contribute meaning to Dylan's work and to also reveal some ways that his work has directly and indirectly contributed to the goals of the civil rights movement. The civil rights era is when much of Dylan's expansive catalogue of music was created, and many of his lyrics reflect the struggle for social justice. Dylan was one of few artists who used his platform to speak out against social injustices committed against Black people. He wrote the song "The Death of Emmett Till" (1962), which describes the grisly and inhumane way that adolescent Till was abducted and murdered by a group of white men who received no punishment whatsoever for their crimes. Dylan wrote "The Lonesome Death of Hattie Carroll" (1964) to describe the senseless murder of a fifty-one-year-old mother of ten who was working as a barmaid when she was beaten to death with a walking stick by Charles Devereux "Billy" Zantzinger, a twenty-four-year-old wealthy tobacco farmer. Dylan's song did much to generate public outrage over Zantzinger's laughable six-month prison sentence. Another influential song, "Hurricane" (1975), protests the wrongful imprisonment of middleweight boxer Ruben Hurricane Carter (1937–2014), who spent nearly twenty years in prison for a 1966 murder that he did not commit. While Dylan never believed that Carter was guilty, many others did not even care. Dylan was very instrumental in obtaining Carter's release from prison. In addition to writing the epic song "Hurricane," detailing Carter's story, Dylan also wrote letters to public officials and lawmakers, visited Carter frequently while he was incarcerated, and helped him to obtain legal representation. Dylan wrote "Oxford Town" (1962) to address the racial hatred experienced by Blacks throughout sundown towns across Mississippi. One may easily argue that all of Dylan's music will always reflect the 1960s in one way or another because it is when he strove to grow into his own as a musician, and he did so as the nation struggled to grow into its own as a people. Dylan expresses the essence of this struggle in *The Times Are A-Changin'* (1964). People recognize an air of wisdom in Dylan's words, so much so, that even the phrase "The Times Are A-Changin'" from his third studio album has grown to function much like a proverb in and of itself. When it is heard, people immediately associate it with Dylan and the civil rights era. The words "the times are-a changin'" express knowledge that social change in America is inevitable. When imagined within the context of the song, it implies the didactic message that those who fight against socially progressive change will ultimately sink like the proverbial stone in the song.

In some of his current music Dylan still offers much reflection on the social and political climate of the civil rights era. One of his most recent songs, "Murder Most Foul" (2020), is about the assassination of the nation's thirty-fifth president, John F. Kennedy (1917–63). In addition to details regarding the JFK shooting, "Murder Most Foul" provides sweeping cultural commentary. Dylan portrays the Kennedy assassination for what it actually was: a heinous crime committed in front of thousands of unsuspecting onlookers, many of whom were obviously devastated by what they had just witnessed. President Kennedy was shot by Lee Harvey Oswald as his motorcade traveled slowly through Dealey Plaza in downtown Dallas, Texas. The proverbial expressions used in the first stanza of the song point directly to the irony of being killed on such a widely respected public platform. Dylan compares the last public appearance of Kennedy to a ritual sacrifice, saying he was "being led to the slaughter" like a proverbial "sacrificial lamb," and just a few lines later, a variation of the proverbial expression "to die like a dog" is suggestive of the inhumanity involved in the situation. The proverbial "unpaid debt" mentioned in the song may refer to increasing attention that Kennedy was paying to issues regarding civil rights in America. Months leading up to his death, Kennedy garnered a lot of attention for promoting what would become the Civil Rights Act of 1964. Kennedy was also known for inviting civil rights leaders to the White House, and for racist people, any concessions made on behalf of Black America was often automatically equated with the abandonment of white America. The fourth stanza reads: "Don't ask what your country can do for you / Cash on the barrel head, money to burn / Dealey Plaza, make a left hand turn / Go down to the crossroads, try to flag a ride" (bobdylan.com). Dylan incorporates the first part of the famous Kennedy proverb, first spoken during Kennedy's televised inaugural address, "Don't ask what your country can do for you, ask what you can do for your country,"[4] to invoke the largely positive image that Kennedy left in the minds of many Americans. The double entendre evoked by the pairing of the age-old proverbial expressions "cash on the barrelhead," and "money to burn" insinuates that there is huge debt to be paid. Dylan may also be highlighting class disparity between shooter and victim. The proverbial expression "cash on the barrelhead" was once a literal statement frequently used by bartenders when payment was due. In nineteenth-century bars and saloons where wooden barrels were used in place of tables, if credit was being refused, bartenders would say: "cash on the barrelhead." The proverbial "crossroads" is a general folklore reference to the liminal space between the spirit world and the corporeal world. The crossroads also simultaneously functions as a blues folklore reference (Gussow 2017). According to blues legend, the crossroads (usually a dark and secluded place in the Deep South where two dirt roads meet) is where blues legend Robert Johnson, also known as the King of the Mississippi Delta Blues, supposedly met the Devil to exchange his soul for uncanny musical talent. Thus, Dylan invokes spiritual liminality and Black America by mentioning the crossroads. The line that follows also suggests what Kennedy symbolized at the time of his death. The speaker says: "That's the place where Faith, Hope and Charity died." Mentioning the Roman Catholic saints Faith, Hope, and Charity (c. 200 AD) points to the fact that as a political martyr, faith, hope, and charity are the things that JFK and his Civil Rights Act would represent for many Americans. The fourth stanza continues: "Shoot 'em while he runs, boy, shoot 'em while you can / See if you can shoot the Invisible Man / Goodbye, Charlie, goodbye Uncle Sam, Frankly, Miss Scarlet, I don't give a damn" (bobdylan.com). These lyrics give voice to several different narratives all at once. On the one hand, the lines suggest possible motives for Oswald's crime. On the other hand, Dylan's lyrics actually constitute a detailed sequence of events which gives at least some credence to the popular saying: "People don't listen to Dylan, they study Dylan" (Rogovoy 2009). The opening lines of the fourth stanza emphasize the fact that for Oswald, a poor, disgruntled, twice court-martialed Marine veteran with a history of mental health issues, JFK represents the military from which he may have sought retribution for being punished and imprisoned. Thus, Dylan insinuates that Oswald or "Mr. Charlie" may have had his own reasons for murdering the president or "Uncle Sam." Dylan also invokes Ralph Ellison's celebrated novel *Invisible Man* (1952). In a literal sense, it highlights the fact that Oswald became an invisible man when he hid from the world after killing the president. In considering the possibility of a postcolonial subtext, one must consider the fact that Ellison's *Invisible Man* is also a work of fiction portraying psychological issues faced by a young Black man coming of age in the Jim Crow South. This part of Dylan's commentary gives further voice to irony, hinting at the irony involved in the fact that JFK's death could be viewed as political backlash for attempting to remedy a racist political system which has obviously done psychological harm to both Blacks and whites alike. The popular proverbial expression "Frankly, Miss Scarlett, I don't give a damn" from the film *Gone with the Wind* (1939) also gives more voice to the literal chain of events that take place after the Kennedy killing. To authorities, Oswald seemed to be gone with the wind, that is, until he fatally shot a Texas police officer. Afterwards, he attempted to hide in a crowded movie theatre where he was later apprehended. Thus, the novel and lines from the famous film are both literal and figurative references. The lines which follow—"What is the truth and where did it go/ Ask Oswald and Ruby—they oughta know" (bobdylan.com)—provide subtle clues to the shocking and paradoxical outcome. Oswald is shot on live television by a nightclub owner, Jack Ruby, as he is being held in the basement of Dallas police headquarters. The line that follows, "shut your mouth," is a testament to the astonishment and disbelief obviously felt by anyone hearing the story, while the phrase "wise old owl" may signal the concluding proverb: "Business is business and it's murder most foul" (bobdylan.com). The proverb "business is business" (Bryan, et al. 2016: 116) may accurately sum up the attitude of either Oswald or Ruby, especially if they both felt justified in their own actions.

Dylan wrote "Murder Most Foul" (2020) nearly six decades after writing "Only a Pawn in Their Game" (1964), a song about slain civil rights leader Medgar Evers (1925–63). Written at the young age of twenty-two, "A Pawn in Their Game" also illustrates Dylan's penchant for rhyme and storytelling while also exemplifying his ability to provide accurate and insightful social and political commentary. The song does not contain proverbs, but it has become so well-known that for many, the title when used as a phrase in and of itself, functions very much like a proverb in that it conveys the same moral lesson implied in the song's lyrics. Dylan is bringing attention to the fact that racism is an important aspect of capitalism. In other words, wealthy capitalists will always take advantage of the poor. Dylan ends each stanza with the refrain "he's only a pawn in their game," and throughout the song, the poor, white uneducated killer is portrayed as a proverbial "pawn" and a proverbial "tool" to be used by the hands of the wealthy elite. Dylan deals with the assassinations of Medgar Evers and JFK in similar ways, but it is clear that "Murder Most Foul" displays a level of skill and mastery which surpasses some his previous work. Some people who were alive in the 1960s say that they can recall exactly where they were and what they were doing when they first received news that JFK had been assassinated, and after hearing "Murder Most Foul," there is no doubting the fact that Dylan is among those people. It is even more fascinating that those who were not alive in the 1960s and 1970s can still turn to Dylan's music to find out what the civil rights era was like.

The focus of chapter five is on an individual who may be far lesser known, and yet is no less important to American civil rights history: Septima Poinsette Clark (1898–1987). As an educator, she could not have had a more contrasting life. As opposed to being a high-profile public figure like Dylan and some of the other figures included in this study, Clark functioned behind the scenes, well out of the reach of the media and the general public. It was primarily in privacy, behind closed doors, where she shared her inspiring words of wisdom in the form of proverbs and proverbial expressions to all of the students and civil rights activists she sought to inspire.

Chapter Five

"EACH ONE, TEACH ONE"

The Proverbs and Proverbial Expressions of Septima Poinsette Clark

One purpose of this chapter is to illustrate the extent that proverbs, sayings, and proverbial expressions are connected to issues surrounding social justice in America. While it is focused on Septima Poinsette Clark and her use of proverbial language, it is not a chronologically organized account of Clark's life or an attempt to document every single proverb or proverbial expression that Clark has ever used. This study offers a distinctive look at the civil rights era due to Clark's unique position as an African American female, and because of the irreplaceable roles that she played. Clark functioned largely behind the scenes throughout the movement teaching Black and white people, many of whom never had the opportunity to receive any formal schooling, to read so that they could become independent thinkers and registered voters. One of Clark's most well-remembered sayings is: "I train people to do their own talking" (Collins). Thus, she was a very outspoken and vocal leader, but she gave very few public speeches. Although Clark uses proverbs and proverbial expressions, and coins several well-remembered sayings, she incorporates proverbial expressions far more often than any other form of traditional language. Furthermore, the proverbial language that Clark uses is documented primarily in her autobiographies, interviews, and through other people's accounts. Clark primarily shared proverbial language as she worked in the background of the movement as an educator, activist, and political organizer, empowering tens of thousands of Black people to stand up to racism and oppression, and to speak for themselves. To understand the traditional language that Clark uses, in the form of proverbs and proverbial expressions, one must first understand some basic information regarding her early life and upbringing.

Septima Poinsette Clark (1898–1987) was born in Charleston, South Carolina, to Victoria Anderson Warren and Peter Poinsette. Warren was a free

American-born washerwoman who was raised in Haiti, but later returned to the US following the Civil War (1861–65). Clark's father, Peter Poinsette, was a man who was enslaved until his early twenties to a wealthy politician and first United States minister to Mexico, Joel Roberts Poinsette, who is most widely known for introducing his namesake, the Poinsettia plant, to American soil from Mexico in the 1820s. Clark's parents had a very strong influence on her life. They both valued education highly, and though it is unknown exactly how much education they each received, they were very successful in instilling this value in their children. Warren often flaunted the fact that she was born "free issue," and she kept her vow to never become anyone's slave. Warren was known for her very light complexion, religious piety, and her fiery temper. When her patience was tested, she would sometimes say, "I'm a little piece of leather, but I'm well put together" (Charron 2009: 33, 456), which insinuated that she would fight if need be.

Charleston was a segregated city in the late nineteenth and early twentieth century. Likewise, racism kept Blacks and whites separated, while colorism and class discrimination kept Black communities divided, and despite being a family of modest means, Clark's parents were very race-conscious and class-conscious. As a dark-skinned former slave, Peter Poinsette was fully cognizant of the low position that he held on Charleston's social ladder, which is one of the reasons why he chose to keep his slave name—he enjoyed the sense of prestige that it brought him. Likewise, Warren refused to let her daughters date and hang around with what she called "two-for-fives" or commoners, and she expressed disdain for all white people and very dark-skinned Black people. While Clark embraced her parents' educational values and determined spirits, she did not take on any of her mother's class or color conscious ways. In fact, Clark was determined to succeed, not because of her parents' background, but rather despite it (Charron 2009: 48).

Clark became an impressive figure in American history for several reasons. She is known affectionately as the "grandmother" of the civil rights era (1954–68) because it is a movement that she gave birth to. Clark is also known as the "teacher" of the civil rights movement because the adult education schools that she established enabled tens of thousands of Black people to become literate and politically active. Clark's teaching career spans many decades. In the early 1900s, Clark was one of the very first educators to endorse adult literacy training solely as a means of civic empowerment for scores of illiterate and disenfranchised people in the state of South Carolina and across the South who were barred from voting in several ways, including physical violence, the implementation of complicated literacy tests, poll taxes, land-owning requirements, and other means. Throughout the twentieth and twenty-first centuries, Clark's teachings and teaching methods have continued to have positive impacts on countless numbers of African American people who became engaged in the political process because of Clark's literacy and civic education programs, either through voting, running for public office, or becoming teachers in these programs themselves. There were very few people who were involved in the civil rights movement who taught as long as Clark or had the pedagogical skills and knowledge base that Clark had acquired. Since Clark began teaching in 1916 on Johns Island, she worked diligently to establish a blueprint for teaching the poor, illiterate, and dispossessed Black and white people of the South basic skills such as reading, writing, and arithmetic, so that they could become literate, independent, self-sufficient, and civically engaged. Clark wanted Black people in the South, many of whom still lived on the same plantations that their ancestors were forced to work, to be able to vote, to run for office, and to ultimately take part in shaping their own destinies from a political standpoint, and she did not believe that anyone who lacked these basic skills could become politically active in any meaningful way. Likewise, Clark felt that getting dispossessed and underserved populations educated would then enable them to perform the political work that would be necessary to eventually bring an end to segregation throughout the South and the rest of America. Clark also felt that educating the masses would also help to alleviate other problems in the African American community such as unemployment, homelessness, and widespread poverty.

At the age of eighteen, after having just received her teaching certificate from the highly acclaimed Avery Normal Institute, Clark was assigned to teach the rural poor in a dilapidated, run-down, one-room shack on Johns Island. The practice of assigning young Black teachers to poor rural areas was common in South Carolina. Also, keep in mind that Clark could have easily been a victim of the same inadequate and racist public school system that she would later work for. In a recorded interview with civil rights historian Jacquelyn Dowd Hall, Clark described the harrowing experience of trying to learn in Charleston's Black public schools at the turn of the century. Clark says:

> In 1904, I can remember, we moved to 17 Henrietta Street, and there I must have been about six years of age at that time, and I started going to school. I went to what they called Mary Street School, and at that school they had what they called at that time an ABC gallery where the children of six years were placed. There must have been a hundred children on that gallery; it was like a baseball stadium with the

bleachers. You sat up on those bleachers. And the only thing I could see the teachers could do was to take you to the bathroom and back. By the time she got us all to the bathroom and back, it was about time to go home. We didn't learn too much, and my mother was aware of that so she took me out of that public school, and there were numbers of elderly women in Charleston who kept little schools in their homes. And so I went to one on Logan Street, where the Fielding Funeral Home is today. And at that school, run by a Mrs. Nuckels, I learned to read and write. And she taught us a very hard way. If you couldn't spell a word that she asked you, why, she whipped every letter in your hands. This was the way we learned to spell. (Hall 1976: 1)

Clark's experience at Mary Street School more than likely introduced her to the psychological damage that poorly funded schools often inflicted on Black children. Likewise, the private school of Mrs. Nuckles more than likely provided her with her first real example of how not to teach. Clark's mother was proactive in seeking out private instruction for her child, and Clark realized that many of her first pupils would never have that same luxury, so she did the best that she could. Like other Black teachers, Clark had far too many students, very little pay, and very few resources to work with. In fact, a large portion of the adult population was illiterate. "J. B. Felton, the second state agent for African-American schools, praised the 'unselfish service' of black teachers and the 'missionary spirit' with which they approached 'the removal of illiteracy'" (Charron 20009: 77). Felton also acknowledged that without state funding, Black educators like Clark were essentially "making bricks without straw" (Mieder 2001: 142; Charron 2009: 78). Despite all the setbacks and challenges that Clark faced in her early years as a teacher on Johns Island, she continued to develop, and later in her career, Clark developed an adult education program that eventually proliferated all over the South.

Clark's successful approach to activism and adult education was influenced by several factors. First, as the previous passage from a 1976 interview illustrates, Clark had her own childhood experiences in a racist and segregated school system to draw from. Second, she was always focused on professional development and on advancing her own education. In addition to earning her teaching certificate at Avery, she earned a BA from Benedict College and an MA from Hampton Institute, respectively. She sought out additional teacher education training at Columbia University and Clark Atlanta University. Third, Clark was also influenced and taught by several important leaders during her lifetime, including South Carolina adult education pioneer Wil Lou Gray (1883–1984), whom she worked for during the 1930s, and the world-renowned sociologist, W. E. B. Du Bois (1868–1963), whom she was taught by in the 1940s. Fourth, Clark gained much of her political organizing experience throughout her career as she participated in and sometimes led local branches of organizations such as the National Association of Colored People (NAACP), the Palmetto States Teacher Association (PSTA), the South Carolina Federation of Colored Women (SCFCW), and the Young Women's Christian Association (YWCA). By the time the civil rights movement began in the 1950s, Clark's education, teaching experience, and advanced training had already supplied her with an overabundance of confidence. All in all, Clark was well-versed in pedagogy, civics, and political organizing, but one thing that is often overlooked by scholars is the traditional language that she used to communicate. It is a fact that Clark employed traditional language in the form of proverbs and proverbial expressions as a way of communicating important ideas and concepts. Of the countless numbers of definitions of the term "proverb" that exist, paremiologist Wolfgang Mieder most effectively tells us what they are. Mieder's concise definition is derived from an extensive frequency study that he conducted in the 1980s of words contained in more than fifty proverb definitions: "A proverb is a short, generally known sentence of the folk which contains wisdom, truth, morals, and traditional views in a metaphorical, fixed and memorizable form and which is handed down from generation to generation" (Mieder 2004: 3; Mieder 2008: 11). In examining Clark's biography, autobiographies, interviews, and articles, one may notice that some of the proverbs, sayings, and expressions that Clark uses stand out like jewels of wisdom that convey a multitude of ideas concerning her personal values and beliefs. Additionally, they are used to convey her teaching philosophy and the unique ways that she conceptualizes notions such as freedom, equality, and justice.

In working with the young or old, Clark relied on several personal principles that have been preserved as proverbs or proverbial expressions that help to define her legacy. One of Clark's most well-known personal proverbs is the simple three-word phrase "literacy means liberation," and this proverb communicates a philosophy that Clark spent her entire life teaching (Collins; SNCC Digital Gateway). The idea that literacy education was a prerequisite to political and economic autonomy is a tenet that Clark stood by, and it is also a practice that Clark had down to a science.

One of Clark's favorite proverbial expressions was first made famous by the African American ex-slave and education leader Booker T. Washington during his famous 1895 Atlanta Exposition speech. The proverbial phrase to "reach a person where they are" reflected the way Clark approached her work and people remembered Clark for this fundamental tenet. Civil rights activist Victoria Gray says: "One of the things I learned [from Clark] early on . . . is never underestimate the intelligence of *anyone* in the community . . . always try to meet people where they are and receive them at *whatever* point" (emphasis in original) (Charron 2009: 326). Clark later expounds on this very same point in an interview. She says: "And I saw the same thing with Stokely Carmichael. He went into a community with his thinking up high, and theirs was still down low, and so he couldn't get anything done. You can't get it done unless you get the people sensitized to the fact of what you would like to see happen. This is my feeling" (Hall 1976: 77). Clark always met the people where they were by focusing on the needs of her students and the needs of the community, and she demonstrated an unwavering amount of patience in the classroom as many of her students came to her with no literacy skills at all. Additionally, Clark also aimed to instill in her pupils that each student is responsible for passing along the knowledge that they receive to others, which Clark best communicated proverbially as "each one, teach one" (Doyle et al. 2012: 250). For centuries, this saying of African origins has been used to describe the process by which a single individual learns a skill such as reading or writing, or to perform some other skill, and in turn, shares this knowledge with others. "Each one teach one" is similar in meaning to the proverb "it takes a whole village to raise a child" (Doyle et al. 2012: 268; Speake 2015: 355), which also has African origins, being Nigerian, specifically Igbo and Yoruban (Speake 2015: 355). Ella Baker, in her organizing efforts, sometimes used the Swahili term "fundi" or "mfundi," which is identical in meaning but sometimes required further explanation since it is not a proverb (Ransby 2003: 419). "Each on teach one" expresses the fact that Clark took pride in the fact that she did not speak for her students. Instead, she said she "trained people to do their own talking" (Charron 2009: 315). The people were then empowered in the sense that they were able to communicate the same literacy lessons and political lessons to other people. For Clark, the axiom "each one, teach one" illustrates her "folk"-centered approach to learning, and it is a powerful philosophy by which Clark enabled entire communities throughout the South to become literate and politically involved.

Proverbs and proverbial expressions are a very important component in Clark's verbal and rhetorical repertoire, and there is evidence that there are practical reasons why they are one of the primary ways that Clark chose to express herself. When Clark first began teaching on Johns Island in 1916, she was able to succeed because she came to the island with a clear understanding of the Gullah language (Work 1919: 441–42; Mieder 1989: 126–27), which is a major reason why students, parents, and community members alike trusted her. Years later when Clark returned to Johns Islands to recruit adult students to be trained and educated in literacy and citizenship at Highlander Folk School (HFS), it was again her familiarity with Sea Island culture and language that helped her to gain the community's confidence. Unfortunately, this same sentiment was not always extended to outsiders. For example, her white colleague, Myles Horton, who founded HFS in Monteagle, in the early 1930s to help poor and disenfranchised coal mining communities in the Tennessee mountains, frequently ran into proverbial brick walls when trying to communicate with Black Gullah community members. Horton did not understand their language including the plethora of expressions that they used, and he often wished that instead of incorporating so many expressions in their conversations, that Johns Islanders would be more direct (Charron 2009: 250). Clark explains Horton's difficulty: "Dedicated as he was, it was hard for him to hear them say, 'Now this happened the night that that cow had its calf on such-and-such a moon.'... He wanted them to come right to the point and they wouldn't do it'" (Charron 2009: 250). Thus, throughout Highlander's existence, Horton depended heavily on Clark and her niece Bernice Robinson to be his mediators and facilitators in developing the adult education program curriculum and in getting the Johns Island community involved in it. Clark says that Robinson was her proverbial right arm (Clark 1962: 140: Bryan and Mieder 2005: 352) at Highlander, but ultimately, the literacy program that Highlander would implement, ran through Clark.

Many of Clark's proverbs, sayings, and proverbial expressions illustrate her deep connection to the Gullah people of the South Carolina Sea Islands. In *Echo*, Clark says: I've been all over the United States and I love this country its differing dialects and geographies and customs. But nowhere else have I found an atmosphere and a people—to me, understand—comparable to the atmosphere and the folk of my native section. The Low Country, I suppose, gets into your blood. More probably, indeed, it's in it when you're born" (Clark 1962: 47–48).

Clark also explains an important point concerning the evolution of Gullah culture. She says that the language spoken on Johns Island is a mixture of the French spoken by white Huguenot settlers and the many African languages of the Black people who were brought there as slaves. People from all over the world traveled to South Carolina to participate in what were the largest known slave auctions in America. According to public records, as many as 600 slaves were auctioned at one time (Davila). Thus, there is ample evidence that the Gullah language and dialect are the result of a copious cultural contact zone created by a variety of people that have inhabited the South Carolina Sea Islands for centuries since the onset of the transatlantic slave trade (c. 1500–1800). Consequently, Gullah linguistic and dialectical influence extends to many Black and white people all over the state of South Carolina.

Clark even gives readers a unique glimpse into some of the Gullah folk terminology and expressions that have influenced her the most. One obvious example is the word "echo" from which her first autobiography, *Echo in My Soul* (1962), derives its namesake. Clark explains what the word means in Gullah. She says: "You might say to a Gullah woman in speaking of a certain song that you wished her to sing. 'Sing it your way,' you might tell her, and she would reply, 'Well this is my echo.' By *echo* she would mean *tune*. Others may say, 'This is my *air*.' This latter sounds old-English to me, but I never could figure out how they got *echo*" (Clark 1962: 47). The word "echo" is most used in reference to literal sounds that reverberate, but Clark applies it as an expression to her own undying passion for social justice. Near the end of *Echo*, Clark reveals that the phrase "echo in my soul" is also featured in a Quaker folk song which is one of the twenty-two freedom songs included in a song booklet published by Highlander Folk School. Throughout the civil rights era, Black and white members of HFS held hands and sang after every meeting as a way of bonding. Clark describes the song as "an early Quaker hymn that originated long ago when George Fox and other founders of the Society of Friends were being imprisoned for their beliefs" (Clark 1962: 242). The verse that contains the phrase reads: "My life flows on in endless song above earth's lamentation; I hear the real through far-off hymn that hails a new creation; Through all the tumult and the strife I hear the music ringing. It sounds an echo in my soul; how can I keep from singing!" (Clark 1962: 242).

Another popular Gullah idiom involves the substitution of the word *signal* for the word *denomination*, as in religious denomination. As Clark explains, a person might ask the question, "'Are you going to the preaching at the Methodist church tonight?,' and one's reply might be 'No, that is not my signal'" (Clark 1962: 47). Thus, the term "signal" may also be equated with the word *preference* or *liking*.

Furthermore, according to Clark, many people who are not from the SC Sea Islands do not understand the folk expression "too dear," which simply means that an item is too lavish or pricey for one to afford. She says that a person may ask, "'Are you going to buy that hat—or cow, or boat, or pig, or dress?' And the person may respond 'Py God, no! It is too dear!'" (Clark 1962: 47). Clark's example is accentuated by the exclamatory phrase *Py God* which Gullah people often uttered to express anger or surprise.

Clark's familiarity with and appreciation for Gullah language illustrates that she treasured the Sea Island's linguistic and dialectical traditions, and her affinity for Gullah language and culture, more than likely played a major role in shaping the way that she incorporates proverbs and proverbial expressions into her own discourse. Throughout *Echo* Clark employs proverbial language largely when addressing issues that are very important to her such as education, civil rights, freedom, and equality. In fact, one of the very first proverbs that she uses in *Echo* appears as she is explaining the unconventional methods that she uses to gain an education while growing up in a segregated Charleston, South Carolina, during the early twentieth century. As Clark explains, her mother, Victoria Warren, a washerwoman with little disposable income, was determined to enroll young Clark into the prestigious Avery Normal Institute, but she had no idea how she would raise enough money to pay the expensive tuition fee. To sum up her mother's attitude towards the situation Clark says: "It has always been my contention that there's much truth to the old adage that where there's a will there's a way" (Clark 1962: 23). Clark then explains that she took a job babysitting for wealthy Black newlyweds who lived in her neighborhood to make enough money to attend high school at Avery. The proverb "where there's a will there's a way" (Whiting 1989: 683; Mieder 2001: 511–12; Mieder 2008: 115; Speake 2015: 346) helps Clark to explain to her audience that her will to work for what she wanted allowed her to succeed at Avery. Additionally, she describes Avery as a proverbial "paradise," where she instantly "fell in love with reading and exploring the wonderland embraced in the covers of countless books" (Clark 1962: 24). Clark also enjoyed learning from Avery's many "dedicated teachers" (Clark 1962: 24). Avery is where young Clark discovered that her life passion would be teaching.

Clark uses proverbial language to describe another significant turning point in her life, which is when she began to work closely with Myles Horton and Highlander Folk School. Clark as an outspoken leader of the Parent Teacher Association (PTA), invited Horton and his wife, Zilphia, to conduct a workshop on integration in which "twenty-two communities were represented, and some ninety persons participated" (Clark 1962: 112). Horton, who was already known as a "race agitator," would be the group's keynote speaker, and during the workshop, information about HFS and the National Association for the Advancement of Colored People (NAACP) was shared. Clark knew beforehand that the unpopular move would garner plenty of negative attention among some of her moderate colleagues who did not want her "stirring up any trouble," but she had already decided that she would simply ignore them. Clark brushes their disapproval aside with a proverbial expression saying: "I just resolved in my mind to wear whatever criticism came along simply as a loose garment" (Clark 1962: 115). Despite Clark's resolve to wear criticism as a proverbial "loose garment," she still describes this event as the proverbial "final straw" that leads to her being fired by the Charleston school board in 1956 (Clark 1962: 112). As a result of the controversial workshop, Clark generated a lot of attention from the local media. After seeing Clark's name splashed across headlines, a local principal admonished Clark for holding this meeting with a well-known proverb. The principle tells Clark that only "fools rush in where angels fear to tread" (Clark 1962: 115; Mieder 2008: 96). In other words, the principal felt that Clark would only cause trouble for herself and others by getting involved with the social activism of Highlander and the NAACP. As Clark explains, even though there were those who were afraid for her job security, she remained undaunted because she knew that she was only doing the right thing by aligning herself with other advocates of integration and social justice. While her decision would ultimately lead to her firing, it also led her to work full-time at Highlander Folk School as a teacher and later as director of programs. The adult education programs that Clark would implement eventually reached tens of thousands of students across at least a dozen states.

At another point in the narrative of *Echo*, Clark explains that Highlander was initially established on private land gifted to Horton by retired professor, former college president, and founder of Western State Teachers College for Women, Dr. Lilian Wyckoff Johnson (1864–1956), and it was initially designed through the collaborative efforts of Johnson and Horton in the 1930s to help improve the living conditions for the hundreds of poor coal mine workers and their families who lived in the Grundy County, Tennessee, area by educating them about their rights and making them aware of the many political decisions that affected them daily. Once the coal-mining industry abandoned Monteagle, Tennessee, it was not replaced by any other industry, which left much of the Grundy County community poor and on welfare. Due to this unfortunate circumstance, many mountain-dwellers would leave to find work in factories in larger cities such as Chicago and Detroit only to return after a short time (Clark 1962: 129). Clark employs a revealing proverb to characterize this predicament: "You simply can't get the mountains out of the people even though the people leave the mountains" (Clark 1962: 129). Clark employs this well-known proverb construction (Speake 2015: 33) to better characterize the mountain population of Grundy County as a close-knit and friendly group. Clark's characterization of the "friendly mountain folk" is important because of the information that she conveys next, which is that despite Highlander's continued focus on social justice and economic empowerment, Highlander's stance on integration always presented a barrier to reaching people. In fact, the community and the State of Tennessee did not become hostile toward HFS until Clark achieved success in recruiting larger numbers of Black participants. The negative attention that the integrated workshops garnered, prompted the state to raid the facility in 1956 and to eventually close it in 1961. Horton, who remained a steadfast believer that HFS was an "idea" and thus could never truly be destroyed, relocated the school to Knoxville, Tennessee. Afterwards, upon the request of the Reverend Dr. Martin Luther King Jr., the operation of Highlander's adult education program was transferred to King's organization, the Southern Christian Leadership Conference (SCLC). There it continued as the Citizenship Education Program (CEP), a major component of SCLCs Crusade for Citizenship, under the leadership of Clark and Student Nonviolent Coordinating Committee (SNCC) founder, Ella Baker. In one interview, Clark sheds more light on the logic behind her philosophy of "reaching her students where they are" as she explains some of the political struggles that each community faces:

> To [teach] them to read and write so that they could register and vote. Because, see, all of these states had these stringent registration laws. They had to write their name in cursive writing here in Charleston and read a section of the election laws. In Georgia they had thirty questions they had to read and give answers to. In Mississippi they had twenty-four questions. And in Louisiana there were thirty questions that they had to read and answer. Now eastern Texas did not have that; in eastern Texas they had to pay poll tax, and we had to work with them to get them not to pay the poll tax. And they had to do that each year. So we had these differences all around. And in each state we had to do different things. (Hall 1976: 79)

Highlander's stance on politics and integration was not very popular especially among racists, which is why Clark defends HFS throughout *Echo*. HFS was attacked because many people believed the vicious lies that were being spread by the media who frequently portrayed HFS as a communist organization, an illegal bootlegging operation, and an immoral group that welcomed and promoted interracial sex—even on their front lawn. Of course, those who were familiar with HFS knew that it was none of these things, and in *Echo*, Clark capitalizes on this point saying: "The school that Myles established with Dr. Johnson's help was to be an instruction conducted on Christian principles and on an interracial basis; a place, as her home had been, where brotherhood would be felt, emphasized, and practiced. And that is what drew me to Highlander and made it a place of light and hope and refreshment of the spirit" (Clark 1962: 131–32). Clark emphasizes Highlander's theme of Christian brotherhood even further using a proverb in the process:

"I like to think of Highlander as a place where the simple but profound ideals of Christianity were not only preached but practiced" (Clark 1962: 132). Not only did they teach brotherhood, but they also "practiced what they preached" (Whiting 1989: 510; Speake 2015: 254; Bryan and Mieder 2005: 606). This proverb helps to dispel any untruths regarding the purpose of the school or Horton's character.

Clark was instrumental in expanding Highlander's adult education program to Johns Island, South Carolina. She would then utilize the program to recruit and train other teachers, who would then go on to open their own schools in the area and on neighboring Sea Islands. The program sought to reach all people, but they were primarily concerned about reaching the poor, disfranchised, illiterate African American populations. They taught many adults to read and write for the very first time, many of whom were still living and working on the very same plantations that their ancestors had been enslaved upon. Some participants did not even know how to hold a pencil, and some could not even recognize their own names in print. One of Clark's biggest fears is that without knowing how to read, they would never be able to pass the complicated literacy tests that were required of most Black people who wanted to register to vote. After mastering basic reading and writing skills, students learned more about civics, and about their rights as American citizens, including how to register themselves as voters and how to actively participate in other political processes such as running for a public office. As Clark explains, the adult literacy program at Highlander was very well-structured and implemented with a great deal of expertise. Highlander offered them educational opportunities most never had since they usually performed agricultural work nearly year-round just to make enough money to survive as sharecroppers. Despite having access to new learning opportunities some of the Sea Islanders still had little interest in book learning or even voting. In fact, at one workshop two participants, a Black undertaker from Georgia and a white woman from North Carolina pointed out to Clark that it was difficult to interest most Black people in voting, thus it would be best to just "let sleeping dogs lie" (Clark 1962: 184–85). To just "let sleeping dogs lie" (Whiting 1989: 176; Speake 2015: 288; Bryan and Mieder 2005: 220) is a bit of proverbial advice that is memorable enough for Clark to include it in her narrative, but had she taken its message to heart, the program would not have continued to flourish. Likewise, Clark also had to contend with potential participants' fear of violent attacks from racists and their fear of being fired or driven away from their plantations for affiliating with Highlander. Therefore, some of the programs were limited to very few participants. "Don't need no education to work in the fields" was a sentiment sometimes voiced by Black tenant or sharecropping parents, especially within earshot of the white landlords on whom their livelihoods depended" (Charron 2009: 53). Clark uses a proverb from scripture to describe her attitude towards the conundrum of having to start out with very few students saying: "Nevertheless, as the Scriptures point out, often a small bit of yeast will be the leaven that raises the large loaf" (Galatians 5:9 KJV; Clark 1962: 159). At another point, in describing the growth of the schools, she alludes to yet another proverb. Clark says: "You see, one thing spreading out starts others. It's like the pebble thrown into the mill pond" (Clark 1962: 162; Whiting 1989: 412; Charron 2009: 259). More proverbial language, which mirrors the same exact message, comes from Clark biographer and historian Katherine Mellon Charron, who says: "Septima Clark discerned that seeds scattered sometimes disappear into the wind, but others take root and yield a bountiful harvest" (Charron 2009: 350). These sayings reflect Clark's religious upbringing, the agrarian lifestyle to which she remained close her entire life, and the farming communities that she served daily. Furthermore, these proverbial insights are evidence that Clark was fully aware of the fact that many people would not be on board with her, and they emphasize the idea that having just a few enthusiastic students was more than enough to continue to expand the program.

Clark closes *Echo* with two more proverbs from scripture. At the end of the last chapter, she expresses optimism that the activism that has taken place throughout her lifetime will gradually bring about social justice in America saying: "Yes, but the new year will be better. And the years after it better, and better. I so desperately hope that they will be, I so earnestly pray that they will be, I have complete and utter faith if we falter and faint not, if we continue in good will and outreaching love the good fight, the truth some early day if not tomorrow will make us free" (Clark 1962: 242–43). "If we falter and faint not" is an allusion to a proverb from scripture which reads: "If thou faint in the face of adversity, thy strength is small" (Proverbs 24:10 KJV). Likewise, Clark employs an extended variation of the biblical proverb "the truth shall set you free." The original verse reads: "And ye shall know the truth, and the truth shall make you free" (John 8:32 KJV; Mieder 2001: 8). This is certainly evidence that Clark had a propensity for using biblical proverbs and sayings. Additionally, in an interview conducted by historian Robert Penn Warren in 1964, Clark uses another proverb from scripture as she explains to Warren that she does not believe that America will ever become decent or even stable without exercising basic Christian principles. Clark articulates her vision for America's future as she invokes the proverbial Golden Rule (Mieder 2001: 184–92; Mieder 2008: 198–99; Bryan and Mieder

2005: 322; Mieder 2020: 30) by saying: "When I say the Christian principles . . . I mean just that . . . I mean that doing unto others as we would like to be done by. This is what I consider the Christian principles that I feel we'd have to take with us everywhere" (Warren). In the Bible, the proverb reads: "Therefore all things whatsoever ye would that men should do to you, do ye even so to them: for this is the law and the prophets" (Matthew 7:12 KJV). In examining Clark's proverbial language there is no doubt that religious faith is a driving force in her life and one of the main reasons why she refused to stop fighting for the equal rights of all people.

In the very same interview, Clark also displays her knowledge of American history as she quotes a proverb that was made famous by President Abraham Lincoln. Warren asks Clark how she feels about Lincoln, and she responds:

> I can't help but think that he was a wonderful president. I can remember one thing that I admire him for and that is when he was campaigning and this fellow Stanton was his arch enemy and talked against him. When he got ready to find the Secretary of War, he decided that this was the man to be the Secretary of War and he appointed him. All the members of his cabinet felt that this should not be, but he stood up and said, gentleman I've looked over the nation and I know that this is the best man for the job. It wasn't too long a woman stood beside him and said, Mr. President, you must be losing your mind, this man even talked about your personal appearance, and he said, madam, the best way to destroy your enemies is to make him your friend. And when he died many years after that many great things were said about him, but the greatest thing that was said was the thing that was said by Stanton, the Secretary of War, he said, this was a great man and his name will go down in the ages. So both of them went to their graves as friends and not as enemies. (Warren)

The proverb "the best way to destroy your enemy is to make him your friend," and the anecdote that she shares along with it, both illustrate an important lesson, one that depicts some of the values that Clark lives by such as friendship, togetherness, and to do as Lincoln and Stanton demonstrate: to work alongside others to solve difficult problems. Throughout Clark's lifetime she made far more allies than enemies. When Warren asks Clark if she knows that Lincoln was racist, Clark responds in the negative saying:

> I don't know any of the things that he said that makes me feel that he was a racist. I heard of his 10% plan to free the slaves. I heard of him

going down to Mississippi on a barge saying that when he became a man that he was gonna strike a blow that would stop this slavery cause he saw the slaves chained there on barges. I can't remember any of the [racist] things that he said. (Warren)

Despite any controversy surrounding Lincoln, Clark does not believe that Lincoln was racist, and this impression was more than likely garnered in part by some of the proverbial wisdom that Clark attained by studying and remembering the president's words. The fact that Abraham Lincoln, as a child, vowed to one day strike a proverbial blow against slavery obviously made a huge impression on Clark, and there is at least some evidence that the attitude exhibited by young Lincoln's strong proverbial language helped to motivate Clark as she continued to shape her own life and fight against racial injustice and oppression (Mieder 2001: 229–31). In fact, Clark uses the very same proverbial expression as she describes her own calculated and measured approach to practicing social activism, saying: "Each time I pass through a new crisis . . . the sun is barely peeping through the storm clouds . . . I patiently wait to strike the blow when my inner self whispers, 'Now is the time'" (Charron 2009: 241–42). Most would agree that in speaking of striking proverbial blows against racial injustice, Clark is clearly stepping outside of prescribed gender roles for her time. However, Clark was still mild-mannered, soft-spoken, and kind, as most women were expected to be in a male-dominated society in the 1950s. Nevertheless, she was also cognizant of the fact that teaching literacy for the purpose of promoting political engagement in Black communities is considered by most to be a very militant and radical act, and if it had garnered more attention, it could have easily cost her life. In fact, Clark uses what historian Katherine M. Charron refers to as the "tactical invisibility" (Charron 2009: 350) that most Black women possessed to their advantage, and it allowed Clark and the other Black women to continue to help manage the transformative education programs that she created. Charron's insights and the idea of Clark patiently waiting for decades to strike proverbial blows in the name of social justice provides further evidence that Clark knew she was no passive role player, but one of the masterminds behind the civil rights movement.

The sense of "tactical invisibility" that Charron explains was built in part because of the subservient roles that Black women were expected to play in the community and in Black churches. Black women were largely viewed as organizers, nurturers, protectors, and moral support to male clergy, and they were generally expected to be seen and not heard. This tradition of subservience also carried over to the church affiliated clubs and organizations.

Consequently, women such as Clark, Baker, and other female leaders knew that they were being radical on several different fronts when they held high-ranking positions in Black organizations and when they openly attacked white supremacy by themselves instead of waiting on their male counterparts to do it for them. Clark explains this scenario using the proverbial expression to live in a "man-made world" in an interview as she acknowledges the fact that she was constantly reminded that her presence was disrupting the long-held tradition of male dominance among clergy (Walker 1976: 11). Clark says that when Dr. King appointed her to the executive board of the Southern Christian Leadership Conference (SCLC), her authority was always questioned simply because she was a woman: "Many times we'd go into the meeting and [Reverend Abernathy] always wanted to know why was I a member of that trustee board?" (Walker 1976: 12), Clark sums up the problem best as she employs the popular proverbial expression saying: "Well I think that we live in a man-made world, and because of that, as a man, he didn't feel as if women had really enough intelligence . . ." (Walker 1976: 11). In another instance, Clark explains a time when Dr. King gave an SCLC secretary the proverbial devil for allowing Clark to award certificates to program participants in place of himself (Bryan and Mieder 2005: 207):

> I found out that they didn't respect women too much. I went into a small community down here, and, we were getting affiliates started. And I don't know where Dr. King was, but I presented the certificates to the people who had joined. And he asked his secretary about it. And I wrote a letter thanking them for their help, and I showed it to her. And Dr. King, he too, wanted to know about me as a woman. So I had a copy of the letter, and I showed him that I said in the name of Dr. King, I'm presenting these certificates and so forth. And the little secretary was just fine and wondered why [he had] given her the devil for not letting him be the person to present these certificates. I said, "Well, of all the [nerve]." (Hall 1976: 81–82)

Clark turns to the proverbial expression "man-made world" again as she explains that male chauvinism was one reason that led Baker to leave SCLC after initiating the Student Nonviolent Coordinating Committee (SNCC) in 1960. She says Baker "was concerned about not being recognized in a man-made world, and it didn't bother me" (Hall 1976: 80). Clark reiterates: "And this is a man-made world we've been living in all these years. We're just coming to the forefront" (Hall 1976: 80). Likewise, living in a "man-made world" caused Clark to be openly critical of Black male leadership whenever they seemed to lack enough courage to stand up to white supremacy. In *Echo*, she uses another popular proverbial expression as she explains a time when she expressed this very sentiment. In 1955, as school integration debates heated up and Black boycotts of white businesses proliferated, due to outside pressure, the president of South Carolina State University threatened to expel any student that participated in a planned NAACP meeting on campus despite the university being historically Black. Clark says in a letter to her close friend Mrs. Warring, that although she is very proud of the young students' activist spirit, the university president's actions are a prime example that there is "no spine in the backbone of the professionals" (Charron 2009: 239). In the letter, she also expresses full confidence that "the younger generation" will "ride over this [proverbial] hump" (Charron 2009: 239). While Black male leadership often lacked a "spine" or "backbone," she acknowledges the fact that Black women contrarily have always been the "backbone" of the church and civil rights movement (Hall 1976: 91; Mieder 2001: 117–18; Mieder 2009: 168; Mieder 2010: 217).

On at least two separate occasions, Clark uses variations of the proverbial expression "to jump out of the frying pan into the fire" (Whiting 1989: 244). Clark's mother wanted her to marry a wealthy, light-skinned, and upstanding member of the Black community, since in early twentieth-century Charleston, having lighter skin and wealth could easily gain a newly married Black woman open access to all the most elite Black social circles. Likewise, doing the opposite could just as easily get one barred from the very same groups. In an interview, Clark explains her difficult decision to turn down a marriage proposal from a well-off and popular Black minister, and instead choosing to marry a dark-skinned and relatively poor unknown sailor, against her mother's wishes. She says: "My mother was so strict and had all those strict religious ideas, and I'd felt that I'd be jumping into another frying pan if I went into [being] a minister's wife. I didn't know you know, how I could live and please all the people, because I didn't feel as if I wanted to do all those things. And preacher's wives had to endure so much, you know. I didn't think that I could do it" (Hall 1976: 44–45). Shortly after being married in 1921, Clark discovered that her new husband, Nerie Clark, also remained married to another woman and when she confronted him about the matter, he asked her to leave their home. To add to her misfortune, they had a child, a girl named Victoria Irma, who died in infancy. She later gave birth to a healthy son, Nerie David Clark Jr., who would never know his father because Nerie Sr. would die from liver failure at the age of thirty-five, before his son's third birthday (Charron 2009: 107–10). To make matters worse, her mother, Victoria Warren, never actually forgave Clark for marrying Nerie Sr. even though Warren and Clark would later mend their relationship. This series of unfortunate events caused Clark to believe that she was being cursed by God for going against her mother's wishes, and for some time the deep spiral of depression that she found herself experiencing was pushing her towards committing suicide. Widowed at the age of twenty-seven, teaching the poor on John's Island and engaging in activist efforts to improve social and economic conditions for Black people in Charleston were among the ways that Clark overcame this difficult time in her life. She also uses a variation of the proverbial expression to describe what it was like to live with her in-laws after the death of her husband, saying: "My mother-in-law was of the same type as my mother; in the two families they made the decisions. So actually I had jumped from the frying pan into the fire. And since I was living under the roof of my in-laws, I felt that I should obey the rules of the household" (Clark 1962: 71). It is rather telling that she would use this proverbial expression to describe one of the most difficult times in her life on at least two separate occasions that span nearly fifteen years. Perhaps in using the proverbial expression "to jump from the frying pan into the fire" (Whiting 1989: 244), Clark is signaling to her audience that the most difficult years of her life ultimately functioned as a rite of passage that ultimately helped her to value her own education, independence and voice as a teacher and civil rights activist.

Clark also uses other sayings that involve fire. In *Echo*, she includes a proverb that was uttered by a man who was very much against Clark inviting Mrs. Elizabeth Warring, to speak before a YWCA annual meeting in Charleston. He was against the move because Warring was a white woman from the North who was an outspoken supporter of integration. She was also a staunch critic of all southern white women whom she believed to be inherently racist. In a phone call, the director of the United Givers Fund, a major source of funding for Charleston's YWCA, warns Clark of controversy surrounding Warring. He says: "I live nine miles from her in Litchfield, Connecticut, and I can tell you there is fire where you see all that smoke" (Clark 1962: 97–98; Speake 2015: 290). As a result of Clark's decision to invite the integrationist to speak at the meeting, the YWCA executive director attempts to force Clark to sign a statement saying that the information was false, and Clark vehemently refuses. In describing the media's reaction to this news, Clark says:

> Well, the fat was in the fire! Letters and calls began to pour into the newspapers, and a reporter called me. The reporter wanted to know if these reports were true—did I say this and that, did I tell the executive secretary of the United Givers Fund that his paths didn't cross with

Mrs. Waring's, did I tell them that I would not sign such a letter, did I refuse to sign the statement the trustees had written. I told him that I had refused to sign them, and I answered frankly and truthfully all his questions. The newspapers carried stories, the telephones buzzed, the gossipers had a field day. Never, I'm sure, had a YWCA annual meeting had more advance publicity. (Clark 1962: 98)

Clark uses the expression "the fat was in the fire" (Whiting 1989: 215), but she is certainly not alarmed by the proverbial field day that the media is having. In fact, she says to one close friend that she had determined that the issue would have to remain a proverbial "hot potato" (Clark 1962: 96; Whiting 1989: 508) because while it angered YWCA leaders and members, Clark did not feel comfortable rescinding a speaking invitation to a federal judge's wife whom she felt could be a much more useful ally than donors or even timid Black leaders. Despite the controversy that it caused, Mrs. Warring spoke at the meeting, and it became known as the 1950 Coming Street YWCA "Shock Treatment Speech." Throughout the speech, Warring praised Black Charleston women for their activist efforts and she also vehemently attacked white southerners whom she described as being "sick" and "confused" (LDHI). Clark remained friends with Mrs. Warring and her husband, Judge Waties Warring, for long after Mrs. Warring gave her renowned speech, although Clark never shared Warring's views of southern white women. For years they continued to break social norms by having integrated meetings and social gatherings at one another's homes, and in the process, angering groups such as the Ku Klux Klan (KKK) and the all-white Citizen's Council (CC). These hate groups continually issued death threats. Once during a meeting they even attempted to intimidate Clark and Warring by throwing a brick through a front window of the Warrings' home.

Clark and her colleague Myles Horton took careful notice as sit-in protests, initiated by four students from North Carolina Agricultural and Technical State University in Greensboro, North Carolina, on February 1, 1960, proliferated across most of the southern states in a matter of weeks. Clark says on one occasion that in her view, the protest "spread like a wild prairie fire . . . to more than one hundred cities across the South" (Charron 2009: 290). Clark's use of the proverbial expression "to spread like a wild prairie fire" may be a biblical reference used to express excitement for the movement's new direction. A passage from Psalms reads:

> Like swarming bees, like wild prairie fire, they hemmed me in; in God's name I rubbed their faces in the dirt. I was right on the cliff-edge,

ready to fall, when God grabbed and held me. God's my strength, he's also my song, and now he's my salvation. Hear the shouts, hear the triumph songs in the camp of the saved? "The hand of God has turned the tide! The hand of God is raised in victory! The hand of God has turned the tide!" (Psalm 118:12–16 MSG)

No matter what version of the Bible one is reading, the verse is an exaltation of victory in the face of attack, and Clark's use of the proverbial expression brings attention to how fast the movement spread, and to the fact that the group of student protesters stood their ground in a very dangerous situation. The protestors from Greensboro included Joseph McNeil, Franklin McCain, Ezell Blair Jr. (a.k.a. Jibreel Khazan), and David Richmond. They became known as the A&T Four, and the sit-in movement that they initiated encouraged Horton to reposition his thinking on Highlander's future role in the civil rights movement. While Clark already had confidence in the youth due to several successful integration workshops and conferences that she held at Highlander throughout the 1950s, Horton still held the perspective that Highlander should remain primarily focused on adults, but because of the exponential growth of the largely student-led sit-in movement, Horton began to think more about how to get young people involved (Charron 2009: 290). This is when Clark decided to call Ella Baker of the Southern Christian Leadership Conference (SCLC) and together, they organized a three-day conference at Shaw University that lasted from April 1 through April 3 and it included "forty-seven African Americans, thirty-five white students, representing twenty colleges in nineteen states and three foreign countries" (Charron 2009: 290). At the conference, Clark and Baker helped the students to outline the goals and philosophy of what would be known as the Student Nonviolent Coordinating Committee (SNCC), the first and only Black organization to be organized and led entirely by students. Clark and Baker's guidance and tutelage helped to guarantee the students that their proverbial "wild prairie fire" (Psalm 118:12–16 MSG; Mieder 2010: 310) would continue to grow.

Additionally, Clark uses a plethora of proverbial expressions that communicate ways that she conceptualizes American ideals such as the right to education, freedom, justice, and equality. In Clark's later years she refers to education as the proverbial "tree of life." Clark retired from the classroom in the 1970s, but she never retired from the movement as she continued to work on behalf of the Black community in Charleston, South Carolina, by serving the public school system as the first female African American Charleston school board member. Thus, the very same school system that fired her for belonging to the NAACP in 1956 sought out her wisdom and council throughout the 1970s and 1980s (Charron 2009: 345). When the school board tried to distribute a pamphlet on American government that did not include any information about Black political accomplishments at all, Clark quickly brought this issue to the school board's attention. In speaking of the incident Clark says: "I wanted to know who the black children would have to look up to in that book. There was nothing in there that would help black children to feel that they had a right to the tree of life, and I know how important that is" (Charron 2009: 345–46).

Another revealing proverbial expression from *Echo* appears in a letter from someone who donated money to Highlander Folk School after it was raided by the State of Tennessee and all assets and property were seized and auctioned off, forcing Myles Horton to relocate the school to Knoxville, essentially starting all over again from scratch. In addition to sending a charitable donation, the contributor writes:

> The wheels of justice certainly operated in this case on a bent axle. I am sure that you feel as I do that nothing is to be gained by looking backward—only forward, and if determination, courage and vision are needed to create a new Highlander, you are endowed in abundance with all three. I can only stand in awe of what you have done and are willing to do. I hope that within a few weeks I will be able to add to this contribution and help you in whatever way I can to rebuild Highlander. (Clark 1962: 230)

Out of the nearly five hundred letters that were written in support of HFS, Clark chose to include this letter in its entirety due in part to its proverbial wit and wisdom. There is quite a bit of humor and irony displayed in the idea of America's proverbial wheels of justice operating on a "bent axle." Furthermore, the humor and irony are tempered by the phrase "nothing is to be gained by looking backward—only forward" (Clark 1962: 230). These are the kinds of messages that Highlander needed during its time of calamity, and by including it in her narrative, Clark knew that it would only motivate more people to support the cause.

In addition to America's proverbial "wheels of justice," Clark also makes reference to America's proverbial "lamp of freedom" (Clark 1962: 233). As Clark is reflecting on all the friends that she has made during her nearly decade long tenure at Highlander, she laments the fact that HFS is being forced to close:

These things and these faces I can never forget, and as I pray for the lamp of freedom to burn incessantly, I know that I am not weaving my life's pattern alone. Only one end of the threads do I hold in my hands; the other ends go many ways linking my life with others, my country with others. My pattern and my country's pattern will depend largely upon the awareness, the insights, the skills, the personal goals and the incentives of those who hold the other ends of those threads. (Clark 1962: 233–34)

In addition to the proverbial "lamp of freedom," Clark's extended weaving metaphor further highlights the fact that she knows that she is not alone in the struggle for social justice and equality. In fact, she views it as a struggle that she shares with the entire world.

Clark also refers to America's proverbial "fruits of democracy," and a part of what makes this proverbial expression so interesting is the way that Clark builds up to the proverbial language and uses it to heighten her message:

So I work among the Negro people, who, we must agree, have the fewest of the democratic freedoms and many of whom have inadequate education or none at all, who live constantly under the fear of intimidation, insult and violence, I am reminded that here is the continuing test of our democratic form of government. In the recent rise of the image of hope for the segregated black man and his deliverance from this state of pseudo-slavery I see clearly the form of challenge. If permanent social patterns are to be created that are truly democratic, I maintain, then the most lowly being must enjoy equally with every other American the fruits of democracy. Only then will the Negro, and particularly the Negro parent, see the glimmer of light ahead, only then will he see a way out of his dilemma. (Clark 1962: 236–37)

Clark saves all the proverbial language for the very end of her statement so that it may help the reader to realize the enormity of the situation that she is describing. The idea that drastic change is the only thing that can facilitate a process that will still only take place gradually is her overall implication.

When Clark uses the proverbial expression "laws of the land," it is to point out the government's own political and social wrongdoing and its failure to practice humanitarianism. One instance of the expression being used appears near the end of *Echo* as she invokes another popular hymn that was sang at

HFS. It just so happens that this hymn, entitled *Black and White*, is as critical of the government as Clark is. It reads:

> The ink is black, the page is white, together we learn to read
> and write, to read and write;
> And now a child can understand this is the law of all the land;
> The ink is black, the page is white, together we learn to read
> And write, to read and write. (Clark 1962: 241)

The hymn promotes integrated education as the best way to encourage America's youth to believe in freedom and equality. Additionally, Clark repeats the proverbial expression "laws of the land" when she quotes a statement taken from a Highlander press release that she wrote. The statement is so important that she includes it twice in *Echo*, saying it once near the beginning and then later near the end. In both instances, the proverbial expression "laws of the land" is also accompanied by variations of two proverbs regarding freedom that were popularized by Martin Luther King Jr., whom she also taught at Highlander:

> Highlander was established three decades ago it had been fighting for the rights of all people, whatever their race, religion or political persuasion, to meet together and discuss their problems, And it is because of this meeting together, and only because of this, I insist, that Highlander intermittently has been attacked by forces that oppose not only the principles of human brotherhood, but also the very law of the land as interpreted by our highest courts. (Clark 1962: 11, 207)

Clark then adds that despite the attacks, HFS will continue to serve all people. This statement is then followed by two proverbs that were largely popularized by King although it is unknown if King or Clark used the proverbs first. Clark says: "Freedom has always been lost by a people who allowed their rights gradually to be whittled away. The threat to silence and to keep forever silent the voice of Highlander is a threat to the very existence of every organization in this nation and to the basic freedom of thought and expression of every American" (Clark 1962: 11, 207). The proverb "freedom has always been lost by a people who allowed their rights gradually to be whittled away" and also her variation of the proverb "a threat to justice in one place is a threat to justice everywhere" (Mieder 2010: 354–56) may not have been proverbs when she first publishes her press release or *Echo*, but they were popularized greatly by her former student, Dr. King, as he attracted a great deal of attention whenever he spoke in public.

There are other proverbial expressions that Clark uses in reference to social justice. In *Echo* she refers to the proverbial "good fight" (Clark 1962: 242). Historian and Clark biographer Katherine M. Charron discusses the fact that Clark garnered much self-satisfaction from fighting proverbial good fights and winning them. In fact, early in her career she did so on at least two separate occasions—once in 1919 when she worked with the NAACP to have more Black teachers hired in the city of Charleston, and then when she worked with NAACP lawyers (including Thurgood Marshall) to force the cities of Columbia and Charleston to pay equal salaries to Black teachers. With Clark's help, the NAACP won their case against the city of Columbia in 1944, and they later won their case against the city of Charleston in 1945 (Charron 2009). As a result of the court's verdicts and as a form of backlash, the Columbia school board expanded their control over Black educators by requiring all teachers to take recertification exams that would then determine their level of pay. Some teachers refused to take the exam, choosing to resign instead. Others performed so poorly on the test that their pay either stayed the same or they only saw marginal increases. Only a small number of Black teachers performed well, and Clark was among them. She expresses a tremendous amount of confidence as she employs a proverbial expression to motivate her colleagues to "fight the proverbial good fight" and take the recertification exam. At a meeting, as Palmetto States Teacher Association (PTSA) president, Clark says to distraught members: "If you say that you are not going to take that examination in the morning . . . I will be with you. But if some of you say tonight that you are on the fence on this proposition, then I know you will be the first ones there to take it. So I will let you know right now that I am going. I'm not afraid to take that examination" (Clark 1962: 83). This statement depicts a very self-reliant Clark, who demonstrates nothing but poised confidence as she tries to empower her colleagues to not straddle the proverbial fence on this one important issue. Clark says that her "activists' efforts 'paid off,' not only in the satisfaction of having made the good fight, but also in actual cash" (Charron 2009: 177). After earning an A on the recertification exam, Clark's formerly meager teacher salary tripled. Likewise, Clark also makes it known that there is still a proverbial price to pay (Mieder 2009: 286–88; Mieder 2020b: 172–73) for anyone who wishes to engage in any form of activism. She says: "I feel that before a person goes into work of this kind, he must search his soul and decide once and for all that this is the price he may have to pay for the freedom he is trying to establish"

(Clark 1962: 11, 12). Clark was always aware of the personal sacrifices that she made to stay involved in activism. The work that she did often left little time for friends or family. Additionally, there was the constant threat of violent retaliation from racists, so much so that her immediate family was often afraid for Clark's life. Likewise, some of her friends were at times afraid to even be associated with Clark. Once at an event in her honor, some of her own sorority sisters, AKAs, refused to be photographed with her for fear of losing their jobs (Charron 2009: 245). Clark would continue to "pay the price" on behalf of her race and all people throughout her entire career.

There is also another proverb that Clark uses in acknowledgement of her calculated and measured approach to political organizing. In the early 1960s, as Clark's Citizenship Education Programs became increasingly popular, Black organizations throughout the South requested training for their own members. Organizations such as the National Association for Colored People (NAACP), the Student Nonviolent Coordinating Committee (SNCC), and the Congress of Racial Equality (CORE) began to realize that if they wanted to empower the Black communities from a political standpoint that they must heed Clark's philosophy and first focus on education. People would then be able to use the basic literacy and civic skills that they have acquired to fill out voter registration forms, vote for the most viable candidates, and even run for political offices themselves. Clark was not surprised by the sudden upswing in Citizenship Education Program participation, and she likely realized that the tens of thousands of newly registered Black voters would be hard for any organization to ignore. She uses a popular proverb to convey her belief that success was to be expected saying: "The acceptance of these services by other civil rights organizations says that great designs are based on method not madness" (Charron 2009: 319). "Great designs are based on method not madness" is an appropriate proverb that attests to the program's positive results (Whiting 1989: 408; Bryan and Mieder 2005: 505).

Additionally, there are at least a few other statements made by Clark that have become well-known sayings that most people easily attribute to her. One such saying conveys the fact that Clark believed ignorance to be a far more immediate threat to humanity than some of its consequences such as racism or even segregation. In support of this conviction, Clark famously states: "We need to be taught to study rather than believe, to inquire rather than to affirm" (Charron 2009: 341). This saying emphasizes the fact that she was always proud of teaching her students to think and conduct research for themselves.

Finally, in her eightieth year Clark was content that she had devoted nearly her entire life to fights for civil rights and social justice and she was satisfied with all that she had accomplished. In fact, she says in her second autobiography, *Ready from Within* (1990), that old age is "the best part of life" (Clark 1990: 124). Clark then shares her reason for having this attitude, with a brief sentence which has since become a popular saying: "It's not that you have just grown old, but it is how you have grown old" (Clark 1990; Charron 2009: 12). As Clark continues, she also alludes to a proverb: "I feel that I have grown old believing there is always a beautiful lining to that cloud that overshadows things" (Clark 1990: 124–25). This statement is an allusion to the well-known proverb "every dark cloud always has a silver lining" (Mieder 2008: 12; Doyle et al. 2012: 39). Clark then delivers another brief sentence that has since become her most famous saying: "I have a great belief in the fact that whenever there is chaos, it creates wonderful thinking. I consider chaos a gift, and this has come during my old age" (Clark 1990: 125). The saying "whenever there is chaos, it creates wonderful thinking" at first glance seems like an oxymoron or paradox. Many consider the civil rights era to be the most chaotic years in American history, but it is also an era that Clark learned to navigate. Amid chaos, Clark demanded basic rights like the freedom to vote and equal pay for Black teachers, and with the calm, meticulous, and observant air of a veteran teacher, she taught others how to demand freedom and equality also. Thus, it only makes sense that Clark would view chaos as a gift. Perhaps our present generation of Americans may benefit from viewing chaos as a gift also.

Chapter six delves into the life of one of Clark's more widely known contemporaries, Malcolm X (1925–65). Like Clark and the other proverb masters included in this text, Malcolm X was a voracious reader for most of his adult life which undoubtedly increased his exposure to proverbs. However, Malcom X's life also greatly contrasts with the others. For instance, Clark discovered her love for literature as a child at the prestigious Avery Institute, while Malcolm X would hone his literary and oratorical skills in a federal penitentiary. Despite his unconventional road to wisdom, Malcolm X would eventually teach multitudes of Black youth to take pride in themselves and their communities during a time when anti-Black rhetoric permeated American society. Today Malcolm X is primarily remembered by the multitudes of public talks and speeches that he gave at universities around the country and for his televised interviews. In fact, Malcolm X's entire career of activism was heavily documented by news reporters and television cameras. One thing that chapter six illustrates is that Malcolm X sometimes used his public platform to communicate his philosophy and different aspects of his worldview in the form of proverbs and proverbial expressions.

Chapter Six

"YOU CAN'T HATE THE ROOTS OF A TREE AND NOT HATE THE TREE, YOU CAN'T HATE AFRICA AND NOT HATE YOURSELF"

The Important Proverbs, Sayings, and Proverbial Expressions of Malcolm X

Malcolm X (1925–65), also known as Malcolm Little and El Hajj Malik El-Shabbazz, was born to Louise Helen Norton Little and Earl Little in Omaha, Nebraska. "Malcolm was the seventh of his father's ten children, including three by a previous marriage" (Wainstock 2009: 5). Both of Malcom's parents were members of Marcus Garvey's Universal Negro Improvement Association (UNIA). The UNIA was founded in 1914 by Garvey (1887–1940), a Jamaican-born Black nationalist who was widely known for initiating the global "back to Africa" movement. He espoused the notion that ultimately only Africa would be suitable for Africans and all its descendants due to the racial violence and discrimination which plagued the US and other colonized nations (Payne 2020: 32–37). Malcolm's parents were likely drawn to the UNIA because of Garvey's self-help approach to solving racial issues. Garvey wanted Black communities to be politically and economically independent, and the Little family worked to help spread this message. Malcolm's father was a UNIA minister and president of the Omaha chapter, while his mother, Louise, wrote articles for the UNIA newspaper, *Negro World*. Malcolm seemed to be his father's favorite child, and he would take him with him as he preached in different places around the country. Malcolm's early exposure to public speaking most likely had a profound effect on him later in life. The family also faced constant threats and harassment from the Ku Klux Klan, which wanted Earl to stop preaching and vacate their family home. Sometimes the Klan would vandalize the Littles' property or issue harsh verbal warnings, but the family never relented. Earl's preaching eventually took them to several places. The family would live in Milwaukee, Albion, and Lansing, Michigan. Additionally, Earl would take Malcolm on solo trips to preach in different places around the world like Philadelphia and Canada. The Little family continued to preach the UNIA message of Black nationalism even though they faced constant threats from the Ku Klux Klan. In fact, Earl was on his way to a speaking engagement when he died in 1931. He was accidentally killed after he slipped and fell underneath a railway car (Payne 2020: 81–93).

In the wake of the Great Depression (1929–39), Louise had a very difficult time providing for all her children. Furthermore, the self-help philosophy which she practiced became a debilitating factor. She rejected help from several outside sources including neighbors, and the welfare agency. The mental and physical strain of caring for such a large family eventually became too much for her, and she had to be admitted to a mental institution while the children were placed with relatives and in foster care. Malcolm would bounce around to different foster homes as an adolescent until he went to live with his older sister, Ella, in Boston. As a fifteen-year-old living in Boston, Malcolm proved to be a very bright student, earning some of the highest marks in his class, but he quickly became disillusioned with education after one of his favorite teachers told him that his goal of becoming a lawyer was not a realistic option for a Negro. Being the only Black student in the class probably added to his embarrassment, rendering any aspirations that he previously held feel utterly hopeless. Subsequently, in the eighth grade Malcolm dropped out of school and quickly discovered that being unusually tall for his age made it very easy for him to pass for an adult. Malcolm quickly became enthralled with city street life, which included staying out late at night, dancing with pretty women in lavish night clubs, wearing fancy zoot suits, and adopting wild conk hair styles. The sleep-by-day, party-by-night lifestyle that Malcolm had adopted eventually became too much for his older sister, and he went to live with another relative in Detroit where he worked a series of odd jobs as a dishwasher and railway porter. He would also sell drugs, gamble, dabble in the prostitution trade, and take part in a robbery ring which targeted upscale white neighborhoods. Malcolm lived a dangerous lifestyle, and by his own accounts he barely escaped death several times. Malcolm became very street savvy, but he was no crime boss by anyone's standard. Illegal side hustles were quite typical in Black inner-city neighborhoods throughout the 1940s and 1950s, when job discrimination and redlining had many Blacks trapped in slums and ghettoes, working menial labor positions for very low wages. Consequently, the side hustles were used to supplement miniscule wages. Unfortunately, this practice also led many African Americans to the federal penitentiary, and Malcolm's case was no different. Malcolm served seven years for burglary (1946-52), and while incarcerated, he was introduced to the Nation of Islam (NOI) by his brother, Reginald, who convinced him to begin practicing some of NOI's most important tenets, including abandoning drugs, alcohol, and smoking. Furthermore, he would adopt the NOI practice of eliminating pork from his diet and praying daily while facing eastward. However, the most profound influence on Malcolm X was a fellow prisoner named John Elton Bembry (Payne 2020: 222-26), who noticed that Malcolm was smarter than most inmates. Bembry was considered a model prisoner, and he always took advantage of Norfolk prison's enhanced education system, which included library access, and a debate team which competed against students from several Ivy League schools. Malcolm sometimes read casually to pass the time, mostly from cowboy novels, until Bembry introduced him to a much more serious and disciplined style of learning. Bembry encouraged Malcolm to read from a range of subjects including philosophy, American and world literature, and history. He also inspired Malcolm to work at expanding his basic vocabulary, which he did by copying and memorizing entire dictionaries. Ultimately, Bembry helped shape Malcolm's worldview even more so than his correspondences with NOI leader, Elijah Muhammad (1897-1975), who also encouraged Malcom's studies.

When Malcolm was finally released from prison, he was appointed by Elijah Muhammed to be minister of NOI Temple No. 7 in Harlem, while he also worked diligently to grow NOI membership around the country. He often traveled to major cities such as Philadelphia, Boston, and Detroit to help initiate new branches of the organization. Malcolm X helped NOI membership grow from hundreds to thousands in a relatively short amount of time. Malcolm's oration was charismatic, fiery, and spellbinding, and many young Black people were drawn to him and NOI's self-help philosophy.

After being released from prison, Malcolm X spent twelve years with NOI. He endured a prolonged and complicated divergence from the group when he discovered that Elijah Muhmmad was engaging in extramarital affairs. Muhammad fathered ten children with seven of his teenage secretaries, whom he immediately had excommunicated from the organization and left without financial support or guidance (Payne 2020: 431-33). Furthermore, Malcolm came to the realization that NOI's cultish and racist philosophy had nothing to do with true orthodox Islam which was practiced in many Middle Eastern nations for centuries. During Malcolm's tenure, he helped Elijah Muhammad grow to become a very wealthy and powerful leader. As a result, Muhammad had also grown intensely jealous of Malcolm's speaking ability and his popularity. Furthermore, Muhammad did not like the fact that news media outlets around the country always wanted to know what Malcolm thought about issues surrounding race, class, and politics in America—topics that Malcolm felt very strongly about even though speaking out on such issues went against NOI policy (Payne 2020: 535). These difficult circumstances made Malcolm's split from NOI inevitable. When Malcolm split from NOI in 1963, he founded two organizations, Muslim Mosque Incorporated (MMI) and the Organization of Afro-American Unity (OAAU). Malcom's plan for MMI was to adhere to all tenets of true Islam while also expounding on the orthodox principle of universal brotherhood amongst Muslims of all races (Payne 2020: 454). The OAAU, named for Africa's Organization of African Unity, promoted Black nationalism. Its ultimate purpose was to connect all civil rights organizations around the United States and in Africa with hopes that the Black struggle for equality would be viewed as an international human rights issue effecting all people as opposed to being viewed as only a domestic problem. Malcolm knew that his philosophy was considered a dangerous threat to NOIs stronghold in Black communities. He also understood that he would be killed as a result, but he never ran or expatriated because he believed that death was a small price to pay for justice and equality. After many threats and failed attempts on his life, he was eventually assassinated on February 21, 1965, gunned down as he stood to deliver a speech to a small audience of OAAU supporters in Harlem's Audubon auditorium. He was killed at the hands of the same organization responsible for making him famous.

How did Malcolm X rise through the ranks of the NOI so quickly? At the height of his career, he was the most sought out public speaker in America, giving countless interviews and speaking at nearly one hundred universities around the country. What made Malcolm X's speeches and talks so engaging? One source of Malcom X's oratorical efficiency was his use of proverbial language. Throughout his life of public speaking, Malcolm made many poignant and profound statements using proverbs, proverbial expressions, and sayings. This chapter is not an inventory of every proverb or proverbial statement, but it emphasizes the fact that proverb use often accentuated the strongest points in his oratory. Malcolm sometimes used proverbs from scripture (the Holy Bible, the Hebrew Bible, and the Koran). Several things often go unmentioned regarding Malcolm's rhetoric. Firstly, scholars have mentioned the presence of animal imagery in Malcolm's rhetoric (Flick et al.: 1988) without discussing the fact that his animal imagery is often accompanied by other agrarian literary elements such as symbolism, proverbs, and proverbial expressions. Secondly, scholars often ignore some possible reasons *why* Malcolm chose to employ pastoral language so often. Malcolm's aim wasn't simply to use animal imagery or proverbs to disparage *all* white people as some may believe. Malcolm simply aimed to vilify Jim Crow Law and those who advocated for it. Third and lastly, scholars often ignore the fact that the agrarian elements of Malcolm's proverbial rhetoric (including the animal imagery) reflect the agrarian lifestyle that he lived as a young child growing up in rural Lansing, Michigan before his father died, when he was surrounded by wilderness, farm life, and much free time to himself. According to Malcolm's autobiography, he would spend many hours reclining on his back among grassy hills studying the clouds and having "pre-visions" of what his future might hold (DeCaro 1996: 48). Malcom says: "Out behind our house, out in the country from Lansing, Michigan, there was an old, grassy 'Hector's Hill,' we called it. . . . I used to lie on the top of Hector's Hill, and look up at the sky, at the clouds, moving over me, and day-dream, all kinds of things" (DeCaro 1996: 48). It is clear from his description that he cherished those times, as DeCaro explains further:

> Malcolm's youthful moments of meditation may have entailed more than simple childhood fantasy. In contemplation, both before and after his father's death, he began to feel the stirring of a certain sense of purpose in his life. His continuing fascination with the sky and clouds, though certainly a childlike characteristic, held for Malcolm a deeper meaning that he carried with him throughout life, and even sought to explain in the closing pages of his autobiography. (DeCaro 1996: 49)

The preadolescent years of his life may represent the most comfortable years that he would ever enjoy, and by the time Malcolm reached adulthood, he clearly wanted to remember those years, and draw wisdom from them. This may partially account for why he frequented agrarian proverbs and sayings so often in his rhetoric, even in the most difficult of circumstances.

One agrarian proverb that Malcolm X used at times was "chickens come *home* to roost" (Wilson 1970: 118; Taylor 1985: 10; Harder et al. 1992: 95; Mieder 1993: 52; Prahlad 1996: 217; Bryan and Mieder 2016: 149). To really understand why he used this pastoral axiom on one specific occasion, one must consider some key events of the 1960s. During that decade, America witnessed racial violence take the lives of many important figures, including Medgar Evers (1925–63), Bobby Kennedy (1925–68), and Martin Luther King Jr. (1929–68). Only weeks after the March on Washington for Jobs and Freedom (August 28, 1963), racist backlash precipitated in the form of a

Birmingham, Alabama, church bombing (September 15, 1963), which killed four young Black girls. Then weeks later, on November 22, 1963, President John F. Kennedy was assassinated in Dallas, Texas. Kennedy played a major role in bringing the March on Washington to fruition. Additionally, Kennedy had been promoting a highly publicized civil rights bill for months (which eventually became the Civil Rights Act of 1964). The fact that Kennedy was willing to work with civil rights leaders generated a lot of hostility. Nine days after Kennedy was murdered, on December 1, 1963, Malcolm delivered a speech which he had written one week before Kennedy's assassination entitled "God's Judgement of White America." It wasn't Malcolm's speech that drew ire from the press; rather, it was the statement that Malcom made during the question-and-answer period following his speech. One member of the press asked for Malcolm's opinion on Kennedy, and Malcolm candidly responded "that it was an instance of 'chickens coming home to roost'— . . . Being an old farm boy myself, chickens coming home to roost never did make me sad; they always made me glad" (Marable, et al. 2013: 274–75; Payne 2020: 434). Malcolm's statement alluding to the old agrarian proverb "chickens come home to roost" (Mieder 1993: 52; Bryan and Mieder 2016: 149) was misinterpreted by many and even left some NOI members confused. One NOI member, Captain Joseph, said: "I couldn't understand" (Wainstock 2009: 80). For Joseph, Malcolm's remarks were primarily about "authority, rivalry, and betrayal," meaning that Kennedy was not the focus of the statement (Wainstock 2009: 80). Nevertheless, "they relayed [Malcolm's words] back to the Chicago leadership who then informed Muhammad" (Wainstock 2009: 80).

Historian Rudolph, J. Siebert seems to agree with Joseph's interpretation of the proverb. Siebert also views it as a broad comment regarding racial hatred as opposed to a jab at the president. In other words, it is another way of saying: "The more hate was permitted to lash out, when there were still ways it could have been checked, the more bold the hate became. At last it struck the white man's own kind, including his own leader" (Siebert 2016: 155). Siebert contends that "it was in this context that Malcolm X used the fateful phrase that *Chickens*, i.e., the necrophilic white hate, were, *Coming Home to Roost*" (emphasis in original) (Haley 1992: 347; Marable, et al. 2013: 274–75: Siebert 2016: 155).

The fact that Malcolm broke NOI rules by publicly sharing an opinion on political matters and the confusion and insult brought about by multiple interpretations was used by Elijah Muhammad and NOI to justify silencing Malcolm X for ninety days with the intention of eventually barring him from the organization altogether. Malcolm's statement simply gave them the excuse they were looking for since he had become widely known. Despite the physical and mental stress that it caused him, Malcolm X's ousting from NOI was a necessary step in his philosophical and spiritual development which began with his hajj (or spiritual journey) to the Holy Land of Mecca in 1964 (April 13 to May 21), a journey that all Sunni Muslims are expected to make at some point in their lives. The hajj opened Malcolm's eyes to several important facts. While touring Middle Eastern and West African nations, including Egypt, Lebanon, Saudi Arabia, Nigeria, Ghana, Morocco, and Algeria, he witnessed Muslim people of all races worshipping side by side, and this helped him to realize that white people could not be and have never been the genetically engineered race of devils that NOI doctrine taught. The NOI leader and most of its followers had little formal schooling, and Muhammad capitalized greatly on the ignorance of his followers. The white devil rhetoric isolated NOI followers and kept them out of the arena of politics, specifically all talks surrounding integration. The hajj also helped Malcolm to realize that the NOI wasn't a legitimate branch of Islam. In fact, he discovered that the NOI was detested in the Middle East, in part, because they didn't follow the Koran. Additionally, most Sunni or Orthodox Muslims had never even heard of NOI founder Wallace Fard Muhammad (1877–1934) or even Elijah Muhammad, for that matter. Malcolm was forced to accept the fact that, to true Muslims, Fard was not God in the flesh, and subsequently, as Fard's successor, Elijah Muhammad was not God's "messenger." Malcolm's previous discovery of Elijah Muhammad's numerous infidelities further supported this notion. Shortly after returning from his pilgrimage, a more enlightened Malcolm X (now El-Hajj Malik El-Shabazz) would revisit the "chickens come home to roost" proverb (Mieder 1993: 52; Bryan and Mieder 2016: 149) in a public statement made on January 7, 1965. In this instance, the meaning also closely resembles Joseph's earlier interpretation. Malcolm says: "There are many white people in this country, especially the younger generation, who realize that the injustice that has been done and is being done to black people cannot go on without the chickens coming home to roost eventually. And those white people, even if they're not morally motivated, their intelligence forces them to see that something must be done" (Morrow 2016: 219). Here, it is much clearer that Malcolm's proverbial statement has nothing to do with Kennedy, but more so about the dangers of allowing injustice to go unchecked. Malcolm continues:

> And many of them would be willing to involve themselves in the type of operation that you were just talking about. For one, when a white man comes to me and tells me how liberal he is, the first thing I want

to know; is he a nonviolent liberal, or the other kind? I don't go for any nonviolent white liberals. If you are for me and my problem-when I say me I mean *us*, —our people—then you have to be willing to do as old John Brown did. And if you're not of the John Brown School of liberals, we'll get to you later—later. (Morrow 2016: 219)

Malcolm makes this statement in support of his newly adopted philosophy of universal brotherhood. He is asserting that both Blacks and whites have the capacity to become radicalized in the fight for civil rights and equality. Seeing radicalization and violence as two necessary steps, he uses abolitionist John Brown (1800–59) as a prime example of a white man who killed other white people in the name of freedom.

Malcolm uses another proverb in reference to John Brown during a question-and-answer session following an Organization of African American Unity (OAAU) speech on July 5, 1964. One member of his audience questions the fact that Malcolm would now ally himself with whites in the civil rights movement, and Malcolm responds:

Brother yes, I understand what you are saying, I think. There's an old African proverb which I find most enlightening, which says that the enemy of my enemy is my friend. . . . This doesn't mean that you always trust your allies. But as long as they want to ally themselves against the same one that you're fighting against, attach them and let them go ahead and fight against it. (DeCaro 2016: 183)

Historian, Louis A. DeCaro Jr. explains that Malcolm's rationale for being willing to align himself with whites came with stipulations. DeCaro says: "The fact that individual whites like John Brown might prove to be allies did not mitigate the fact that white society as a whole remained inimical toward black freedom in Malcolm's understanding. Under such circumstances, he naturally did not want his words about Brown to be misconstrued by whites either as conciliatory or consolation before they had properly demonstrated the same radical commitment to black liberation that they would express for their own freedom" (DeCaro 2016: 183).

Thematically, "God's Judgement of White America" was based on another agrarian proverb from scripture, although it reflects the very same idea that he seems to express with the "chickens come home to roost" (Mieder 1993: 52) proverb. Malcolm based his speech on this Hebrew Bible and New Testament proverb: "As you sow, so shall you reap" (Siebert 2016: 160). The actual words from scripture read:

> I speak of what I know: those who plow iniquity and sow the seeds of grief reap a harvest of the same kind. (Proverbs 22:8; Siebert 2016: 160)

> Wind they sow, and storm they shall reap. (Hosea 8:7; Siebert 2016: 160)

> Don't delude yourself into thinking God can be cheated: where a man sows, there he reaps: if he sows in the field of self-indulgence he will get a harvest of corruption out of it; if he sows in the field of the Spirit he will get from it a harvest of eternal life. We must never get tired of doing good because if we don't give up the struggle we shall get our harvest at the proper time. While we have the chance, we must do good to all, and especially to our brothers in faith. (Galatians 6:7–10; Siebert 2016: 161)

Based on the previous three religious texts, retribution for perceived injustice is an ancient idea, and throughout the speech Malcolm uses forceful language to reflect the proverbial theme that "one must reap what one sows." Malcolm says: "If the government of white America truly repents of its sins against our people, and atones by giving us our true share, only then can America save herself!" (Malcolm X) Although he was scrutinized and subsequently punished for commenting that "chickens come home to roost," one can easily see that he was extending the very same proverbial theme which he had previously been speaking on. Furthermore, "Malcolm said that 'it was the same thing as had happened with Reverend Medgar Evers, with Patrice Lumumba,' with Fidel Castro, 'with Madame Nhu's husband,' and all emancipatory movements that had been attacked by America" (Haley 1992: 347; Siebert 2016: 161). Thus, Malcolm's focus was on America as a colonizing entity.

On May 29, 1964, the Militant Labor Forum of New York held a symposium on "What's Behind the 'Hate-Gang' Scare?" (Breitman 1990: 64). Malcolm X spoke at this symposium to dispel the erroneous rumor being spread around by the press that young Black, negro Muslims were organizing themselves to "maim and kill" whites around the city (Breitman 1990: 64). Malcolm, having just returned from his pilgrimage, had adopted antiracist views, but he still harbored strong feelings against colonialism, imperialism, and capitalism, which, he felt, were all intrinsically connected to racism and so deeply engrained in American democracy that real social equality would never exist for Blacks unless the system was completely changed. In the speech, Malcolm returns to his agrarian roots as he evokes another convincing analogy involving proverbial chickens, and this time he also includes ducks. He says:

Because people will realize that it's impossible for a chicken to produce a duck egg—even though they both belong to the same family of fowl. A chicken just doesn't have it within its system to produce a duck egg. It can't do it. It can only produce according to what that particular system was constructed to produce. The system in this country cannot produce freedom for an Afro-American. It is impossible for this system, this economic system, this political system, this social system, this system, period. It's impossible for this system, as it stands, to produce freedom right now for the black man in this country. And if ever a chicken did produce a duck egg, I'm quite sure you would say it was certainly a revolutionary chicken! (Breitman 1990: 68–69)

According to historians, John H. McClendon III and Stephen C. Ferguson II, when Malcolm X utters the statement, "It's impossible for a chicken to produce a duck egg," he is bringing "to our attention how the imperialist interests of the United States government and its ruling class—today often framed on the rhetoric of global capitalism/empire and the ruling one percent-in systematically hegemonic fashion remains dialectically part and parcel of the conditions of African American political impotency, social oppression, and economic exploitation. In his now well-known speech, 'The Ballot or The Bullet,' Malcolm explicitly states that Black people are 'the victims of Democracy" (McClendon and Ferguson 2016: 38). The statement "it's impossible for a chicken to produce a duck egg" is not a proverb, but it is a remarkably innovative and appropriate saying that displays Malcolm's disappointment and frustration with the state of America. It also demonstrated that underneath Malcolm's well-educated, urban persona, he still had not forgotten his country roots.

Proverbial chickens and ducks are not the only animal imagery that Malcolm worked into his speeches. On occasion he also employed sayings involving mules, foxes, wolves, and goats. Abolitionist, Frederick Douglass's use of wolf and sheep imagery to describe the cruel institution of slavery has been well documented (see Mieder 2001: 43). Like Douglass, Malcolm used agrarian sayings as a way of putting complex political issues into simpler terms. In a speech in 1963 at Venerable Bushnell Hall in Hartford, Connecticut, Malcolm addresses the complicated issues of integration and miscegenation, two things that were outlawed in the Jim Crow South at the time. According to historians Les and Tamara Payne, Martin Luther King Jr. "usually sidestepped [the miscegenation] component of his drive for integration" (Payne 2020: 400). However, the NOI "didn't hesitate to play it for all it was worth in advancing Elijah Muhammad's call for black unity" (Payne 2020:

401). Malcolm first criticized famous Black entertainers who were known to have white spouses, including Eartha Kitt, Ralph Bunch, and Harry Belafonte (Payne 2020: 401). He then draws a stark comparison between Connecticut governor John Dempsey and Alabama governor George Wallace. He states that Wallace represents the "mule-headedness of the South" while Dempsey represents "the deception of the North" (Payne 2020: 401). "To be stubborn as a mule" (Whiting 1989: 433) is a rustic proverbial expression that many people from the South are familiar with. Malcolm's criticism doesn't end there. He has a rhetorical question for his Hartford, Connecticut, audience, many of them white college students and professors. Les and Tamara Payne describe the scene best: "With his right index finger darting over the podium, he stabbed at Governor Dempsey as a Northern liberal hypocrite: 'how can the fox point the finger at the wolf?'" (Payne 2020: 402). According to Hank Flick and Larry Powell: "While such [animal] imagery had the effect of awakening and rousing feelings within an audience, it also served to transform an audience from a passive to a more active state" (Flick and Powell 1988: 444). The audience's response reflects Flick and Powell's rhetorical analysis perfectly. Malcolm's metaphors were quite effective, and with that comparison he "stirred the college students in the audience as only the most legendary of their professors could have done" (Payne 2020: 402). In fact, he moved the Bushnell Hall audience so much so with his sustained metaphors involving proverbial animals that some students had further comments and questions following the speech. Payne describes the scene in the auditorium:

> One local white college student reacted sharply to Malcolm's biblical assertion that it would soon be "harvest time" when the goats, which he implied were whites, would be led to the slaughter. Accordingly, Malcolm had stressed the impracticality of "woolly haired sheep [Blacks] lying down with straight haired goats." How could Malcolm X, speak so bluntly about blacks as sheep and whites as goats when his light complexion clearly indicated that he himself had mixed blood? Flashing that impish smile, the minister canted his head, ran his right hand slowly over his close-cropped hair and said, "I still have a lot of sheep in me." (Payne 2020: 405)

Malcom may have been simply putting his own spin on Isaiah 11:6 which reads: "The wolf also shall dwell with the lamb, and the leopard shall lie down with the kid" (KJV). Nevertheless, Malcolm's talk at Bushnell Hall created quite a stir with the local press. The *Hartford Courant* published at least two separate articles; one headline reads, "Malcolm X States Creed of

Muslims at Bushnell" (Payne 2020: 405), while another *Hartford Courant* newspaper reporter simply framed the same talk given at a different location as an animal fable: "Malcolm X Tells About White Fox" (Marable et al. 2013: 261). The story reads: "Malcolm X, a leader in the Negro Black Muslim movement, Friday told 4,000 University of California [Berkeley] students the parable of 'the white fox of the North' and 'the white wolf of the South.' The 'white fox,' he said, is a symbol of the so-called white liberal who strangles Negro efforts by infiltrating our groups and posing as our friends. At least, he said, the Negro knows where he stands with the 'white wolf' of the South" (Marable et al. 2013: 261).

Even when Malcolm had broken away from NOI, he still had a penchant for employing fox and wolf analogies in creative ways, the proverbial fox and wolf often representing two evil sides of the same coin. In Cairo, Egypt, while lobbying for the Organization of African Unity (OAU) to bring the issue of American mistreatment of Black citizens before the United Nations as international human rights issues, he compares Jim Crow in the US to apartheid in South Africa. He says: "South Africa is like a vicious wolf, openly hostile towards black humanity. But America is cunning like a fox, friendly and smiling, but even more vicious and deadly than the wolf. And if South African racism is not a domestic issue, then American racism also is not a domestic issue" (Payne 2020: 449). The previous quote is important because it demonstrates that Malcolm would employ the proverbial wolf and fox to explain a variety of topics, in part, because it forced people to think critically about social and political issues. According to historians, Hank Flick and Larry Powell, "Malcolm's use of highly charged imagery was a tactic by which future adjustments to new situations could be brought about, and by which disparate positions could be identified, illustrated, examined, and made more intense" (1988: 444).

Malcolm was critical of all the political parties in the US, but he was even more critical of Blacks who allowed themselves to be influenced by phony political rhetoric. As Malcolm states: "The black man in North America was sickest of all politically. He lets the white man divide him into such foolishness as considering himself a black 'Democrat,' a black 'Republican,' a black 'Conservative,' or a black 'Liberal'" (McClendon and Ferguson II 2016: 45). In one speech Malcolm states: "A fox and a wolf are both canine, both belong to the dog family. Now you take your choice. You going to choose a Northern dog or a Southern dog? Because either dog you choose, I guarantee you'll still be in the doghouse" (McClendon and Ferguson 2016: 46). McClendon and Ferguson contend that "with his analysis of the two-party system and how it operates as a *racist institutional reality*, Malcolm brings into bold relief why this political system locks out the masses of African Americans from effectively engaging in the political process as means for capturing the necessary power to change their real material (life) circumstances" (emphasis in original) (2016: 46).

Malcolm used another proverbial expression in response to a question regarding rumors that the Johnson administration would be appointing a Black cabinet member. Malcolm's response may be slightly satirical, but the point he makes in 1966 is quite serious. He says:

> I just read where they planned to make a black cabinet member. Yes, they have a new gimmick every year. They're going to take one of their boys, black boys, and put him in the cabinet, so he can walk around Washington with a cigar—fire on one end and fool on the other. And because his immediate personal problem will have been solved, he will be the one to tell our people, "Look how much progress we're making: I'm in Washington D.C. I can have tea in the White House. I'm your spokesman, I'm your leader." But will it work? Can that one, whom they are going to put down there, step into the fire and put it out when the flames begin to leap up? When people take to the streets in their explosive mood, will that one, that they're going to put in the cabinet, be able to go among the people? Why, they'll burn him faster than they burn the ones who sent him. (McClendon and Ferguson 2016: 47–48)

The phrase "fire on one end, fool on the other" (Tréguer) is an old proverbial expression dating as far back as 1841, and Malcolm could not have chosen a more appropriate time to use it. In referencing proverbial "flames" and "fire," one must consider the fact that Malcolm could foresee that growing dissent among Black inner-city youth would continue to culminate into disastrous events such as the Watts Riots (1965), Detroit Riots (1967), Newark Riots (1967), and many others that sprang up around the nation following his death. Malcolm was putting to rest the ridiculous notion that one white-appointed Black politician could ever appease angry Black masses: "Why, they'll burn him faster than they burn the ones who sent him" (McClendon and Ferguson 2016: 47–48). Communist Bill Epton agrees that Malcolm had a talent for summarizing "complex social, political, and cultural developments in succinct phrases and explain[ing] them in clear everyday language that the masses could easily understand" (McClendon and Ferguson 2016: 48). Malcolm's expression of wit in the form of proverbs, brief sayings, and proverbial expressions is one reason why his political rhetoric has captured the attention of politicians, scholars, and historians alike.

Malcolm also uses a proverb which illustrates that he had real talent for knowing his audience; meaning that he had a feel for who would really buy into NOI philosophy and who wouldn't. In writing about being a young NOI minister in his autobiography, he asserts that it was the lower-class Black people, working menial labor jobs who were most receptive to what he had to say, and Malcolm uses a proverb to express this sentiment. He says: "You've heard that saying, 'no man is a hero to his valet,'... Well those Negroes who waited on wealthy whites hand and foot opened their eyes quicker than most Negroes" (Whiting 1989: 399; Bryan and Mieder 2016: 382; Payne 2020: 290).

Malcolm delivered an untitled speech in Detroit, sponsored by the Afro-American Broadcasting Company on February 14, 1965—the very same day that the NOI firebombed his home in East Elmhurst, Queens. Unharmed, Malcolm, his wife, and four daughters barely escaped (Breitman 1990: 157). Malcolm was still able to deliver a powerful message to his audience despite being shaken up by the unfortunate event that took place earlier that morning. Throughout the speech, Malcolm continues to promote his post pilgrimage message of anticolonialism and Black nationalism. He emphasizes this message using an agrarian proverb, and in doing so, Malcom is again using nature symbolically to explain things in the corporeal world that are sometimes difficult for people to comprehend. The effect is that he creates another flawless analogy, and even the buildup is important. He says:

> Now what effect does [the struggle over Africa] have on us? Why should the black man in America concern himself since he's been away from the African continent for three or four hundred years? Why should we concern ourselves? Number one, you have to realize that up until 1959 Africa was dominated by the colonial powers. Having complete control over Africa, the colonial powers of Europe projected the image of Africa negatively. They always project Africa in a negative light: jungle savages, cannibals, nothing civilized. Why then naturally it was so negative that it was negative to you and me, and you and I began to hate it. We didn't want anybody telling us anything about Africa, much less calling us Africans. In hating Africa and in hating Africans, we ended up hating ourselves, without even realizing it. (Breitman 1990: 168)

He then says: "Because you can't hate the roots of a tree, and not hate the tree. You can't hate your origin and not end up hating yourself. You can't hate Africa and not hate yourself" (Breitman 1990: 157). The statement "you can't hate the roots of a tree and not hate the tree" has all the markings of a true proverb. It is a succinct, metaphoric statement being expressed as one complete sentence, and its meaning is certainly "didactic" (Mieder 1993: 20). Since this famous statement can only be attributed to him, it is safe to conclude that it is a personal proverb that he coined himself. What Malcolm says about dishonest portrayals of African culture is equally important because it contributes additional meaning. Malcolm emphasizes the importance of harboring a positive perception of Black people and Black culture in America when he says: "When you let yourself be influenced by images created by others, you'll find that oftentimes the one who creates these images can use them to mislead you and misuse you" (Flick and Powell 1988: 440). According to historians, Les and Tamara Payne, Malcolm's proverb, "['You can't hate the roots of a tree, and not hate the tree'] . . . speaks directly to today's youth across the United States as they challenge the media's beauty standards to be more inclusive" (Payne 2020: 524). It also reflects the spirit of the 1960s when young Student Nonviolent Coordinating Committee (SNCC) members popularized the saying "Black power," and the proverb "Black is beautiful" became a permanent part of the African American lexicon.

World travel made Malcolm more aware of the need for young Black girls and women to see Africa and its descendants as beautiful. It also motivated Malcolm to add another feminist objective to his agenda. What he witnessed overseas made him more aware of the need for Black women to be formally educated and assertive in the various organizations that they were a part of. He says: "In every Middle-East or African country I have visited. I noticed the country is as 'advanced' as its women are, or as backward as its women, . . . Thus, in my opinion, the Muslim religious leaders of today must re-evaluate and spell out with clarity the Muslim position on education in general and education for women in particular. And then a vast program must be launched to elevate the standard of education in the Muslim world" (Payne 2020: 454). Malcolm then uses a powerful proverb to emphasize this point. He says: "An old African proverb states: 'Educate a man and you educate an individual; educate a woman and you educate an entire family'" (Payne 2020: 454).

Right after Malcolm formally announced his break from NOI, he proposed a plan for improving economic conditions in African American communities that closely reflected his Black nationalist philosophy. He explains the plan in his speech, "The Ballot or the Bullet." Malcolm alludes to an old proverb in the process of outlining his strategy. He says:

> The economic philosophy of black nationalism is pure and simple. It only means that we should control the economy of our community.

Why should white people be running all the stores in our community? Why should white people be running the banks in our community? Why should the economy of our community be in the hands of the white man? Why? If a black man can't move his store into a white community, you tell me why a white man should move his store into a black community . . . Our people have to be made to see that any time you take your dollar out of your community and spend it in a community where you don't live, the community where you live will get poorer and poorer, and the community where you spend your money will get richer and richer. (Breitman 1990: 38; McClendon and Ferguson 2016: 79)

The proverb that Malcolm X alludes to in the concluding line, "the rich get richer, and the poor get poorer" (Bryan and Mieder 2016: 637), is a well-known proverb that was first recorded in 1921 in a song entitled "Ain't We Got Fun" written by Raymond B. Egan and Gus Khan (Bryan and Mieder 2016: 637). The song's theme of having good times and being happy and content in the absence of any material wealth contrasts Malcolm's point drastically, and the phrase helps him to make his point, although it is unlikely that he had the song in mind when he made the statement.

"The Ballot or The Bullet" is filled with all kinds of proverbial language. In one paragraph, Malcolm X makes the point that many Black youths are becoming disillusioned with the civil rights movement by way of the biblical proverbial expression "turn-the-other-cheek" (Matthew 5: 39). Malcolm says: "The young Negro's coming up. They don't want to hear that 'turn-the-other-cheek' stuff, no. In Jacksonville, those teenagers were throwing Molotov cocktails" (Breitman 1990: 31). Malcolm explains to his audience that Black people in the inner-cities are tired of waiting for the end Jim Crow, and they are demanding that change take place immediately. Emphatically stressing this point further, he says: "It'll be ballots, or bullets. It'll be liberty, or it will be death. The only difference about this kind of death—it'll be reciprocal" (Breitman 1990: 32). Malcolm, plotting his course carefully, borrows a phrase from Patrick Henry's famous speech from 1775, "Give Me Liberty, or Give Me Death" (Meade 1969). By invoking Henry, he is using American history to underscore a foundational precept in his philosophy: the notion that revolutions have always involved some degree of violence. Malcolm then summons another revolutionary from history when he says: "I find you can get a whole lot of small people and whip hell out of a whole lot of big people. They haven't got anything to lose, and they've got everything to gain" (Breitman 1990: 32). It is certainly not a mistake that he chooses to mirror the words of German philosopher Karl Marx, who famously said: "Workers of the world unite, you have nothing to lose but your chains" (Marx 1996). By making this portion of his speech reflect the language of Henry and Marx, he is justifying his position and providing the audience with more reasons to align themselves with his cause. Furthermore, it makes his audience aware that his ideas reflect some of the very same ideas which have been expressed for centuries. Malcolm closes this part of the speech by invoking more of the slick style of rhetoric that he developed during his hustling years, and he uses another proverb in the process. He says: "It take two to tango; when I go, you go" (Breitman 1990: 32). The proverb "it takes two to tango" (Doyle et al. 2012: 266; Bryan and Mieder 2016: 805) helps describe his revolutionary mindset.

In another portion of the speech, Malcolm makes it clear that he is no advocate of senseless violence. He says:

> I don't mean go out and get violent; but at the same time you should never be nonviolent unless you run into some nonviolence. I'm nonviolent with those who are nonviolent with me. . . . Any time you know you're within the law, within your legal rights, within your moral rights, in accord with justice, then die for what you believe in. But don't die alone. Let your dying be reciprocal. That is what is meant by equality. What's good for the goose is good for the gander. (Breitman 1990: 33–34)

When Malcolm makes this statement, he is thinking of the thousands of nonviolent protesters who have been killed, maimed, and murdered as they marched and protested peacefully. Malcolm doesn't see an end to this deadly trend unless civil rights activists begin to defend themselves when necessary. The rustic proverb "what's good for the goose is good for the gander" (Speake 2015: 276) punctuates his statement on self-defense and equality perfectly.

One of Malcolm's most famous statements which has turned proverbial is "a man who stands for nothing will fall for anything." Malcolm is known to have uttered this personal proverb in interviews at times, some of which have been made available on YouTube, and it has grown to become one of his most well-remembered statements. Marable even includes this proverb on the cover of *The Portable Malcolm X Reader* (2013). Regardless of its origin, the proverb still rings true to many people, even over half a century after his death. In retrospect, it applied to himself because he was killed as he promoted causes that he believed were worth dying for, and he wanted his followers to feel as strongly about those causes as he did. It is for this reason that he frequented the saying "by any means necessary" (Breitman 1990:

201, 203) the motto for his Organization of Afro American Unity (OAAU). Malcolm X explains his rationale for using it as a motto best. In his final interview (Malcolm typed his responses to several questions on the eve of his assassination), he says: "With the Muslim Mosque we are teaching our people a better way of life, and with the OAAU we are fighting on an even broader level for complete respect and recognition as human beings for all Black Americans, and we are ready and willing to use any means necessary to see that this goal is reached" (Payne 2020: 538). These statements still seem powerful enough to inspire future generations of revolutionary leaders.

Chapter seven explores the life of one of Malcolm X's most important associates, Stokely Carmichael (1941–98). Carmichael was not Malcolm X's protégé. He most often worked beside King and Clark. Nevertheless, Carmichael made it no secret that he and other activists looked up to Malcolm X, even seeking his counsel at times. Thus, chapter seven includes several important Malcolm X proverbs shared by Carmichael in his autobiography, *Ready for Revolution* (2005). Carmichael says that he greatly valued the proverbial wisdom that he was able to derive from strong leaders like Malcolm X, and as chapter seven demonstrates, he internalized those proverbs, and considered them words to live by.

Chapter Seven

"BLACK POWER" AND BLACK RHETORICAL TRADITION

The Proverbial Language of Stokely Carmichael

Stokely Standiford Churchill Carmichael (Kwame Ture, 1941–98) played many important roles during the civil rights era (1954–68). Carmichael was a political activist, an effective community organizer, an author, a valuable teacher (who taught voting rights, literacy, and Black history in the Deep South), a dynamic public speaker and philosopher, and a ground-breaking revolutionary. Another important talent and aspect of Carmichael's life that often goes unmentioned by scholars is that he was also a master of proverbs or "concise traditional statements of apparent truths with currency among the folk" and proverbial language, and he used this inimitable skill in at least three unique ways (Mieder 2004: 4; Mieder 2019: 264). Firstly, his proverbial mastery helped him to learn and impart important life lessons, meaning that he internalized the proverbial wisdom of others and then shared these axioms liberally throughout his entire life through conversation, and through his speeches and writings. Secondly, his use of proverbial language is used as an overt expression of the pride that he had in his Black identity, and because Carmichael attributes many of his sayings to Black people from all over the world, including Trinidad, Jamaica, West India, Nigeria, Egypt, Ghana, Guinea, and the American Deep South, they simultaneously demonstrate his belief in Pan-Africanism or the notion that all Black people around the world share in one common struggle against forces of colonialism and imperialism. Thirdly, Carmichael's proverbial language is an important tool that he used to establish and reinforce relationships with family, friends, colleagues, students, and audiences.

The most important expression that Carmichael is remembered for is "Black power." He unveils the expression at the Meredith Mississippi Freedom March (1966). Many who know of Carmichael associate him with this slogan, but many others cannot determine why he is so important to the civil rights movement. Carmichael's own son, Bokar Ture, would not learn much about his famous father's life as a political activist until he went to college and did his own research. In the CNN documentary *Black in America 2* (2008), Ture explains his predicament. He had no idea that his father had become a symbol of Black militancy because, like so many survivors of the civil rights era, Carmichael did not discuss it: "He never told me what he did, really. He just told me what was good to do: 'Work for your people'" (Blake 2008). Carmichael's son goes on to explain that he had internalized many of the same misconceptions about the movement as others. He says:

> I had not understood how brutal the movement was. I saw it as a Disney movie—people marching in the sunshine, King speaking, and victory. But it was war. Many of these front-line activists lived under the constant threat of death. Several lost friends. Some were tortured in jail. Several were disowned by their families. Their memories were too painful to share with their children. (Blake 2008)

Fortunately, today Carmichael's connection to the movement is well documented, and by examining some of the material, one can easily determine why, after so many decades have past, the expression "Black power" still retains so much of its historical significance.

The saying was first heard at the Meredith Mississippi Freedom March (1966), which began as the Meredith March Against Fear. It was established by James Meredith (1933–), the first African American to be admitted to the University of Mississippi. On the historic day that he was admitted (October 1, 1962), it would take dozens of federal troops to keep the peace. Meredith's admittance would be a small victory in an ongoing war against what Carmichael defines as "institutional racism" or "racism [which] relies on the active and pervasive operation of anti-black attitudes and practices" (Ture and Hamilton 1967: 4). The march came about because Meredith wanted to demonstrate that it was possible for a Black man to walk through the Deep South without being afraid of racial violence. Meredith embarked on the 220-mile trek from Memphis, Tennessee, to Jackson, Mississippi, alone, aside from some onlookers and a few members of the press. On the second day of his journey, Meredith was attacked and badly wounded by an angry shotgun wielding racist. After hearing about the ordeal, the Student Nonviolent Coordinating Committee (SNCC) decided to continue the march on Meredith's behalf, only this time there were two major changes. Firstly, they renamed it the Meredith Mississippi Freedom March. Secondly, as opposed to a single person or a single organization, SNCC would be joined by thousands of Black people from a range of different organizations, universities, and church groups, one of the most important attendees being the Reverend Dr. Martin Luther King Jr., who started the march "by reading a contentious manifesto that describes Mississippi as a living symbol of 'every evil that American Negroes have long endured'" (Joseph 2014: 108). In *Ready for Revolution* (2003) Carmichael recounts the moment that he decides to utter the expression that would gain him international attention: "As I passed Mukasa [Willie Ricks], he said, "Drop it now. The people are ready. Drop it now" (Carmichael and Thelwell 2003: 507). The famous speech is not recorded, but it is recounted by SNCC member Cleve Sellers (1944–), who attended the event. Sellers asserts that after taking the podium, Carmichael says:

> "This is the twenty-seventh time I have been arrested—and I ain't going to jail no more!" The crowd exploded into cheers and clapping. "The only way we gonna stop them white men from whuppin' us is to take over. We been saying freedom for six years and we ain't got nothing. What we gonna start saying now is Black Power!" The Crowd was right with him. They picked up his thoughts immediately. "Black Power!" They roared in unison. Willie Ricks [1943–], who is good at orchestrating the emotions of a crowd as anyone I have ever seen, sprang into action. Jumping to the platform with Stokely, he yelled to the crowd, "What do you want? Black Power! What do you want? Black Power! What do you want? Black Power!! Black Power!!! Black Power!!!!" Everything that happened afterward was a response to that moment. (Carmichael and Thelwell 2003: 507)

Before that moment, it was a phrase SNCC activists would exchange with one another from time to time around the office and sometimes when engaged in "internal debates over strategy and organizing approaches" (Johnson 2022a: 31), but in that moment, for Carmichael and the other protesters, "Black power" became a call against Carmichael's unjust incarceration. It was also a call against the constant harassment by police and state troopers who beat marchers and hit them with tear gas on a number of occasions in efforts to force them to give up the march. By demanding "Black power" as opposed to the traditional chant of "freedom," he is connecting the civil rights struggle to his broader philosophical notion, Pan-Africanism. Furthermore, Carmichael is making a demand for "political, economic, and cultural self-determination" (Joseph 2014: 115). Previously, the expression "Black power" had a history that spanned at least a decade. According to Johnson:

Some SNCC members used the slogan "Black Power for Black People" during the Alabama voting rights campaigns of 1965. In Harlem, leaders including Congressman Adam Clayton Powell, Jr., and tenant organizer Jesse Gray had also used the phrase "Black Power," as had Richard Wright, who published a travelogue of his time in newly independent Ghana with that title [in 1954]. It was SNCC activist Willie Ricks, however, who began using the phrase in speeches throughout the South, often asking from the podium, "What do you want?" to audiences, who shouted back, "Black Power!" (Johnson 2022a: 29)

Carmichael's use of the expression "Black power" gained the glare of publicity on a national and global scale. According to historian Peniel E. Joseph, "Carmichael's speech on June 16th, 1966, instantly transformed the aesthetics of the black freedom struggle and forever altered the course of the modern civil rights movement" (Joseph 2014: 115).

"Black power" is the expression Carmichael is most widely known for, but it is not the only powerful expression in his vast array of meaningful traditional communicative language. Carmichael uses many proverbs, sayings, and expressions that he learns from a number of different sources. In fact, some proverbs that Carmichael learned were first heard in his own home. As a young child in Trinidad, Carmichael spent the majority of his time with his paternal grandmother, Cecilia Harris Carmichael, and she was full of proverbial wisdom. Of Grandma Cecilia, Carmichael says:

> Grandma Cecilia was the major influence on my young personality, the adult with whom I spent most of my time and with whom I was closest. She was a devout woman. A pillar of Trinity Anglican Church, close friend and adviser to the parish parson, she was entrusted with the baking of the communal wafers each week. My earliest and most enduring ethical instruction came from her. (Carmichael and Thelwell 2003: 24)

Carmichael then shares some of the lessons that he learns from Grandma Cecilia: "'Don't ever lie, always speak the truth. Think of others always. Remember the less fortunate. Never waste food. Never waste anything that someone else might need. Waste not, want not.' And so forth. And the 'memory gems' so much a part of any respectable colonial child's training" (Carmichael and Thelwell 2003: 24, 25). The fundamental lesson about frugality contained in the proverb "waste not, want not" (Mieder et al. 1991: 641; Speake 2015: 341) is very important to Carmichael, so much so that it brings to mind two more important "memory gems" of Grandma Cecilia which he feels are equally significant: "If you in the morning throw minutes away, you can't pick them up the course of the day" and "Whatsoever you set your hand to do, do it with all your might" (Carmichael and Thelwell 2003: 25). The possibility that the recollection of one proverb may lead, or even help one to remember others has been considered by other proverb scholars. According to folklorist Betsy Bowden, "Rumination upon one proverb might lead into the depths of personal experience. Thereby a thinker comes to reconstruct other oral or written contexts containing that same sentence: relevant stories, sermons, commentaries, and so on . . . one proverb can lead to recall of other ones memorized along with it elsewhere and lead ultimately to all of those other proverbs' additional contexts as well" (Bowden 1996: 442). If what Bowden says is correct, then proverbs may have served as important mnemonic devices that helped Carmichael to remember scenes from his eventful life as he constructed his autobiography.

Carmichael's father also liked to share precepts in the form of proverbs. Adolphus Carmichael, a hard-working and skilled carpenter, valued honesty and integrity and he tried to instill these principles in his son: "My father was so scrupulously, resolutely, and unambiguously honest man. 'If you didn't work for it,' he'd say, 'don't look for it. If you didn't sweat for it, don't even think of it.' In all the time we lived together, I never knew him to deviate in the slightest from that principle" (Carmichael and Thelwell 2003: 69). Another saying that his father liked to use seems so didactic and moralizing that young Carmichael spends ample time ruminating on its meaning: "My late father had a much used saying that, because it seemed so unforgiving, puzzled me greatly as a young boy. It occurs to me that . . . it was about: integrity. 'You can tell the truth every day of your life,' my father would say, 'and if, on the day of your death, you tell a lie . . . that is what will matter'" (Carmichael and Thelwell 2003: 71).

Adolphus Carmichael did not have much formal education, but he did value learning, and he instilled this value in his children as well. His father also did not waste words, and he knew how to deliver extraordinarily strong messages by using brief sayings. In the following passage, Carmichael describes his father's often-repeated lesson on learning:

> His words were always thoughtful. He was not verbose, but we always knew that whatever our father said in his quiet voice, he truly meant. We never disobeyed him. At dinner he'd always ask each of us, "Well, what did you learn today?" If someone came up shaky, he'd shake his head. "You know, the day on which you learned nothing is a wasted

day. Enough of those and what've you got? A wasted life." (Carmichael and Thelwell 2003: 77)

Even when his father was faced with difficult problems on his job as a carpenter, Adolphus could remedy the issue with an axiom: "Nothing, and in particular, no problem in carpentry or craftsmanship ever seemed to intimidate him. 'Well now,' he'd say as he studied the problem. 'There's always more'n one way to skin a cat.' Sooner or later he came out with an approach—often not the conventional one—but one that would get the job done, and often more efficiently" (Carmichael and Thelwell 2003: 78). The proverb "there is always more than one way to skin a cat" is used by Carmichael to describe his father's unparalleled confidence as a carpenter, and it also effectively describes the thinking process that his father applies when faced with complex issues (Mieder et al. 1991: 644; Speake 2015: 342). Carmichael learns a number of important values from his father and the proverbs that Adolphus used helps Carmichael to remember the lessons and the man.

Carmichael also uses the proverbs and sayings of several famous political leaders. According to paremiologist Wolfgang Mieder: "All political leaders are faced with addressing heterogenous audiences, and they must find a common denominator in their rhetoric that will be grasped and appreciated by the largest possible number of people both here in the United States and throughout the world" (Mieder 2019: 58). Based on this information, it is no surprise that Carmichael frequents proverbs and sayings from such an eclectic mixture of leadership. He employs the proverbial language of leaders such as Elijah Muhammad (1897–1975), Malcolm X (1925–65), the Reverend Dr. Martin Luther King Jr. (1929–68), President John F. Kennedy (1917–63), Oliver Wendell Holmes (1841–1935), Rabbi Hillel (110 BC–10 AD), African president(s) Sékou Turé (1922–84) and Dr. Kwame Nkrumah (1909–72), and Italian diplomat Niccolò Machiavelli (1469–1527). In some cases, he frequents the proverbial language of leaders as an ode to the leadership qualities that they possessed, their political instruction, and in some cases their friendship, such as in the case of Dr. King. In many instances, proverbs from important leaders provide some keen insight into issues that may plague Black communities.

Malcolm X was one leader who was known for imparting such words of wisdom to anyone who would listen. Carmichael recounts an anecdote that illustrates a moment when Malcolm X offers an important point of cultural criticism to some Black youth who appear to be wasting their lives hanging out on street corners. The insightful cultural criticism that Malcolm X shares is then punctuated by a proverb from Elijah Muhammad:

According to the story, Malcolm was driving along and saw a group of young brothers shooting craps on a sidewalk. He stopped the car and approached the game. He either seized or put his foot on the dice. Of course, the players started to get into they bags. Malcolm froze them with that look he had. My young brothers, you know what this building is? He asked. Yeah, I thought so. You don't know, do you? This is the Schomburg Collection. It's got damn near everything ever written by or about black people. And what you doing? Instead of being inside learning about yourself, your people, and our history, you out here in darkness shooting dice. That's what's wrong with us, why Mr. Muhammad says: "If you want to hide something from the black man, put it in a library." (Carmichael and Thelwell 2003: 105)

The famous saying of Elijah Muhammad, "If you want to hide something from the black man, put it in a library," has become so well-known that it is indeed regarded as a proverb. Carmichael was not there to watch this fascinating scene unfold, but simply hearing the story from others and remembering the saying was enough to encourage young Carmichael to frequent the library as often as he could: "Now, I was not among those crapshooters. But the story impressed on me the importance of the Schomburg and I began to spend many a profitable hour there" (Carmichael and Thelwell 2003: 105).

Another anecdote involving Malcolm X appears at a point in the narrative when Carmichael discusses a march that is staged by SNCC in order to bring the senseless murder of SNCC Summer Project volunteer, Louis Allen, to the attention of US Attorney General Bobby Kennedy (1925–68). SNCC planned to march from the Howard campus to the Justice Department, carrying a coffin and deposit the coffin on Kennedy's desk. As SNCC and just over a thousand students are in route to their destination, they notice Malcolm X watching, so they invite him to join the march. After Malcolm X respectfully declines their offer, a SNCC member asks Malcolm X what he thinks about the march. Malcolm X then shares an analogy with them that is punctuated by a proverb: "Now, if I see a long line of cats and mice all marching toward the same hole? If the cats ask me 'How we doing?' I gotta say it sure look like you doing fine, right. But now, if the mice ask me . . . well, now, you know I gotta give 'em a different answer" (Carmichael and Thelwell 2003: 356). After hearing this brief analogy involving animal imagery, the SNCC members aren't quite as confident about their mission. If Malcolm X's brief anecdote injures their pride, the proverb that Malcolm X shares with them next does not do them much good either. Malcolm X then says: "Remember now, just because you see a man throwing worms into the river, don't necessarily mean he a friend to the fish" (Carmichael and Thelwell 2003: 356). In employing the proverb, Malcolm X is basically warning them to proceed with caution because politicians often have ulterior motives. The marchers are not discouraged enough to abandon their mission, but due to Malcolm X's parable and proverb, one must imagine that they proceeded on that afternoon with much more discretion.

In October of 1969, Carmichael writes a speech that is delivered on his behalf by Howard Fuller for the opening ceremony of Malcolm X Liberation University in Durham, North Carolina. In the speech, Carmichael asserts that the African race will never be strong unless they educate their own people. For Carmichael, the suppression of Black thought is at the heart of what he believes is an ensuing race war evidenced by the widespread racial violence that overtook much of the country in the 1960s. He employs a proverb from Malcolm X to make his point:

When we begin to move militarily on all fronts, it will be an all-out race war, Africa versus Europe. This may not seem pleasant to some of our brothers and sisters, but it is a question of who is going to survive—them or us. I think that the natural law of survival will answer that, even for those of us who recoil and do not want to face what is coming. I am reminded of what Brother Malcolm said in Chicago, way back in 1962: "What's good news for some is bad news for others." (Stokely 1971: 179)

The proverb from Malcolm X—"What's good news for some is bad news for others"—is used to try to instill a sense of militancy in his audience. He wants them to feel motivated to take control of their own destinies by making Malcolm X Liberation University a successful enterprise. Carmichael believes that if Black people do not educate themselves, Black culture will ultimately be wiped out. In this instance the proverb underscores Carmichael's "us or them" attitude.

Another Malcolm X saying appears in *Stokely Speaks*, in chapter fourteen, which is entitled "Pan Africanism." In this chapter, Carmichael explains some of Kwame Nkrumah's philosophical tenets. He argues that Nkrumah embodies Pan-Africanism and that his leadership in Ghana was deposed by colonial forces for this very reason:

I know you would not understand this because you haven't been allowed to read books by Kwame Nkrumah. There must be a reason for that. They called him a traitor, they called him a tyrant, they called him everything that is bad in the world, but Brother Malcolm X told you when they say something bad about a man then that's the man you should run to. The white boy seeks to destroy the leaders in our movement. (Carmichael 1971: 216)

The Malcolm X saying "when they say something bad about a man, then that's the man you should run to" is used to explain the nature of the political coup in Ghana that displaced Kwame Nkrumah. According to Carmichael, Nkrumah was deposed for refusing to be an ally of colonial forces that sought to further exploit African natural resources. The Malcolm X saying also calls attention to the fact that political slander was the primary tool that they used to facilitate the overthrowing of the Ghanaian government.

At another point in Carmichael's narrative, he says that young activists of his day liked powerful proverbs and sayings that spoke to the spirit of the civil rights revolution that was ensuing. He describes the scene on the campus of Howard University in 1960 when he arrived there as a freshman:

One thing that reflects the spirit of the times among that generation of activist youth—white and black—is the recurrence of certain favorite quotations, ideas that spoke to collective human responsibility. These quotes were prevalent during my high school and early college years. Later in the decade these would be replaced by more overtly revolutionary slogans from people like Che, Malcolm, and Uncle Ho. But when I was a freshman, a lot of the people I knew would have some combination of these high-minded quotes up somewhere in their room. I remember three of these quotations. (Carmichael and Thelwell 2003: 144)

The three quotes that Carmichael largely remembers gracing the walls of Bronx Science and Howard University dorm rooms must have made a huge impression on him in order for him to remember them so many decades later. He says:

One was from Dr. King's *Stride Toward Freedom* to the effect that "If a man hasn't discovered something that he will die for, he isn't fit to live." The second was from the white jurist Oliver Wendell Holmes: "As life is action and passion, it is required of a man that he should share the passion and action of his time at peril being judged not to have lived." But the most common one—which I would later occasionally use to end speeches—was Rabbi Hillel's famous quote: If I am not for myself, who is for me? And when I am for myself what am I? And if not now, when? (Carmichael and Thelwell 2003: 144)

In many ways these sayings collectively describe Carmichael's attitude as he took part in the activism that the Nonviolent Action Group (NAG) and the Student Nonviolent Coordinating Committee (SNCC) became known for.

On another occasion, Carmichael employs a proverb from King to justify SNCC taking a position on the 1967 Arab-Israeli War. Many people including the media felt that to take a position on the situation in the Middle East was not SNCC's role and that they should stay silent on the issue. Carmichael employs a proverb from King to rationalize the need for the group to be vocal against Zionism. He says:

So obviously, there would be a price to pay. It would have come down to priorities. But as Dr. King said, "There comes a time when silence is tantamount to consent." But in any event that discussion never took place. Had the process not been short-circuited, I'm sure the overwhelming sentiment would have been to make a statement, a moral statement, on justice for the Palestinian people while trying hard not to offend or alienate our Jewish friends on a personal level. (Carmichael and Thelwell 2003: 561)

Carmichael contends that he is neither anti-Semitic nor anti-Judaic, but like many others, Carmichael believes that Zionism should be equated with colonialism, and that it is imperative for any political organization committed to social justice to speak out against it. Carmichael also references an anti-Zionist saying from G. Neuberger that he first heard in 1976 while attending an international conference in Libya: "If one is a good Jew, one cannot be a Zionist. If one is Zionist, one cannot be a good Jew" (Carmichael and Thelwell 2003: 562). Carmichael asserts that while Neuberger's words are not absolute truth, they do speak to the pain and destruction from war that has been caused in part by Zionist thinking in the Middle East.

Carmichael often referenced the words of President John F. Kennedy. Like Malcolm X and other Black Americans, Carmichael was very skeptical about the effectiveness of both of the major political parties in the United States, but one may assume that he must have seen wisdom in some of Kennedy's language, or perhaps he noticed an air of authenticity in Kennedy's statements because he references him on several occasions. At one point Carmichael says:

In January of 1960—I was still in high school then—the administration in Washington changed. Democrats replaced Republicans. A "vigorous, progressive, young" president, so they told us, took over. He proclaimed a new challenge of energetic and progressive activism when Americans should "ask not what your country can do for you; ask what you can do for your country." It was a great speech . . . until you really studied what he was saying. But many of us heard what we wanted to hear. And some of us believed him. So, soon indeed, we would test the sincerity of those words about defending freedom and paying any price. (Carmichael and Thelwell 2003: 177)

Each time that Carmichael references Kennedy's language, it is indeed as if he is testing the limits of Kennedy's political stances. For instance, when he discusses Kennedy's reluctance to enforce laws banning segregation in facilities used for interstate travel such as gas stations and rest stops, he invokes another Kennedy statement that has also grown to become proverbial: "The new Kennedy administration had come into office mouthing rhetoric about the national government's responsibility toward the constitutional rights of all Americans. CORE's plan would test their sincerity and their resolve, for in JFK's famous phrase, was not 'sincerity always subject to proof?'" (Carmichael and Thelwell 2003: 179).

The Congress of Racial Equality (CORE) plan that Carmichael discusses would be known as the 1961 Freedom Rides. The Freedom Riders were a group of integrated students and civil rights activists that challenged laws which banned integrated facilities for interstate travel in the South. To force systemic change, they simply boarded busses and traveled along highways in the South where segregation was most vehemently enforced. They also stopped at several illegally segregated establishments. While their efforts gained them international attention, they also suffered many indignities and abuses. They were often attacked by racist whites and Ku Klux Klan members who were eager to: impart physical and verbal abuse, throw fire-bombs, and pummel Freedom Riders with sticks and bottles as they exited busses. In Jackson, Mississippi, Carmichael and eight other riders were arrested and sent to the infamous Parchman Prison Farm in Sunflower County where they remained jailed for forty-nine days. They also suffered verbal and physical abuse at the hands of the prison guards. Carmichael was a nineteen-year-old freshman at Howard when this happened and while it was his first time being arrested in the name of the movement, it would certainly not be his last. Carmichael would be arrested dozens of times before his life as a political activist would end.

Carmichael also invokes Kennedy's famous plea to the nation as he describes the process of organizing the Freedom Rides. The Congress of Racial Equality's (CORE) initiated efforts to organize an integrated group of college students from around the country to participate in Freedom Rides to desegregate all public facilities along Route 40, which was the main interstate out of DC. They receive such an overwhelming turnout of white supporters at a Baltimore church that Carmichael is certain that Kennedy's famous maxim is a motivating factor: "Students from schools across the Northeast—Brandeis, Harvard, Yale, Cornell, New York University, and Johns Hopkins—answered CORE's call. When we and the Morgan State students arrived, the church was already half filled with white students (good ol' CPT?). I suspect many of these white students were youthful 'New Frontiersmen,' inspired by JFK's injunction to 'ask what you can do for your country' and eager to put an end to their president's international embarrassments" (Carmichael and Thelwell 2003: 164–65). Carmichael believes that progressive white students, inspired largely by Kennedy's language, sought to dedicate themselves to redeeming their country's tarnished image through activism.

At another point in Carmichael's narrative, he again uses Kennedy's famous saying about serving the country, but this time it is to express pure skepticism concerning the government's intentions when the Freedom Riders are invited to meet with Attorney General Bobby Kennedy:

> Even while some of us were still penned up in Parchman, Bobby Kennedy's emissaries had begun sending out feelers to the student movement? Git outta here. What was he up to? Was he now talking to "extremist on both sides"? Maybe it was "ask not what your country can do you for you; ask what you can do . . ." time, huh? I wasn't about to cut him any slack at all, Jack. On Parchman death row, we had talked about him like a dog. Hey, wasn't it because of their failure to enforce their own laws that we were sitting in that hellhole in the first place? And for what, buying a ticket and riding a bus? C'mon. Gimme an ever-loving break, bro. That hadn't been everyone's reaction, but it was most people's and it sure was mine. (Carmichael and Thelwell 2003: 218)

The notion of continuing the Freedom Rides is abandoned after SNCC meets with the Kennedy administration. They are promised funding and support if they stop and take up the cause of voter registration instead, which they agree to do. Subsequently, SNCC would remain committed to the cause of voter registration for the entire duration of the civil rights movement. In the summer of 1964, many SNCC members embark on the Mississippi

Summer Project, which is designed to help disfranchised Mississippians and impoverished sharecroppers (many of whom were illiterate) to register to vote, but first SNCC conducts interviews to determine if volunteers are mentally and physically fit to serve. They only want intelligent volunteers who knew exactly what they were getting into, due to the physical dangers, including the possibility of death, which southern racism poses in the Mississippi Delta. Carmichael says:

> We ended up with an impressive group of young Americans at their most idealistic. Interesting people, serious people, political activists, Peace Corps volunteers, seminarians. No pun intended, but in 1964 the country's "best and brightest" were headed for Mississippi, not Southeast Asia, and were genuinely to "ask not what your country can do for you; ask what you can do for your country." Y'all remember that? (Carmichael and Thelwell 2003: 359)

This time there is a tinge of irony and sarcasm in Carmichael's words as he again invokes Kennedy's famous saying. While the US government was recruiting scores of young Americans to fight against the spread of communism in the Vietnam War (1969–73), SNCC was recruiting young people of all races to fight against racism and social and economic injustice here in the United States.

Chapter seven in *Stokely Speaks*, entitled "Dialectics of Liberation," describes the negative impact that colonization had on Zimbabwe, and Carmichael employs an important saying from Italian diplomat and philosopher Niccolò Machiavelli in the process:

> If a few settlers left England to go to Zimbabwe, there was no reason for them to rename that country Rhodesia, after themselves, and then force everybody to speak their language. If they'd had respect for the cultures of other people, they would have spoken the language of those people and adopted their religions. But the West was powerful—that's the word nobody wants to talk about, power. It was only power that made people bow their heads to the West. They didn't bow because they liked Jesus Christ or because they liked white folks. Machiavelli said a long time ago that "people obey masters for one of two reasons. Either they love them, or they fear them." I often ask myself whether the West believes the Third World obeys them out of love. (Carmichael 1971: 81–83)

The Machiavellian saying—"People obey masters for one of two reasons. Either they love them, or they fear them"—is employed to help his audience to conceptualize the effects that colonialism and imperialism has on the African psyche. Carmichael wants Black people to see the negative consequences of European exploits on other continents, and he wants to identify them as causes for many of the world's problems.

Carmichael also uses proverbs and sayings from his mentor, Dr. Kwame Nkrumah (1909-72), who was the president of Ghana. In 1969, Carmichael would expatriate to Africa where he learns more about political organizing as a personal assistant to Nkrumah who was named copresident of Guinea by President Sékou Touré (1922-84) after Nkrumah was deposed by a US-backed coup in Ghana. Sékou Touré worked tirelessly to make a return to power in Ghana possible for Nkrumah, but this vision would never fully materialize. Nkrumah (also known affectionately as Osagyefo, redeemer of his native land) is most famous for his ideas concerning the liberation of the African continent which he expresses in his *Handbook of Revolutionary Warfare* (1968). To advance his vision of a unified African continent, free of colonial and imperial exploitation Nkrumah and Sékou Touré launched the All-African People's Revolution Party (AAPRP) which had memberships from sixty-two African countries. As an ode to the African leaders, Carmichael changed his name to Kwame Ture. Carmichael's move to Africa ultimately helps him to expand his mentor's philosophy of Pan-Africanism, the notion that all Black people around the world, as members of the Black diaspora, had a responsibility to share in the struggle to unify and liberate the African continent from colonial powers.

Nkrumah's prolific use of proverbs may reflect an increased value placed on proverbs in African societies. According to paremiologist and folklorist Anand Prahlad: "proverbs have traditionally played a much more central role in the everyday speech of Africans than in that of African Americans. All researchers of African proverbs seem to agree on the absolute proliferation of items throughout individual [African] societies" (Prahlad 1996: location 426). Additionally, proverbs are commonly employed in Africa as "verbal art, and are used in all manner of situations as a means of amusement, in educating the young, to sanction institutionalized behavior, as a method of gaining favor in court, in performing religious rituals and association ceremonies, and to give and add color to ordinary conversations" (Messenger 1959: 1; Prahlad 1996: location 426). Based on research, Nkrumah, in sharing proverbs, is also passing down his knowledge of an ancient African oral tradition which has many different purposes.

At one point in his narrative, Carmichael discusses the impact that broken promises had on newly freed African Americans during the Reconstruction Era (1865–77), invoking a saying from Nkrumah in the process:

> And we should not lightly dismiss that forty acres and a mule either. Later Kwame Nkrumah would tell me, "All liberation begins with land." Working in the Delta, we began to see clearly how the withholding of those forty acres had been no trivial blow. In fact, almost exactly a hundred years later, the lasting, visible, painful consequences of that betrayal were still indelibly etched in our people's condition. Of the many, many betrayals and disappointments Africans had suffered at the hands of this republic, I began to see how Congress's failure to make good on its promise of those forty acres to the freedmen was arguably the most far reaching and injurious. No doubt about it. (Carmichael and Thelwell 2003: 288)

Nkrumah's axiom that "all liberation begins with land" is used to explain why it was necessary for SNCC volunteers to travel to the Mississippi Delta in the first place. They were there to help liberate Mississippi's poor Black population by teaching them how to procure political power through the voting process, but as Carmichael asserts, Black Mississippians would have already had political and economic independence if their one request following the war had been granted. The forty acres and a mule the freedmen originally sought was promised to them by Union General William Tecumseh Sherman at the end of the Civil War in 1865. The order is known as Special Field Order No.15, but it was quickly reversed after Lincoln's assassination.

Carmichael also describes the impact that the killing of one his closest friends, SNCC volunteer Jonathan Daniels had on him and the movement. Daniels had been working alongside Carmichael and other SNCC members as an organizer and instructor in Freedom Schools which were designed to teach Mississippi's uneducated poor, literacy, civics, Black history, and voting rights. Daniels was a dedicated Episcopal seminarian who was murdered in cold blood by an enraged shotgun wielding racist as he shielded another SNCC volunteer, seventeen-year-old Ruby Sales, from gunfire. Afterwards Daniels became a martyr of the civil rights movement. His murder caused Carmichael and other SNCC members to reconsider the role of white volunteers in the movement because they were targeted more intensely. In reference to Daniels's killing, he says: "The Osagyefo [Kwame Nkrumah] used to tell me, 'The only people who never make mistakes are people who never do anything.' I've made mistakes and I'm sure I'll make some more 'cause I'm not finished working. We made a mistake with Jonathan. One that I always remember with regret" (Carmichael and Thelwell 2003: 470–71; Speake 2015: 166). Carmichael shared responsibility for Daniels's murder with the rest of the SNCC organization who felt that they should have done more to keep Daniels out of harm's way, but as Carmichael explains, Daniels's murder "backfired" on the angry racists who wanted to scare SNCC into abandoning their organizing efforts in Lowndes County:

> Organizing the [Lowndes County Freedom Organization] became much easier after that. Now all of the people could see that the Democratic Party—"Hey them ain't nothing but some night-riding, cross-burning, no-count, low-life snakes"—was not for them. Could be that I channeled my anger into work, but I became tireless, almost driven. I was determined that this evil system had to be destroyed, and that only the people themselves could do it. (Carmichael and Thelwell 2003: 471)

Due to Daniels's murder, the people were able to see a clear need for new political representation, and Carmichael became even more determined to help them bring this dream to fruition. From these examples one can see how the sayings of Kwame Nkrumah help Carmichael to formulate a new perspective by which he is able to view his experiences as a political organizer in the Deep South.

After becoming a full-fledged Pan-African revolutionary, Carmichael returned to America from Africa only to have his passport seized by the US government. While sidelined in the US, he was determined to continue his mission of organizing for the political organizations, United Front, and the All-African People's Revolution Party (AAPRP). To explain his rationale for continuing his work, he employs another saying from his mentor Nkrumah:

> I didn't have time to worry about the government's little games. I mean, what was this passport seizure supposed to do? Intimidate me? Demonstrate their power and control over me? American *baasskap*? What? All it meant is that I wouldn't be returning to Guinea as quickly as I had planned, that's all. Hey, I had plenty to occupy me in America. Until the passport situation was resolved with the lawyers, I'd just keep on working . . . Nkrumah always said, "A revolutionary makes a positive out of a negative." (Carmichael and Thelwell 2003: 640)

The Nkrumahism, "a revolutionary makes a positive out of a negative," is a mantra that Carmichael would live by his entire life. He was always willing to work with a limited amount of resources and he frequently took advantage of opportunities to organize and to deliver political speeches on behalf of the Party in any place that he visited.

In one of their first meetings, Nkrumah explains to Carmichael that the two greatest threats to the All-African People's Revolution Party (AAPRP) are a lack of consciousness and a lack of unity. Nkrumah asserts that people need to be aware that "the Afro-American struggle is inextricably linked to the struggle in Africa and vice versa" and that this is the primary reason that capitalist forces such as the media profit by keeping Black people "confused and divided" (Carmichael and Thelwell 2003: 674–75). Carmichael punctuates this message with another one of Nkrumah's universal apothegms: "There is another maxim the Osagyefo [Nkrumah] was fond of: action without thought is blind; thought without action is empty" (Mieder et al. 1991: 6; Carmichael and Thelwell 2003: 675). This proverb speaks to the need for Black activists to be organized and united, and to be fully aware of the organization's purpose. As Carmichael asserts, without organization "we leave ourselves open to the oppressors' tactic of 'divide and conquer' or 'divide and rule'" (Mieder et al. 1991: 112; Carmichael and Thelwell 2003: 678).

When Carmichael expresses his desire to help Nkrumah return to power in Ghana, Nkrumah tells him that an effective political organizer sometimes needs to demonstrate patience. Nkrumah communicates this message to Carmichael using a brief story which he then accentuates with a saying that Carmichael presumably remembers for the rest of his life:

> But y'know, you do remind me of a man standing on the shore watching a boat approach. Now he *knows* the boat is coming. He can clearly see it coming. But he is impatient. He must wade out to meet it. Which in no way speeds up the boat's arrival. At best, the man is soaked; at worst, he drowns. The boat's progress is not affected in the slightest. All impatience is selfishness and egotism. Remember that. (emphasis in original) (Carmichael and Thelwell 2003: 691)

Carmichael again repeats the saying "all impatience is selfishness and egotism" as he ruminates over Nkrumah's untimely death from cancer and his own bout with cancer, and how the possibility of death would ultimately affect the Pan-African movement:

And, you know, a lot of my attitude toward the cancer comes from his influence. Let me reflect carefully because I've never said this publicly. . . . But when I look at all his movements, I really think that Nkrumah knew—long before we did—that the cancer he had would not allow him to return to Ghana. But he was confident that the African revolution would triumph, whether he was here or not. (Carmichael and Thelwell 2003: 694)

At this point, Carmichael reminds the reader of Nkrumah's wise words and the meaning behind them:

I told you his example of the boat approaching and me wanting to plunge in and him saying, "All impatience is selfishness and egotism"? His attitude was, look, this is a struggle. The enemy will do anything in his power to target generals. If you are out front, you must expect to be attacked. Survival is not guaranteed, but whatever happens to you personally, the struggle will go on. I think about his attitude often. (Carmichael and Thelwell 2003: 694)

Ultimately Nkrumah's saying "all impatience is selfishness and egotism" does at least three things for Carmichael: (1) it helps Carmichael to understand more fully his place as a leader in the Pan-African struggle; (2) it demonstrates an appropriate attitude to have as a political organizer; and (3) it provides Carmichael with an effective model for coping with his own bout with cancer.

A number of proverbs and sayings that Carmichael uses come from Nkrumah, but his other political mentor, Sékou Touré, does not seem to communicate using aphorisms. A language barrier more than likely prevented Carmichael from communicating with Sékou Touré on the same level as Nkrumah. Touré primarily spoke French while Carmichael did not, but they were still able to understand one another to some extent with common political terms such as "Marxism," "socialism," and "democracy," because they are essentially the same in any language. Despite the language barrier, Carmichael incorporates one important saying into his narrative which he uses to characterize the political philosophy of Touré. Carmichael says: "Culture is politics; politics is culture" (Carmichael and Thelwell 2003: 702). He then says that he really began to understand what this saying meant when he moved to Guinea and witnessed the philosophy in action firsthand and saw that Guinean president Sékou Touré valued African culture so much that culture and politics were intrinsically connected in Guinea:

> The party clearly understood that the traditional culture was a key element from which to mold an African character to the revolution. So they took concrete steps to preserve, develop, and institutionalize nationally many, many traditional forms. So they supported dance groups and schools, musicians, artists, and the famous griots and so on. But not just the arts, also the ethics and values of traditional culture, an *African* sensibility that I called African humanism. (Carmichael and Thelwell 2003: 702)

At another point in *Stokely Speaks*, Carmichael is explaining the rationale behind Pan-Africanism:

> We must understand the concept that for us the question of community is not geography, it is a question of us black people, wherever we are. We have to consciously become a part of the 900 million black people that are separated over this world. We are separated by *them*. We are blood of the same blood and flesh of the same flesh. We do not know who is our sister, who is our brother, or where we came from. They took us from Africa and they put thousands of miles of water between us, but they forgot—blood is thicker than water. (Stokely 1971: 128)

Carmichael employs the biblical proverbial expression "blood of the same blood and flesh of the same flesh," and then reinforces his message of Black unity with the proverb "blood is thicker than water" (Mieder et al. 1991: 57; Speake 2015: 31). The imagery invoked by Carmichael's proverbial language is striking. Together, they imply that one's ties of kinship are far more important than any physical distance. In the minds of readers, the thousands of miles of water separating African Americans from Africa may become obsolete when one considers the wisdom contained in the adage.

Carmichael also uses several proverbs and sayings that he attributes to other activists and members of the Nonviolent Action Group (NAG) and the Student Nonviolent Coordinating Committee (SNCC) including Junebug Jabbo Jones, Hartman Turnbow (1905–88), Joyce Ladner (1943–), Bill Mahoney, Courtland Cox, Chuck McDew (1938–2018), and Gloria Richardson (1922–). Carmichael includes them in his narrative because they are talented organizers who were important to the movement. Furthermore, remembering the proverbs and sayings that certain SNCC members shared from time to time may have also helped Carmichael to "reconstruct other oral and written contexts" that may be relative to the narrative (Bowden 1996: 442).

One important proverb that effectively characterizes the mindset of the Nonviolent Action Group (NAG) in the 1960s is "a free black mind is a concealed weapon" (Carmichael and Thelwell 2003: 254). This saying, which became proverbial within the group over time, basically describes the value that (NAG) members place on learning and knowledge: "So our generation never expected to find much that represented what Dr. Du Bois had called 'our spiritual strivings' in the American media. The exclusion of racial minorities generally, and militant and intelligent black voices in particular, was near total. We used to say in NAG, 'A free black mind is a concealed weapon.' And someone would always add, 'Yeah, an' the media going make darn sure it *stay* concealed too'" (emphasis in original) (Carmichael and Thelwell 2003: 254). The NAG proverb is similar to the proverb "a little learning is a dangerous thing" (Mieder et al. 1991: 367). By sharing the proverb "a free black mind is a concealed weapon," they are reminding themselves that their education is viewed largely as a threat to white establishments, many of which still support institutional racism despite the growing movement. Ultimately the proverb helps them to motivate one another to succeed.

Another proverb shared by the Student Nonviolent Coordinating Committee (SNCC) also shares a similar message. At one point in Carmichael's narrative, he describes a moment when SNCC spent time debating whether they should speak out about growing tensions in the Middle East: "One of SNCC's mantras was 'Knowledge is power.' So, as we learned, we shared our political education with other field secretaries. We discovered that many SNCC people already harbored serious doubts about the media's official version of events in that region of the world" (Carmichael and Thelwell 2003: 559). In this case the proverb "knowledge is power" (Mieder et al. 1991: 354; Speake 2015: 174) describes the mutual distrust held by most SNCC members concerning the media. Instead of taking the media's information at face value, they instead decide to find out what is happening in the Middle East for themselves before sharing the information with other colleagues. In sharing their research, they are also sharing the power to influence global politics.

Several sayings in Carmichael's narrative are attributed to Junebug Jabbo Jones, an African American southern fictional character that was created and performed by SNCC member, John M. O'Neal (1940–2019) who worked as SNCC's field secretary and coordinator of the Freedom Schools. O'Neal was also a very talented actor and playwright who created and performed as the Jones character. One may say that O'Neal's character *grew out of* and also *with* the movement (SNCC Legacy Project). SNCC worked with many poor sharecroppers who lacked the same educational opportunities as many of the SNCC volunteers (many of whom attended prestigious universities). O'Neal created Jones as a way of expressing the straightforward folk wisdom that sharecroppers demonstrated. One may only imagine how many late-night SNCC meetings were enlightened by insights that SNCC members would attribute to this southern folk persona. The character became so popular that O'Neal would go on to found Junebug Productions, Inc., after his work with SNCC was done.

One of the very first sayings that Carmichael attributes to Jones appears as he is describing the social and political climate at Howard University in the 1960s:

> Howard presented me with every dialectic existing in the African community. At Howard, on any given day, one might meet every black thing . . . and its opposite. The place was a veritable tissue of contradiction, embodying the best and the absolute worst values of the African-American tradition. As Junebug Jabbo Jones (may his tribe increase) loved to say, "Effen yo' doan unnerstan' the principle of eternal contradiction, yo' sho ain't gonna unnerstan' diddly about Howard University. Nor about black life in these United States neither." (Carmichael and Thelwell 2003: 113)

Jones's saying means that as a freshman at Howard Carmichael quickly learned that he was going to have to "take the good with the bad." For instance, one the one hand, there were Black students and organizations at Howard that were extremely class-conscious, only wanting to learn in order to increase their personal wealth. Additionally, some student organizations still practiced colorism, or the notion that lighter skin, in and of itself, carried a higher degree of prestige, therefore barring darker-skinned people from joining their groups. On the other hand, there were also many students like Carmichael, who displayed higher levels of social consciousness and wanted to learn in order to help improve social and economic conditions for all Black people and not just for themselves. Carmichael's proverbial expression "every black thing . . . and its opposite" signals to the reader in advance that Junebug Jabbo Jones's "principle of eternal contradiction" is applicable at Howard.

Carmichael also explains what SNCC members learn from Howard professor Herbert Reed about conducting themselves as young student activists in the Nonviolent Action Group (NAG) and the Student Nonviolent Coordinating Committee (SNCC). After describing some necessary personality traits such as always being goal oriented, polite, and knowledgeable, Carmichael asserts that Reed told them that a good activist should also maintain a good sense of humor. He accentuates his last point concerning humor with another saying from Junebug Jabbo Jones. As Junebug Jabbo Jones (may his tribe increase) says: "What us Africans need most is a lot of patience and a sense of irony" (Carmichael 2003: 149). Carmichael goes on to explain that he and his SNCC comrades would quickly learn that these attributes would only be beneficial at Howard and would not work with "armed barbarians or irrationally savage racists. Or with an inflexible government establishment whose 'interests,' as they understand them, give a low priority to justice for your people or the alleged guarantees of the Constitution. We would have to find that out to our great sorrow" (Carmichael and Thelwell 2003: 149).

Carmichael also describes the process by which he became SNCC chairman. He says that when SNCC members initially voted, John Lewis (1940–2020), who would later become a US congressman representing Georgia, actually won the election. Nevertheless, many members who knew and liked Carmichael wanted him to replace Lewis (whom they felt had become increasingly focused on his own political ambitions), so they forced a recount, and to Lewis's dismay, Carmichael won the election. There is a detailed account of the election debate in SNCC member Julian Bond's biography, which reads:

> The atmosphere was clearly one of dissatisfaction with the old-regime—John Lewis, chairman, and James Forman, executive secretary—who were being eyed with disdain as hopelessly old-fashioned and too moderate for the kind of militance the membership was moving toward. The group opened its balloting for officers on Friday evening around eleven, and the voting continued on through the smoky night until finally, about three o'clock Saturday morning, Lewis emerged still the chairman, winner by a large vote. Then, as the group started to vote on candidates for the executive committee, the proceedings were interrupted by a member who challenged Lewis's victory as illegal, kicking off a renewed and this time more heated debate. Friends turned on old comrades, and bitter tears were shed. Around 6:30 A.M., SNNC voted Stokely Carmichael, who had worked to launch the Black Panther Party in Lowndes County, Alabama, its new chairman. (Neary 1971: 144)

Carmichael described SNCC's new militant direction in his announcement to the press. Carmichael says: "Snick is going to intensify its efforts in the area of independent politics. Our experience organizing in the hard-core racist areas of this country has been one of inaction on the part of the federal government. We will struggle as we have in the past for human rights and join with those around the world who know the same oppression that we know, and the same deception on the part of the so-called United States government in its claims of concern for democracy" (Neary 1971: 144–45). For good measure, Carmichael adds: "Asking blacks to join the Democratic Party . . . is like asking Jews to join the Nazi Party" (Neary 1971: 145). In a side note, the editor, former SNCC activist Ekwueme Michael Thelwell (1939–), describes the discussion that took place between himself and Carmichael concerning the issue of including Lewis's sentiments regarding the election in Carmichael's autobiography. They are ambivalent on the issue. To negotiate, Carmichael employs another popular saying from Junebug Jabbo Jones. Carmichael says: "Okay, Thelwell. We'll hold that one. Leave it the way it is for now. Junebug used to say, 'Inside every Negro there lurks a potential black man.' Let me think about it. Later when we get to that chapter in the book, we can fight about it . . ." (Carmichael 2003: 483). The saying "inside every Negro there lurks a potential black man" insinuates that Carmichael believes that whether Lewis ever expressed any negative sentiments or not, he may still deserve the benefit of the doubt. Carmichael and Thelwell never got the opportunity to "fight about it," but Thelwell's editor's note gives readers a glimpse into their writing process and their mindset.

Carmichael also uses a variation of this saying in *Stokely Speaks: From Black Power to Pan-Africanism* (1971) except in this instance it is not attributed to Jones. In chapter eleven, "A New World to Build," he says: "There's another concept we're trying to put out around the country: every Negro is a potential black man. This concept is not only necessary, it is revolutionary" (Carmichael 1971: 148–49). Here, Carmichael is using the saying to characterize a potential epiphanic moment which may happen when a Black person becomes a revolutionary thinker who fully acknowledges and embraces his African roots. Later in the same chapter, Carmichael presents the proverb as one of three important concepts that Black people must learn in order to resist the culturally divisive forces of colonialism: "(1) We must have an undying love. We must have an undying love for our people. (2) Every Negro is a potential black man. (3) For black people the question of community is not simply a question of geographical boundaries but a question of our people and where we are" (Carmichael 1971: 153). Presented as one of three important tenets, the proverb emphasizes the need to abolish self-hatred in Black communities in America. It also highlights the need to reconsider all of the physical and mental boundaries that are traditionally imposed to demarcate Blackness.

Carmichael also describes the effect that his freshman English teacher, Toni Morrison, had on him as a student at Howard. Years later, Morrison would become a Nobel laureate, and as an editor at Random House she would also edit two of Carmichael's books, *Black Power* (1967) and *Stokely Speaks* (1971). After emphasizing the fact that Morrison was an extremely rare combination of literary talent and good looks, Carmichael uses a saying from SNCC member Chuck McDew to call attention to the assumed luck that the hiring committee at Howard must have had in finding such a genius as Morrison:

> Ms. Toni Morrison was clearly one of the committee's more inspired choices. Brother Chuck McDew sometimes says, "Even a blind pig will pick up a fat acorn evrah now'n den." I hear that Sister Morrison is on record as remembering me as "something of a rascal in class." Perhaps, no doubt. But they say what goes round comes round. Ms. M., don't look now, but your "rascal" just called you the blind committee's "fat acorn." Only metaphorically, of course. (Carmichael and Thelwell 2003: 130)

Carmichael follows up McDew's saying with an age-old aphorism of his own when he says "what goes round comes round." The playful banter that Carmichael sustains through proverbs and sayings illustrates the warm-hearted sentiments that Morrison and Carmichael held for one another.

Another important proverb that Carmichael includes comes from SNCC member Hartman Turnbow as he recalls describing to Turnbow the brutality that some of the Freedom Riders are faced with as they travel through Mississippi: "The one day I told Mr. Hartman Turnbow how three generations of movement women—Mrs. Hamer, Annelle Ponder, and June Johnson (my little sister)—had been beaten in the Winona jail, his face grew overcast, his voice thoughtful. Y'know son," he mused, "water seek de low places but power seek de weak places" (Carmichael and Thelwell 2003: 287). Turnbow's response is meant to both console Carmichael and to help him understand the nature of the political struggle that had consumed much of the Deep South. Furthermore, the proverb is Turnbow's way of communicating to Carmichael that SNCC had become immersed in a battle for power, and much like low-lying water on the Mississippi Delta plains, racist whites sought to absorb and overtake any political influence that SNCC or any poor sharecropper could ever hope to obtain.

The proverb "water seek de low places, but power seek de weak places" communicated such an important lesson to young Carmichael that he refers to it a number of times. At another point in the narrative, he explains some of the complicated logistics behind SNCC's voter registration drive:

Now the bad part. SNCC was entering its third year in voter registration and had staked out the hard places. Those "black belt" counties in the Delta of Mississippi, Arkansas, Alabama, and southwest Georgia. We had agreed that CORE could have Louisiana. We were working where Africans were in the majority and the vote could theoretically make a real difference. Which is why the repression was so desperate. As Mr. Turnbow said when I explained this, "Power seek tha *weak* places, water seek tha *low* places, but SNCC done seek the *hard* places, seem like t'me." (Carmichael and Thelwell 2003: 326)

In this instance, Carmichael extends the proverb by adding his own phrase to the end "but SNCC done seek the *hard* places, seem like t'me" (Carmichael and Thelwell 2003: 326). Carmichael's addition is used to emphasize the extent that SNCC had to contend against racial terrorism. The Kennedy administration made promises of funding and support in order to convince SNCC to abandon the Freedom Rides in favor of voter registration drives, and now that they faced even worse threats of terrorism in the Deep South, "the federal government—the Justice Department, the FBI, those Kennedy liberals who had promised so much—where were they? Nowhere to be found" (Carmichael and Thelwell 2003: 326).

Carmichael would include this proverb at another point in *Ready for Revolution* as an epigraph to chapter twenty-two. The epigraph is attributed to Hartman Turnbow, Mississippi Freedom Democratic Party leader, and reads: "We gotta make this our Mississippi, Jes' as water seek the low places, Power seek the weak places" Carmichael and Thelwell 2003: 501). In this instance, the addition of the phrase "we gotta make this our Mississippi" causes the proverb to read more as a rallying call for African American people to unite for the common cause of political independence.

According to social psychologists Sophia Moskalenko and Clark McCauley, "Slogans are the most basic expression of one side of a political issue. They appeal to widely shared emotions, creating a perception of unity in a crowd of strangers. They prescribe a (simple) course of action that stems from these shared emotions, mobilizing the crowd" (Moskalenko and McCauley 2020: 180). Furthermore, "Research shows that rhymed messages are easier to remember and more persuasive than unrhymed messages carrying the same idea" (Moskalenko and McCauley 2020: 180). This information drawn from research explains the importance of proverbs, sayings, and proverbial expressions that also double as political slogans. As Carmichael demonstrates, SNCC members shared them amongst themselves quite often in all kinds of situations including during large rallies and during private moments of distress. Proverbs and sayings regarding issues dealing with power such as "Black power" and "water seek de low places, but power seek de weak places" serve as effective political slogans because they are simultaneously brief, memorable, and directive. Therefore, they instantly provide members with a renewed sense of hope and purpose by reminding them of the important political objectives of the group.

Carmichael also describes a family like atmosphere that existed among members of the Nonviolent Action Group (NAG) and Student Nonviolent Coordinating Committee (SNCC). The long meetings that they would have were often made longer by disagreements, but as Carmichael explains, the disagreements were a necessary part of their growing process: "But similarities in fundamental attitudes notwithstanding, we were in no way intellectual clones of each other. Folks were stubbornly independent; therefore arguments and disagreements could be fierce, passionate and unending" (Carmichael and Thelwell 2003: 145). He then includes a popular saying from SNCC member Joyce Ladner that effectively describes the intellectual climate of the group: "As Joyce Ladner famously said, 'SNCC folk would argue with a street sign'" (Carmichael and Thelwell 2003: 145). He then adds: "Well, NAG folk would argue with the sign *post*. But the strident rhetoric never managed to conceal a deep mutual respect" (emphasis in original) (Carmichael and Thelwell 2003: 145). Ladner's humorous saying and Carmichael's snappy retort depicts an atmosphere that is mentally challenging on the surface, but also fueled by a strong family-like bond.

Another saying that Carmichael uses comes from SNCC member Bill Mahoney. As Carmichael explains, the process of challenging Howard's administration through organizations like the Nonviolent Action Group (NAG) and the Student Nonviolent Coordinating Committee (SNCC) was a great learning experience that taught him and other members how to negotiate "from a position of no real power" (Carmichael and Thelwell 2003: 147). Additionally, the minor battles that they engaged in with administration would effectively prepare them for far more challenging obstacles. Carmichael uses a saying from Bill Mahoney to emphasize this point: "As Bill Mahoney would sometimes say, 'Today the administration, tomorrow the state'" (Carmichael and Thelwell 2003: 147). It is a brief saying that fully describes the future oriented attitudes of both organizations.

SNCC member Courtland Cox, a fellow Trinidadian from New York, would also popularize a saying. Carmichael describes him as "another big dude . . . who was always thoughtful, deliberate, and given to aphorisms" (Carmichael and Thelwell 2003: 158). The saying that he attributes to Cox reads: "Blackness is necessary. But it is not sufficient" (Carmichael and

Thelwell 2003: 158–59). It is a powerful statement that speaks to the perceived connection between racial identity and political organizing. Some people mistakenly believe that simply being Black qualifies them to speak on behalf of all Black people, but as Cox's aphorism asserts, Blackness is "not sufficient." One must also be willing to gain knowledge from books and other sources about the history of the Black experience.

Another important saying comes from Howard alumna Gloria Richardson (1922–), who led the Cambridge Nonviolent Action Committee (CNAC). Richardson uses a saying as a way of conceptualizing the ramped racial violence that occurred during the Cambridge movement (1961–64). In the spring of 1963, Cambridge, Maryland, had become a virtual powder keg due to a combination of conservatives who were growing increasingly intolerant of Black political organizing in the area, and Black community members who were quick to retaliate. Racial tensions reached a boiling point on July 14, when racist whites began driving through Black neighborhoods firing liberally into Black people's homes. Blacks retaliated with an "organized defense." And subsequently, "sustained fire was returned from various points, off roofs, out of windows, behind cars and trees, etc. That exchange lasted more than an hour" (Carmichael and Thelwell 2003: 339). At a meeting, Richardson would denounce the violence, but she would not denounce Black people who were defending their own lives. Richardson employs a saying to make her point: "When you are attacked by a rabid dog . . . you don't run or throw away the walking stick you have in your hand" (Carmichael and Thelwell 2003: 339–40). This saying was not well received by the press, nor by the Black and white leaders who were proponents of nonviolence, but Richardson had established herself as one of few militant Black females in the movement that could get the Kennedy administration's attention. Subsequently, Richardson and (CNAC) would have several private meetings with Attorney General Robert F. Kennedy. Ultimately, her efforts led to her being one of the signatories of the Treaty of Cambridge, which desegregated all public facilities and implemented provisions to improve equities in housing and education.

Many proverbs and sayings that Carmichael includes in his narrative are attributed to West Indians, Africans, or various African tribes. Some of them involve animals thus reflecting his experiences with agrarian lifestyles that many Black people live around the world. Through these sayings, Carmichael is able to make a number of important points concerning life, truth, and human nature.

One African proverb appears at a point in the narrative when Carmichael is explaining how he and a group of friends at Bronx Science are discussing the Pythagorean Theorem when they are suddenly approached by a man whom Carmichael describes as a "hobo-looking old dude" (Carmichael and Thelwell 2003: 109). The man tells them that the Pythagorean Theorem was not discovered by Pythagoras the Greek, as most people believe. He tells them that the famous formula was instead discovered by Africans in Egypt. Carmichael and his friends initially dismiss the old man as crazy, but after he checks the facts for himself in the library, he realizes that what the man tells him is indeed the truth and he uses two proverbs (one of which is African) and a proverbial expression to communicate this learning experience to readers.

The first mistake that Carmichael says he made is to dismiss the man simply because of his unruly appearance: "Thou seest that man's fall, but though knowest not his wrassling" (Carmichael and Thelwell 2003: 109). This universal proverb that Carmichael does not attribute to any particular person basically means that it is wise not to judge people based on their outward appearances because one has no way of knowing what an individual may have been through. Carmichael goes on to say: "That lesson would be reinforced time and again when as a young man I was organizing sharecroppers in the rural South. Especially with our elders. Knowledge and sometimes wisdom can come from the most unlikely of sources. The stone that the builders rejected" (Cambridge and Thelwell 2003: 109). The proverbial expression "the stone that the builders rejected" further speaks to the notion that one does not have to be formally educated to learn. Knowledge may also be gained through unconventional means. Carmichael then employs an African proverb to accentuate this important message: "And of course, in Africa, in the villages, the same thing. A proverb I heard stayed with me: 'Truth is like a goatskin bag: each man carries his own'" (Carmichael and Thelwell 2003: 109).

At another point in the narrative Carmichael is discussing the overwhelming amount of support that he received after being elected SNCC Chairman. Dr. King congratulates him and tells him that he always believed that Carmichael would eventually be called upon to lead the organization. Contrarily, his former teacher and Congress of Racial Equality (CORE) cofounder James Farmer expresses a more ambivalent attitude towards Carmichael's new role. In fact, he warns Carmichael of some of the perils of leadership. Farmer asks Carmichael if he was familiar with the "West Indian proverb about the high-climbing monkey?" (Carmichael and Thelwell 2003: 485). Carmichael responds: "My grandmother used to say it all the time." (Carmichael and Thelwell 2003: 485; Speak 2015: 151). An editor's side note reveals the West Indian proverb that Farmer is referring to: "The higher the monkey climb, the more he expose he behind." Referencing the proverb is Farmer's way of warning him that as the new leader of SNCC, Carmichael will be under much more scrutiny and observation than he ever was as a regular member. In addition to the West Indian proverb, Farmer also tells him that he must grow "some calluses on [his] soul" (Carmichael and Thelwell 2003: 485), which is a proverbial expression meaning that he would have to maintain a mature attitude when faced with an abundance of criticism. Farmer then leaves Carmichael with another proverb. He asks Carmichael if he recalls the saying "uneasy lies the head" from Shakespeare's *King Henry IV*. (Mieder et al. 1991: 128) The line reads: "Uneasy lies the head that wears the crown." A Shakespearean at heart, Carmichael would sometimes sit in on Shakespeare lectures at Howard, so one may assume that he was well-versed. Carmichael responds by saying: "that [doesn't] apply since SNCC didn't have no crowns no how." In using the proverb reference, Farmer is more than likely testing his former student, and if that is indeed the case, Carmichael passed with flying colors in reminding him of the founding tenet that Ella Baker had established at their first meeting at Shaw University in Raleigh, North Carolina: that SNCC members would lead themselves, and they would organize and empower the communities they served, so that they could eventually lead themselves also (Carmichael and Thelwell 2003: 485).

At another point in the narrative, Carmichael describes a time when he returned home to visit his mother after being away for an extended amount of time. His mother tries to convince him to stay awhile, and after much pleading, he finally concedes to her wishes. He uses an African proverb to justify his decision to take a much-needed break from organizing. He says: "As we say in Africa, 'Why is man better than animals? Because we have kinfolk'" (Carmichael and Thelwell 2003: 731). A variation of this proverb also appears in another section as a caption that accompanies a 1989 photo of Carmichael surrounded by his nieces and nephews. The caption reads: " *'Why are humans better than animals? Because we have kinsmen.'* Igbo proverb" (Carmichael and Thelwell 2003).

As Carmichael explains the effect that his political saying "Black power" had on the media, he says that it is always misinterpreted and attacked by political leaders that do not have a full grasp of its meaning. While Carmichael intends for the slogan to be a rallying cry for Black political, social, and economic independence, many press outlets and politicians misinterpret the call as an overt expression of racial hatred. According to Carmichael: "one famous public intellectual, James Wechsler of the *New York Post*, worried that we 'were killing the dream' . . . that 'the cause of Civil Rights was floundering' . . . 'the visions of the Freedom Movement are imperiled' . . . 'some deeply dedicated [*but obviously confused*] men are setting the stage for the destruction of the noblest cause of our time.'" (emphasis in original) (Carmichael and Thelwell 2003: 525). So many people felt offended or threatened by his new "Black power" mantra that Carmichael had no way of knowing who to attack and employs a proverb to describe the situation. The narrative reads: "West Indian proverb: 'When you throw a stone into a pigsty, the one that bawl is the one you lick'" (Carmichael and Thelwell: 2003 525). The proverb basically describes his attitude towards all the political backlash that he receives. Carmichael clearly believes that the most outspoken opponents are also the enemies who are determined to impede the progress of the movement, and those are the opponents that he wants to reach with his mantra.

At another point in the narrative, Carmichael describes the effect that being SNCC Chairman had on him. While he explains that it did not have a negative effect on his personality or attitude towards the movement, it did pull him away from all of the things that he really enjoyed most such as political organizing and taking part in all of the "day-to-day running of the organization," which ultimately had to be left for others to accomplish because of his heavy speaking and touring schedule (Carmichael and Thelwell 2003: 540). To explain his complicated predicament, Carmichael employs an African proverb which sounds much like Junebug Jabbo Jones's theory of contradiction: "Where one thing stands, something else will stand beside it. That's an African proverb I've always liked. This ancestral wisdom deals with duality and contradiction, complexity. Nothing is ever entirely one thing or even simply what it seems. Another, different thing will stand beside it and behind it. A particular thing will often include its opposite" (Carmichael and Thelwell 2003: 540). The African proverb "where one thing stands, something else will stand beside it" attests to the convoluted nature of Carmichael's issue. Most people assumed that the worldwide attention that Carmichael received as SNCC chairman was what he wanted, but the proverb illustrates that he also had a strong passion to go back to the job that he loved most which was political organizing. Carmichael would eventually return to political organizing after his chairmanship ended, but he never truly gave up one set of duties for the other.

Towards the end of his career when Carmichael receives student papers about the Freedom Movement sent to him by the son of famed sociologist Dr. W. E. B. Du Bois (1868–1963), David Du Bois, Carmichael sends him a thank you letter that describes the experience as humbling. Carmichael is "humbled" by Du Bois's student's interests in the Freedom Movement, and he is also "humbled" by the honesty that the students express in their papers. Carmichael then uses two proverbs, one of which is a favorite of his famous friend and mentor Dr. King and the other he attributes to Egyptians: "But we were humbled to see the honesty of your students in facing contradictions which challenge life-long opinions. That made Martin Luther King come alive with his oft-repeated 'truth crushed to the earth shall rise again.' Or as the Egyptians say, 'struggle is like a rubber ball: the harder it is smashed into the dirt, the higher it rebounds into the sky'" (Mieder et al. 1991: 616; Carmichael and Thelwell 2003: 595–96; Mieder 2010: 512). Carmichael includes these powerful proverbs as a way of saying that the students are now also a major part of the Freedom Movement, and their work is simply a manifestation of this bond.

As a citizen of Guinea, Carmichael explains an ordeal that he experienced when his passport nearly expired. After the death of Guinean president Sékou Touré, Carmichael feared that he would be denied a new passport by the new regime and therefore would no longer be allowed to travel. He says that he was able to obtain a new one from the minister of the interior before it expired by being creative. Due to the fact that he recognized the minister from when the minister was just a low-level officer, he was able to use his knowledge of the man's love for American hip-hop and attractive women to convince him to expedite the handling of his passport. Previously the young man had asked Carmichael to critique the English used in a rap song he had written. The minister remembers Carmichael's favor, and after a few laughs and some small talk Carmichael receives his new passport thereby reducing a process that usually takes several months to only thirty minutes. As Carmichael leaves the minister's office, he promises to send many attractive women to his office in return. Carmichael says: "He was still laughing as I left his office that day" (Carmichael and Thelwell 2003: 724). In addition to this humorous anecdote, Carmichael informs the reader that the same minister was later executed for plotting a government take-over. Carmichael uses an African proverb to describe the young minister's revolutionary spirit. He says: "As the Ashanti proverb says, 'A log may lie in the river for ten years, but it will never become a crocodile" (Carmichael and Thelwell 2003: 723–24). He also adds: "He once was a most impressive young warrior and he taught me a lot. Peace be unto him" (Carmichael and Thelwell 2003: 724). The anecdote and the Ashanti proverb work together to express the notion that if one believes that one is destined to be a revolutionary then that is what one will ultimately become regardless of any title that may be bestowed upon them.

At another point in the narrative, Carmichael describes his strategy for cancer treatment. While he always allowed trusted medical professionals to treat him, he also tried several experimental treatments. He describes his reaction after being exposed to some of these alternative remedies: "I was surprised both at the extent and the variety of these enterprises. It was collectively an underground mini-industry, at least some of which seemed transparently fraudulent, the contemporary equivalents of snake oil salesman preying on frightened people at their most vulnerable. An exploitation of the drowning-man-and-the-straw syndrome, the profit motive at its absolutely most despicable" (Carmichael and Thelwell 2003: 769). The proverbial expression "the drowning-man-and-the straw" is a reference to the proverb "a drowning man will clutch at a straw" (Mieder et al. 1991: 169; Speake 2015: 84). While this may not be attributed to a specific group it helps to prepare the reader for another proverb which Carmichael attributes to Africa:

> But the few that, although unorthodox, appeared to be serious scientific initiatives with some potential to benefit somebody came surrounded by a flotilla of the obviously fraudulent. And how to distinguish between them? The task of sorting out and sifting through fell to Dr. Justice, assisted by Eric, Winky, and my sister Nagib. As our proverb says, "Hungry belly make monkey eat red pepper." Well, necessity has made me an expert on experimental cancer treatment. (Carmichael and Thelwell 2003: 769)

In this instance, Carmichael's use of a proverb and a proverbial expression calls attention to the troubling situation that he was forced into by the insidious disease, cancer, and as the proverb illustrates, desperate times call for desperate measures. Due to the expert care that Carmichael receives after his initial diagnoses, he lived another two years. He lost his life to the disease in 1998.

Carmichael also uses several proverbs and sayings that reflect various disciplines or fields of study such as philosophy, history, English, political science, and engineering. At one point in the narrative he says: "That Greek philosopher Heracleitus was wrong in our case: Africans in America seem always to be crossing and recrossing the same river" (Carmichael and Thelwell 2003: 204). While Carmichael's statement may not be a proverb, it is a reference to a saying that was popularized by Heracleitus who was known for his writings about paradox and incoherence which he argues arises naturally alongside constant change. Heracleitus's original statement reads: "No man ever steps in the same river twice, for its not the same river and he's not the same man." Heracleitus's saying aptly applies to Carmichael, who entered Howard as a premed student, but quickly discovered his passion for philosophy after becoming involved with the movement. Carmichael's reference to it: "Africans in America seem always to be crossing and recrossing the same river" is but one of many examples of Carmichael applying his fervor for philosophical insight to the civil rights struggle.

Another saying that Carmichael incorporates into his narrative which also illustrates his enthusiasm for philosophy appears at a point in the narrative when he describes a need for Black people in the Deep South to have their own political parties that would enable them to elect their own candidates at the local and state levels. Recognizing the limited success of the newly established Mississippi Freedom Democratic Party (MFDP), Carmichael explains that another party is necessary: "The MFDP was one model, but we needed at least a second one. As someone famous said, 'Let a thousand flowers bloom and a thousand schools of thought contend'" (Carmichael and Thelwell 2003: 438). In this case, Carmichael's philosophical aphorism is used to describe a pivotal moment in the movement that would result in the founding of the Lowndes County Freedom Organization (LCFO), which was symbolized on voting ballots by the black panther illustration drawn by fifteen-year-old SNCC field secretary Ruth Howard.

Black Power: The Politics of Liberation in America (1967) includes a proverb that may serve as an explanation for why the MFDP may not have been successful in accomplishing its mission of unseating the racist Democratic Party at the 1964 Democratic National Convention. The passage reads: "Law is the agent of those in political power; it is the product of those powerful enough to define right and wrong and to have that definition legitimized by 'law.' This is not to say that 'might makes right,' but it is to say that might makes law. The MFDP was operating from a base of powerlessness; thus, they could be declared 'illegal'" (Ture and Hamilton: 1967). In this instance, the proverb "might makes right" is used to emphasize the reason why the Mississippi Freedom Democratic Party (MFDP) was not strong enough to unseat the traditional all white racist Democratic Party. According to paremiologist Wolfgang Mieder, "might makes right" is one of the most highly cited proverbs of the English tradition, appearing in the works of figures such as Abraham Lincoln, Frederick Douglass, Martin Luther King Jr., William Shakespeare, and others (Mieder 2019: 269). The proverb means that in the game of politics, it is always the stronger party that wins. This fact is accentuated even further by the antiproverb "might makes law" which proceeds it. Antiproverbs are defined as "those reactions to common proverbs ... which are humorous, ironic, or satirical modifications that contain new insights and generalizations, with the possibility of becoming new proverbs" (Mieder 2019: 15). If the proverb "might makes right" represents any specific field, in this instance, it is unquestionably the field of political science (Mieder et al. 1991: 510; Speake 2015: 207).

At another point in the narrative, Carmichael seems to have a war of words with a reporter or better yet, a war of proverbs. The reporter says to

Carmichael: "You know, Mr. Ture, they say journalism is the first draft of history" (Carmichael and Thelwell 2003: 501). Carmichael, unimpressed, responds: "Napoléon had something to say about that" (Carmichael and Thelwell 2003: 501). The reporter having no clue as to what Napoléon says about history is mocked even further by Carmichael who then says: "You mean you don't know? C'mon, I thought you guys knew everything. [Napoléon] said history is nothing but lies commonly agreed upon. You saying you the first draft of that?" (Carmichael and Thelwell 2003: 501) The reporter who is beginning to feel insulted asks Carmichael if he is accusing him of being a liar. Carmichael responds by saying: "Oh no, but I may be calling you a historian" (Carmichael and Thelwell 2003: 501). This brief exchange illustrates Carmichael's penchant for philosophical thinking and his ability to view academic disciplines from a macroscopic perspective. Carmichael is primarily concerned with learning how different schools of thought function and how that knowledge can be applied to the movement.

Perhaps the previous exchange with the reporter inspires Carmichael to include a similar saying in a speech that he delivers at the University of California, Berkeley, October 1966. In the introduction to the speech, Carmichael says: "Incidentally, for my friends and members of the press, my self-appointed white critics, I was reading Mr. Bernard Shaw two days ago, and I came across a very important quote that I think is most apropos to you. He says, 'All criticism is an autobiography.' Dig yourself. OK" (Carmichael 1971: 45). The saying that he employs in the Berkeley address may be interpreted as an invitation to the media to continue to criticize him and his ideas. He is telling the media outlets that are present, that the negative press that they generate is only contributing to his legacy as a Black revolutionary. The saying may also help to defer any negative criticism that he may receive for that particular speech.

More proverbs and proverbial language concerning Carmichael's philosophical views on history appear in *Stokely Speaks: From Black Power to Pan-Africanism* (1971). In chapter four, "Toward Black Liberation," Carmichael describes the failures of Reconstruction: "We have repeatedly seen that political alliances based on appeals to conscience and decency are chancy things, simply because institutions and political organizations have no consciences outside their own special interests. The political and social rights of Negroes have been and always will be negotiable and expendable the moment they conflict with the interests of our 'allies.' If we do not learn from history, we are doomed to repeat it, and that is precisely the lesson of the Reconstruction" (Carmichael 1971: 37). The use of the proverb "if we do not learn from history, we are doomed to repeat it" speaks to a history of failed promises that the US government has made to Black people since the end of the Civil War. Carmichael uses the aphorism to illustrate the fact that it is one's own responsibility to learn about these unfortunate historical occurrences to prevent them from happening again.

Carmichael echoes the very same point in chapter fifteen, "From Black Power Back to Pan-Africanism." He explains that Black people should learn about the history of Africa that predates the transatlantic slave trade:

> This parochial thinking must cease. Our starting point in history must precede the period of colonialism and slavery; it must precede the Arabic and European invasions. This is not to say we want to rest on the past glory of African civilization, which contributed immensely to world civilization; but in order to map out the future we *must* clearly understand the past. More importantly, this interpretation allows us to view the effects these events had on us. (Carmichael 1971: 222)

The saying "in order to map out the future we *must* clearly understand the past" is nearly identical in meaning to the proverb "if we do not learn from history, we are doomed to repeat it." The main difference is that the former does not attempt to foresee or predict any of the negative consequences that may result from ignoring history. Carmichael's use of the proverb and the saying is indicative of his belief that all revolution begins with education.

Another saying that Carmichael uses a number of times is attributed to the field of engineering. As Carmichael describes some fundamental differences between the Southern Christian Leadership Conference (SCLC) and the Student Nonviolent Coordinating Committee (SNCC), he asserts that SCLC was in some ways pigeonholed because they continued to depend on marches and government support even when federal support was unlikely and even when marches were viewed as being detrimental to the physical and mental well-being of all of its members who were often attacked by racist conservative groups and state troopers. Carmichael uses a proverb to explain the rationale behind this kind of thinking: "You know there is a saying among engineers: "If all you have is a hammer, the whole world will look like a nail to you" (Carmichael and Thelwell 2003: 446; Speake 2015: 142). He repeats this proverb again as he ponders how Dr. King, after leading successful marches in Selma, will alter his political tactics as he prepares to mobilize SCLC to take on northern territories beginning with Chicago. As Carmichael explains, Chicago will require new tactics and it will also pose new dangers. He emphasizes this point to readers using the very same proverb:

The sheer scale of the city, its ethnic neighborhoods, its politics, the infamous Daley machine, the entrenched industrial capitalism. How responsive would these be to SCLC's nonviolent, mass mobilization marches and cries for integration. I wasn't sure. A brother in engineering once told me, "If the only tool you have is a hammer, then the whole world will look like a nail." I wished Dr. King well, but I wondered what tactical changes he was preparing for his first Northern campaign. I had my doubts. (Carmichael and Thelwell 2003: 538; Speake 2015: 142)

This proverb that he attributes to the engineering field is used to explain to the reader that SNCC's purpose was to provide Black people with other viable alternatives that were not being offered by SCLC or other conservative groups. As the proverb implies, a single political organization will never be adequate in all situations.

There are also several proverbs and sayings that equate physical movement with personal growth and development. They are implemented for at least a couple of different reasons. First, they help to characterize the learning process, seeming most appropriate at various points in the narrative when people are faced with difficult learning situations. Secondly, proverbs and sayings regarding motion and movement are used at times to discuss the progress of African people.

One proverb that Carmichael uses that equates movement with learning is "all motion is not progress." The first time that he employs this proverb, he is remembering the annual Carnival celebration in his native homeland of Trinidad, and how much he enjoyed the Calypso music of steel bands, and the float and costume competitions. As a young child, he and his family would view the float-building process and enjoy bickering over which costume would take home the year's grand prize. Carmichael says that the event has now become marred by capitalism: "Today, so I'm told, the steel bands come lavishly attired and equipped courtesy of their multinational corporate sponsors, the marriages of capitalism and local culture. The Shell Oil Invaders and Mobil Corp's Casa Blanca? Somehow it doesn't ring quite right, given the militant history out of which the bands evolved. All motion is not Progress" (Carmichael and Thelwell 2003: 41). The oil manufacturers are products of European colonial forces that sought to exploit the island's people and their natural resources. The steel bands evolved as a form of subversion. When colonists forbade native workers from playing drums, they resorted to secretly designing their own instruments from discarded oil containers. Over the years, the drum-making process evolved into the specialized sounds that can be heard from Calypso bands today. In this instance, the proverb "all motion is not progress" describes the irony demonstrated in the fact that a loved Carnival tradition which was designed to subvert colonial forces, is now, through corporate sponsorship, being used to promote the same colonial forces.

Carmichael uses the proverb again in describing the impact of the landmark *Brown v. Board of Education* (1952–54) decision on the Deep South. On the one hand, many African Americans celebrated the fact that segregation would finally be outlawed, and they looked forward to more opportunities to receive equal education. On the other hand, due to racist backlash (which often appeared in the form of Ku Klux Klan activity, lynching, and mob violence) celebrations surrounding the landmark *Brown* case would be short-lived. Carmichael asserts that the worst part about the deteriorating racial climate was the government's subdued response: "From the rest of the nation and the national government, silence. Things were in fact worse. All motion is not progress" (Carmichael and Thelwell 2003: 175).

In describing the influence that exploitation had on Black people in the film industry, Carmichael contends that there were several positive and powerful images of Blackness in Hollywood in the early 1960s. He names important Black figures such as Harry Belafonte, Yaphet Kotto, William Marshall, Woody Strode, Ivan Dixon, and former NFL running back Jim Brown (Carmichael and Thelwell 2003: 267). He goes on to say that these positive images were quickly overshadowed by stereotypical imagery that became pervasive during the blaxploitation era of the early 1970s. He says: "The . . . wave of blaxploitation films showed us graphically that not all motion is progress. Particularly for black folks in Hollywood" (Carmichael and Thelwell 2003: 267). Carmichael frequently uses the proverb "all motion is not progress" to pinpoint moments in history that are marked by moral regression.

Carmichael also reflects further on the impact that his "Black power" slogan had on the civil rights movement. He explains that the movement was transforming in the 1960s and would have continued to evolve with or without a popular political slogan which could never create change in and of itself. In making this clear to the reader he employs the proverb again:

> Yeah, the movement was changing. Had to change. Struggle is, after all, a dynamic, complicated, and organic process. And not all motion is progress. But, c'mon, gimme a break. We certainly did not change the entire direction of the black movement or the attitudes of black America merely by combining two simple words at a rally in

Greenwood, Mississippi. That's silly and absurd, even for the American media. (Carmichael and Thelwell 2003: 524)

Even though Carmichael's "Black power" saying did not change the movement on its own, it still marks a major turning point in American history. When Carmichael unveils the saying near the tail end of the Meredith Mississippi Freedom March (1966), it basically illustrates that the abuse that marchers suffered at the hands of state troopers only strengthened their resolve. As Carmichael points out, "all motion is not progress," but many Black people were satisfied with the direction that the movement was heading in following that important march.

A motion-oriented proverbial expression that Carmichael uses is "lift as you climb." This expression was also the slogan of the National Association of Colored Women (Ransby 2003: 379). It is an expression that speaks to a sense of unity in the African American community. Carmichael discusses the strong legacy of activism and scholarship that he encountered as a nineteen-year-old freshman at historically Black Howard University in 1960: "In D.C. I was truly in touch for the first time with all aspects of the culture of Africans from the South. While at school I was also being exposed in a systematic and critical way to our intellectual tradition and the history of the struggle of those 'many thousands gone,' who as they proudly said always 'lifted as they climbed.' All of which could not help but have a serious effect on any young person searching for an honorable role for himself and his people in the world" (Carmichael and Thelwell 2003: 133). In addition to author Toni Morrison (1931–2019), Carmichael's professors at Howard included influential thinkers such as sociologist and psychologist Nathan Hare (1933), and poet Sterling Brown (1901–89). Learning about Black culture at Howard from ground-breaking Black scholars was instrumental in shaping his own identity as an activist and Black revolutionary thinker which is why after his freshman year, Carmichael chose to spend each of his three summers volunteering with SNCC before becoming chairman following his graduation in 1966 with his bachelor's degree in philosophy. As both a student and graduate, activism was Carmichael's preferred method of "lifting others up as he continued to climb," and it is a value he tried to instill in others.

At another point in Carmichael's narrative, he discusses his reaction to the book *The Rage of a Privileged Class*. He describes the tone of the book as being completely out of touch with the civil rights movement. He explains that the book's subject is "the anger, frustration, alienation, and despair prevalent among Africans born in America, who although 'supremely qualified' found themselves underappreciated, rarely promoted, and insufficiently rewarded in the American corporate world" (Carmichael and Thelwell 2003: 770). He goes on to discuss some of the sentiments of disappointment expressed by the book's author: "'We accepted *all* their terms,' they wail, 'and *did everything they required* of us: the "right" schools, the "right" degrees, the "right" résumés, so why now do we feel so alienated, underutilized, and isolated?'" (emphasis in original) (Carmichael and Thelwell 2003: 770). Carmichael then explains that what this person is interpreting as racism may simply be a symptom of capitalism which is experienced by many people in the corporate world: "In all likelihood, I thought, a great many of their white colleagues in offices next door who could not claim an ethnic or culturally determined 'glass ceiling' were probably equally victim to the very same ennui and disaffection and for much the same reasons: the craven abandonment of their community and culture in thoughtless pursuit of the sterility of the corporate American dream, cum nightmare, and for *acceptance* and status in that predatory culture" (Carmichael and Thelwell 2003: 770). Here, Carmichael is defining what he considers to be a common attitude found among the Black bourgeoisie. He says that it is an unwarranted feeling of entitlement that is not at all connected to civil rights struggles. He then poses the question: "Whatever happened to 'lifting as ye climb?'" (Carmichael and Thelwell 2003: 770). Carmichael uses the proverbial expression "lift as ye climb" here in order to draw a stark comparison between the effects of capitalism and the effects of racism. He makes it very clear to the reader that they are two very distinct entities.

Another motion-oriented proverbial expression appears as he describes the Student Nonviolent Coordinating Committee (SNCC) at its inception. He asserts that Ms. Ella Josephine Baker (1903–86) at the Southwide Youth Leadership Conference at Shaw University in Raleigh, North Carolina (1960), convinced sit-in movement attendees that their new organization could be independent and operated solely by students. Despite this declaration, there were still many questions left unanswered after the initial meeting. Questions concerning structure, location, and funding continued to arise. Carmichael employs a variation of the proverbial expression "to learn to fly on the way down" to explain their unique predicament: "as Chuck Jones put it, we had to learn to fly before hitting the ground, we also had to decide the style and trajectory of that flight: Just what kind of bird were we, buzzards or falcons?" (Carmichael and Thelwell 2003: 299).

One statement made by Septima Clark gives even more credence to Carmichael's assertion that the young activists were simply "learning to fly on the way down." In an interview, Clark was asked about internal difficulties or fears faced by the young activists and Clark responds:

Well, whenever he [Dr. King] got the executive group together, he would lecture to them about being non-violent. "You can't win," he said. "You can't win if you're going to fight back." And he had Stokely Carmichael to come to his house to dinner to tell Stokely, "You can't win if you're going to send the boys up and down the street to knock out the window glasses of the stores along Morgan Avenue." (Walker 1976: 25)

Carmichael does not mention this private meeting with Dr. King in his writings, but it highlights Dr. King's important role as a moral compass for the younger generation. It also illustrates the appropriateness of Carmichael's proverbial expression. The expression simultaneously depicts the meaning behind the previously discussed proverb, "all motion is not progress." If the young activists were indeed "learning to fly on the way down," who knows what direction the movement might have taken if they navigated their trajectory alone.

Even after SNCC became more established, they still found themselves at times facing situations for which they had no preparation and no planning. As they were organizing their major voter registration drive in the Mississippi Delta (known as Freedom Summer of 1964), they were faced with issues such as communities of Black people who were too terrified to participate due to racial violence. Carmichael explains that it was "another one of those critical moments of decision in which we had no clear guidelines or precedents or guarantees. Another one of those 'learning to fly on the way down' situations" (Carmichael and Thelwell 2003: 354). "Learning to fly on the way down" simply means that they were forced to make important decisions without having any idea of what the results may be.

Carmichael would describe the Black Panther Party (BPP) in the same way. After Eldridge Cleaver and Huey P. Newton gained Carmichael's permission to use the popular panther symbol from Carmichael's Lowndes County Freedom Organization (LCFO), the California-based group spread and grew exponentially across the nation, but as an organization they faced some serious drawbacks. None of the Panther members were well educated at the time and none had previous political leadership experience, and Carmichael declined their invitation to play any significant role aside from allowing them to use him as a figurehead symbol as their Honorary Prime Minister. As he explains, the BPP also suffered from a lack of organization and a lack of leadership:

And the Panthers, what was their interest? At the time they were beginning to have high media visibility, albeit of a dubious kind, and a growing national image. As a consequence, the Black Panther Party was spreading rapidly among Northern African youth who'd grown up listening to Malcolm, seeing SNCC on TV, and feeling deprived of their opportunity to be involved in the kind of struggle SNCC and Dr. King had waged in the South. But the Panther leader lacked real political experience. This was an organization literally with no history and no precedent in American politics. (Carmichael and Thelwell 2003: 661)

Carmichael contends that the Black Panther Party suffers from many of the same ailments that SNCC suffered from in its early days. He then says: "they found themselves in midair, 'learning to fly on the way down'" (Carmichael and Thelwell 2003: 661). Various branches of the Black Panther Party focused on community upliftment, self-policing Black neighborhoods, and educating Black youth. They were no doubt a source of pride for many Black people, but due in part to some of the inefficiencies that Carmichael describes, the organization struggled early on and then eventually dissipated.

A similar moment occurs during Freedom Summer after SNCC activists Mickey Schwerner, James Chaney, and Andy Goodman were murdered by the Ku Klux Klan. Days after they were discovered missing, the charred frame of their vehicle was found. Carmichael accompanied by two other SNCC members embark on a mission to find their friends. Having no clear plan in place for navigating the Mississippi Delta swamps, forest, and farmlands, Carmichael remains optimistic that they can solicit some help from Native Choctaw hunters: "We hoped maybe we could blend in with them on the reservation and take advantage of their knowledge of the terrain. Admittedly not a fully formulated plan, but we were again learning to fly on the way down" (Carmichael and Thelwell 2003: 375). Carmichael and his friends never employ the services of the Choctaw, and they are not successful in locating their friends. However, weeks later, after authorities receive tips from a Ku Klux Klan informer, the remains of Schwerner, Chaney, and Goodman are discovered buried underneath tons of dirt on a farm in Mississippi. Carmichael in explaining what would be described as one of the lowest points of the Freedom Movement, employs the proverbial expression "learning to fly on the way down" to explain the feeling of being thrown into such a desperate situation for which there would be no clear guide for escaping.

At another point in the narrative Carmichael describes the experience of convincing his mentor, Kwame Nkrumah that Nkrumah's Pan-African organization, the All-African People's Revolution Party (AAPRP) should be endorsed heavily throughout the United States as well as Africa. Carmichael is honored when Nkrumah finally agrees to allow him to oversee expanding the party. Their goal is to spread the belief that "all African-descended people living in 113 countries on the continent and in the diaspora ... share history, culture, and common enemies—racism, imperialism, neocolonialism, and capitalist exploitation" (Carmichael and Thelwell 2003: 675). Furthermore, they teach the notion that it is the entire diaspora who endures "disunity, disorganization, and ideological confusion" (Carmichael and Thelwell 2003: 675). While Carmichael realizes that the job of organizing for the party will be no easy task, he expresses optimism, and he captures his sense of hopefulness with a proverb: "Of course, this is ambitious, a vast ongoing enterprise. A general vision, direction, and commitment. The cumulative work of many lifetimes, an incremental and continuing struggle. We understood that clearly. But we were young and, as they say, 'a journey of a thousand miles begins with the first step'" (Carmichael and Thelwell 2003: 675). The proverb "a journey of a thousand miles begins with the first step" equates physical travel with personal growth and it also illustrates that from a mental standpoint, Carmichael is very well prepared for the difficult task of trying to convince Black people around the globe that they share one common plight (Mieder et al. 1991: 594; Speake 2015: 166). The proverb also conveys a sense of accomplishment in even beginning a project of this magnitude. The All-African People's Revolution Party (AAPRP) will provide future generations of revolutionaries with a stable foundation on which they may continue to build.

Carmichael uses an expansive variety of proverbs, sayings, and proverbial expressions. Collectively they illustrate his philosophical growth, and they also demonstrate some of the various ideological revolutions that he experiences throughout his lifetime. While this study is not meant to include every proverb or saying that was ever uttered or written by Carmichael, it does provide one with a sizable sample of the kind of proverbial language that was a part of Carmichael's verbal repertoire.

The important role of proverbial language in civil rights struggles may not be overstated. As Carmichael asserts, activism and political organizing required multitudes of people to think and act as one, and the movement's many proverbs, sayings, proverbial expressions, and mantras helped that to become possible. Whether embracing a humorous saying from Junebug Jabbo Jones or sharing a powerful saying such as "Black power," they helped people to bond, and the insight contained in the messages gave people a shared sense of purpose. Proverbs, proverbial expressions, and sayings were also a way of sharing political strategy and worldview and provided Nonviolent Action Group (NAG) and Student Nonviolent Coordinating Committee (SNCC) organizers with a clear goal and vision for moving forward.

Carmichael's penchant for proverbial language leads one to pose some important questions. Could Carmichael have become such a master of proverbial language if he had not become so accustomed to proverbial language as a child? Likewise, could Carmichael have been such an effective political organizer without applying this unique skill so liberally? Evidence revealed in this chapter points one towards the negative in both cases. As Carmichael demonstrates, proverbs, sayings, and proverbial expressions can become so engrained in the human psyche that they may influence countless other aspects of human interaction including memory, interpersonal relationships, and even an individual's and an entire people's world view. The conclusion will explore an aspect of memory, specifically the extent that proverbs, proverbial expressions, or sayings may encapsulate entire legacies, even if one is not known to have been a proverb master during one's lifetime.

Conclusion

PROVERBS SHAPING LEGACIES

Many important political leaders throughout history have utilized proverbs to communicate important ideas. As Mieder reminds us: "Proverbs in particular can underscore the value system and mentality of the people" (Mieder 2019: ix). However, every important civil rights era pioneer did not use them or rely on them much as a rhetorical strategy. Historian Maegan Brooks Parker notes Fannie Lou Hamer's use of a several biblical proverbs in *A Voice That Could Stir an Army: Fannie Lou Hamer and the Rhetoric of the Black Freedom Movement* (2014). Parker's work illustrates that Hamer's oratorical strength was derived in part from her use of religious symbolism, Hamer's ability to signify, and a limited amount of proverb use. As Patricia A. Turner asserts in the forward to this volume, more research needs to be conducted on the women of the movement. There are several other leaders who seldom used proverbs. This is not to say that they never used them in a speech or writing during their lifetime but that they simply did not use them enough to illustrate any consistent patterns of usage. These leaders include Ella Baker (1903–86), Julian Bond (1940–2015), and Gordon Parks (1912–2006). Nevertheless, there is still at least some evidence that these innovative pioneers recognized the inherent power and influence that proverbs possess and coincidentally their individual legacies will forever be encapsulated by what Mieder describes as brief statements that "contain wisdom, truth, morals . . . in fixed and memorable form[s]" and subsequently they will continue to be "handed down from generation to generation" (Mieder 2004: 3; Mieder 2008: 11).

The above-mentioned were very influential during the movement, but much of their work was performed in solitude. Therefore, they may have placed far less emphasis on rhetorical strategy than someone doing extensive amounts of public speaking. There are several other reasons why one may choose to largely omit proverbs from one's writing. Some may believe that proverbs are cliché. Perhaps, one holding this view may have been preconditioned to harbor disdain for popular or recognizable phrasing—a perspective sometimes encouraged by teachers who may tell inexperienced students to avoid any phraseology which may be mistaken for a common or trite expression. Others may have simply not been exposed to proverbs enough (either through literature or other people) to have any real appreciation for them.

One idea which may be worth considering is the fact that even if a person does not frequently use proverbs to communicate and is not known for displaying this characteristic in their correspondences with others, there is still some possibility that the said individual may still be remembered by specific proverbs, expressions, or sayings. For instance, one brief memorable saying which has since become a proverb through common usage encapsulates the philosophy which Baker is remembered for. Baker was the executive secretary for SCLC and a SNCC cofounder. Baker is widely known for the use of the phrase "bigger than a hamburger" (Moye 2013). It served as the title of the speech she gave at the inaugural SNCC conference held at Baker's alma mater, Shaw University in Raleigh, North Carolina, on Easter weekend of 1960. The conference was inspired by news of the very first staged sit-ins held at a Woolworth's lunch counter in Greensboro, North Carolina. Baker wanted to make her message as plain as possible as she addressed the international audience of students who were eager to begin protesting. "Speaking to the conference Ella Baker told the students that their struggle was 'much bigger than a hamburger.' . . . In presenting this bigger picture and encouraging them to form their own official organization, Ella Baker displayed a talent she had been employing for more than two decades: assisting people to empower themselves" (snccdigital.org/people/ella-baker/). Baker believed that this four-word phrase was significant because she did not want people to equate the movement with materialism. The saying quickly grew in popularity to become another important political slogan. Vernon Jordan (1935–2021), who was director of the Southern Regional Council's Voter Education Project in the 1960s and later an important political adviser to President Bill Clinton, also agreed with Baker's sentiment that the public did tend to associate civil rights activism with materialism. Commenting on the changing complexities of the movement Jordan alludes to Baker's famous phrase. He says: "The target ain't simple no more; it ain't black and white no more; it's grey. The people thought the Movement was about a hamburger." (Neary 1971: 74). Years later, the expression "bigger than a hamburger" serves as an appropriate title for writings and a documentary film about her life (snccdigital.org/people/ella-baker/).

Much like "bigger than a hamburger," Baker's proverb "strong people don't need strong leaders" speaks to the primary objective of SNCC as an organization. Baker was determined that she and other adults such as Septima

Clark and Dr. King would play only secondary roles and the students would lead themselves, each having an equal voice in governance. Likewise, SNCC sought to empower communities to manage themselves and chart their own futures. One of the main reasons there is not a plethora of proverbs and sayings one may attribute to Baker is because she did not speak publicly very often or as frequently as some of the male leaders such as Randolph or King. She worked behind the scenes in various critical organizing roles for SCLC and SNCC, which often required brief and direct forms of communication. Baker's biographers emphasize the fact that she typed and sent important letters and memos, and made hundreds of crucial phone calls, oftentimes using her own money and resources to do so. The fact that Baker's work was underfunded also speaks to the tendency of male leaders to sometimes downplay the important roles that females played (Ransby 2003; Moye 2013). At least the most well-known of Baker's utterances, "strong people don't need strong leaders," insinuates that it was at least partially her own choice to remain in the background, but she certainly did not do so silently.

Julian Bond was the SNCC communications director and editor of the SNCC newspaper, the *Student Voice*. Bond also served as a Georgia state legislator for twenty years after the movement ended (1967–87). He also led the NAACP as its president (1998–2010), and he taught the history of the civil rights movement at several universities. Bond was not widely known for proverb use and neither was his father, historian, and college president Horace Mann Bond (1904–72). However, speaking retrospectively about the movement, Julian Bond mentions a couple of proverbs that he feels best characterizes his political, moral, and philosophical ideals. In what would be his last recorded interview, Bond talks about his moral philosophy and expresses the desire to be remembered as someone who lived wholeheartedly by the Golden Rule. "I want to treat other people the way I want them to treat me. The old Golden Rule is—I really believe in that: 'treat me the way you want me to treat you'" (Leffler 2014: 187). Another proverb which Bond valued was "speaking truth to power." Historian Phyllis Leffler best explains the significance that Bond places on this aphorism. Leffler asserts:

> It is not surprising, therefore, that the 2001 NAACP convention's theme, over which he presided as chairman, was "Speaking Truth to Power." In the opening statement of his convention address, he defined what that maxim means: "It means at all times following your highest sense of right, whatever the consequences, however lonely the path and however loud the jeers.... It is holding on to the power of

truth when everyone around you is accepting compromises." (Leffler 2014: 188)

In the same interview, Bond expounds on the history of the proverb "speaking truth to power." Bond explains that the proverb reflects some of the lessons he learned as a young student at a private Quaker institution in Pennsylvania, where he developed his protestant sense of work ethic and acquired his understanding of egalitarianism. "George Fox, who is one of the founders of Quakerism, used this phrase. I don't think he originated it, but the Quakers were persecuted in England, which is why they came here. He was talking about speaking truth to power. The power is king. We believe we can speak to the king. We can say anything we want to the king" (blackleadership.virginia.edu/28). Bond chose to stay in the background of the movement, but much like Clark and Baker he was not silent. Bond was focused on developing his talents as a reporter and editor through much of the 1960s and this task required a straightforward delivery of "just the facts." In examining Bond's writings, one may draw the conclusion that the terse, straightforward style of reporting which he largely developed in the sixties and seventies became a permanent part of Bond's communication style. Proverb use is very scarce amongst Bond's writings, but he did express the fact that he wanted these two proverbs to characterize his legacy and there is plenty of evidence that his colleagues and students agree.

Gordon Parks is another civil rights era pioneer whose writings do not illustrate a penchant for using proverbs. Amongst other accomplishments, Parks was a self-taught photographer, journalist, filmmaker, composer, and a prolific author. Parks has published over a dozen books, several of which are either autobiographies or memoirs. In *To Smile in Autumn* (1979), Parks describes the experience of growing up poor and Black in America:

> [I have experienced] firsthand the things, the terrible things, poverty and bigotry can do to soul and body. No matter how many rewards the universe bestows upon you, to have undergone stonings, beatings, and being called "shine," "n----r," and "darky," remains unforgettable. But despite all this I had the good fortune of being born to Sarah and Jackson Parks—he, an impoverished dirt farmer. The love they gave to me and my fourteen older brothers and sisters was enough to offset the misery of growing up black in America.... After Momma died and our family broke up, I was shipped off to the cold reaches of Minnesota. And there, at sixteen, I became an expert student of poverty and hunger. Much later, I wrote about the bitterness

of those times—first in *The Learning Tree* (1963) and later, *A Choice of Weapons* (1966), So I go on now to begin where I left off. For me, it suffices that having once foraged in garbage for my supper, I have since eaten watermelon in public. (Parks 1979)

Recalling the moment, a public figure attempted to humiliate him because he was the only Black person at a dinner party thrown by his good friend Gloria Vanderbilt. At the party, Parks shrugged off the man's loud and obnoxious declaration that watermelon was being served. Parks thinking with hindsight juxtaposes that moment with an earlier time in his youth when encountering a racist stereotype, such as the notion that all Black people eat watermelon, may have sent him into a blind rage. He learned early in life that he detested racism, in part due to the numerous physical altercations which he feels fortunate to have survived. Speaking as an older and much wiser individual, Parks is no longer easily insulted by overt bigotry.

In *A Choice of Weapons* (1966), Parks describes an epiphanic moment from his youth when an older cousin, on his death bed, expressed concern over Park's repetitive pattern of fighting whenever he was confronted with racism. He was concerned that Parks would eventually be killed, so he made Parks promise to stop fighting with his fists and use his mind instead. Parks attributes the positive direction that his life took in part to this pact he made with his dying cousin. After struggling with poverty throughout high school and much of early adulthood, Parks was determined to use his mind rather than his fists, eventually deciding that the camera lens would ultimately become his tool for fighting racism and oppression. Historic footage of Parks recounting the significance of this monumental decision can be seen in *A Choice of Weapons: Inspired by Gordon Parks* (2021), a documentary film about his life and the huge influence he had on American culture.

Parks bought his first camera for $7.50 at a pawnshop. After developing his photography skills through reading extensively and practicing, he won a photo submission contest and a fellowship in Washington, DC, taking photos for the Farm Security Administration. Parks's FSA photos (archived by the Gordon Parks Foundation) depict everything from inner-city poverty to the oppressive existence of Jim Crow. Parks's powerful FSA images eventually led to him becoming the first Black journalist to be hired by *Life* magazine. Parks has captured numerous monumental American icons on film including Malcolm X and the NOI, the Tuskegee Airmen, Martin Luther King Jr., Muhammad Ali, and Ralph Ellison. Early in his career at *Life*, Parks covered Carmichael for a story. He shadowed Carmichael as he attended meetings, canvased neighborhoods, and gave talks at community centers, churches, and universities. The first product of Parks's fieldwork was the *Life* editorial (1967) for which Parks would take over seven hundred photos, with only five of them ever making it into print. Why did Parks take so many pictures? As Lisa Volpe, associate curator of photography at the Museum of Fine Arts in Houston asserts in an interview, the pictures were necessary because one of Parks's goals was to counter the negative criticism Carmichael received daily in the press. She says Parks wanted to "cast a different light on Carmichael against the popular white anxieties conjured by the Black Power slogan" (Volpe 2022: 32). More specifically, Parks wanted to use his images to portray Carmichael as the approachable teacher he was and to depict his audiences as students who were in the crowd learning (Johnson 2022). Volpe also points out that there were so many important events happening during the sixties that no amount of photography would have ever been able to capture it all, which is also another reason why Carmichael eventually became the face of the movement, even after his expatriation to Africa and still to this day (Johnson 2022). Another important reason why Carmichael became the figurehead of the Black freedom struggle would be his charismatic oratory. In a draft of the *Life* manuscript, Parks says, "For three months now I had watched him spell bind crowds who flocked to hear him in cities all across the country. His jarring call for black power had exploded emotions everywhere. Among whites—conservatives and liberals alike---it provoked anger and consternation; among Negroes it brought dismay and doubt to some, but to the masses it came as burst of hope" (Volpe 2022: 143). Parks had witnessed firsthand the growth and evolution of "Black power" from a mere phrase or slogan to a full-scale social and political movement during the four months that he shadowed Carmichael.

Another product of Parks's important fieldwork is a book entitled *Gordon Parks: Stokely Carmichael and Black Power* (2022), edited by Volpe. The material for the book was derived in part from Parks's hundreds of negatives, many of which were previously unseen. The same material was also used to create a multifaceted museum exhibit entitled *Gordon Parks: Stokely Carmichael and Black Power*. In her lecture introducing the Parks exhibit, Volpe describes the experience of watching former activist react to seeing pictures and videos of events they lived through so many decades ago. Volpe says:

> Now, it's interesting to note that when I would share the photos with those men and women captured in them, they all had a very similar reaction. Each one of them remembered the scene. They remembered what was being discussed and how they felt. They really had a perfect

recall for pretty much everything within the frame . . . but what was interesting was that they were all shocked to see the photographs. Not a single person I talked to remembered Gordan Parks ever being in the room. Now . . . when he was on assignment, he truly became a fly on the wall in order to get the most truthful images possible. And yes, even speaking to these ladies they did not even notice Gordon Parks, probably three feet in front of them taking their photo. (Volpe 2023)

Volpe is referencing a photo of Sanamu Nyeusi and Hasani Soto of the Ron Karenga–led Us Organization at the Watts rally held at Will Rogers Park in Los Angeles in 1966 (Volpe 2022: 101). Nyeusi and Soto are both wearing matching Malcolm X sweatshirts, smiling, clapping, enjoying the moment, seemingly unaware of Parks. As a proverbial fly on the wall, Parks captured numerous scenes that he may not have been able to capture otherwise.

In conducting an analysis of Parks's writing (namely the autobiography and memoirs) some may easily draw the conclusion that Parks was no proverb master by any stretch of the imagination. However, Parks's writings illustrate that he was a master of metaphorical language. He had a penchant for pun and metaphor as he demonstrates with the title of the *Life* editorial "Whip of Black Power" (Volpe 2022: 156–67). Paired with an image of an angry Carmichael standing at a podium, such a title may invoke hopeful aspirations of a new Black political whip, but it may just as easily invoke the image of a slave whip symbolizing the vile institution of slavery which gave way to the institutional racism still gripping much of the Deep South. Parks did not use proverbs or sayings often, but he did recognize and appreciate this rhetorical strength in Carmichael. In one of the draft manuscripts for the *Life* essay, Parks writes:

> Stokely Carmichael stood at center stage. Beneath an angry sky, with the majestic United Nations building towering behind him; with hundreds of thousands of peace marchers standing ankle-to-ankle in the wide plaza cheering him on, he decided to go for broke. "Vietnam: Hell no! We won't go!" . . . Then a more familiar cry, hostile, unrelenting and razor-sharp, knifed through the chant. "Black Power! Black Power!" A master stroke. He had two of his slogans going at once. He was on fire, spitting his heat into the crowd. (Volpe 2022: 24)

Parks would continue to employ "incendiary metaphors" when describing Carmichael's oratory. As Volpe proclaims, "[Parks] remembered him 'breathing fire' in his speeches, as part of a generation of 'fiery young insurgents,' and, despite his resignation as SNCC's chairman, as a catalyst for change, who predicted that 'across the nation the fires would burn on'" (Volpe 2022: 24).

Both Carmichael and Parks coincidentally attributed their respective choices in career paths to the fact that they were both "born Black," and they both had an appreciation for "the transformative power of images" (Volpe 2022: 13). They also have other things in common. The fact that Carmichael and Parks both chose to use their minds to fight against racism and oppression was perhaps one of the most important things bonding them in the 1960s. In agreeing to work with one another, they combined two separate forms of activism, and this decision would also bond their legacies. Another thing bonding their legacies is the fact that philosophies for which they will be remembered for most are best captured in two short expressions: "a choice of weapons," and "Black power." Both expressions function in much the manner of traditional proverbs. Either expression may invoke memories of the person, the individual's ideology, the civil rights movement, and the influence their work had on the movement and society. These expressions are also a testament to both men's genius. They confirm the wisdom involved in Parks's decision to place value on his own intellect, using his camera as a dangerous weapon against poverty, racial hatred, and oppression. Likewise, the expression "Black power" attests to the wisdom behind Carmichael's realization that obtainment of a collective sense of "political, economic, and cultural self-determination" would be the only way to liberate Black people in America and around the world (Joseph 2014: 115). In conclusion, the legacies of important people may be communicated through proverbs, expressions, or sayings even if these devices were not a widely recognized characteristics of the individual's communication style. Likewise, the expressions "a choice of weapons" and "Black power" function as proverbs and should be used more often as such because of the important legacies they convey and the important lessons they continue to communicate to future generations.

NOTES

ACKNOWLEDGMENTS

1. This is a quote from an email correspondence received by the author on May 22, 2023.

INTRODUCTION: PROVERBS AND SOCIAL JUSTICE

1. Jacquelyn Dowd Hall, "The Long Civil Rights Movement and the Political Uses of the Past," *Journal of American History* 91, no. 4 (2005).
2. Michael Taft, "Proverbs in Blues: How Frequent is Frequent?" *Proverbium* 11 (1994): 227–58.
3. Another version of this chapter appears in *Proverbium* 37 (2020): 315–60.
4. Another version of this chapter appears in *Proverbium* 37 (2020): 281–310.
5. Another version of this chapter appears in *Proverbium* 36 (2019): 371–406.
6. Another version of this chapter appears in *Proverbium* 40 (2023).
7. Another version of this chapter appears in *Proverbium* 39 (2022).

CHAPTER THREE: "WINNING FREEDOM AND EXACTING JUSTICE": A. PHILIP RANDOLPH'S USE OF PROVERBS AND PROVERBIAL LANGUAGE

1. According to historian Cynthia Taylor, "Randolph explained that his 'advocacy of the philosophy of nonviolence as one of the highways for fundamental social change' was inspired by the life of Jesus Christ as well as by Gandhi. But even before he had heard of Gandhi, Randolph attributed his 'belief in the moral and spiritual power of nonviolence from his father who was a minister of the African Methodist Episcopal Church' and a man of 'high moral commitments'" (2006: 158–59).
2. Both Frederick Douglass and Martin Luther King Jr. also used the proverb "if the enemy strikes you on one side of the face, turn the other cheek" (KJV Matthew 5:39) in a variety of ways. In some instances, King uses it to advocate for nonviolent direct action

(Mieder 2010: 246–47) while Douglass uses it most often to characterize what he views as the enslaved African American mind-set (Mieder 2001: 153–54).

3. Henry Louis Gates Jr. also discusses the significance of Randolph and Owen's political cartoons in *Stony the Road: Reconstruction, White Supremacy, and the Rise of Jim Crow* (2019: 276).

4. Patrick Ibekwe also cites a variation of this Yoruba proverb in, *Wit and Wisdom of Africa: Proverbs from Africa and the Caribbean* (1998). It reads: "A wise person who is skilled in the use of proverbs settles disputes" (153).

5. John Messenger, "The Role of Proverbs in a Nigerian Judicial System" (1959), also cites the use of proverbs to settle disputes in Nigerian culture, asserting that they are used in a wide variety of ways including "as a method of gaining favor in court" (64).

6. Martin Luther King Jr. cited the same passage from Donne's *Devotion Upon Emergent Occasions* (1624) profusely. Wolfgang Mieder documents King's use of Donne in at least ten separate speeches and sermons that King delivered between 1955 and 1968. King uses Donne's proverbs much like Randolph; to encourage his followers to join him in the struggle for civil rights. Surprisingly, King attributes the message to Donne in every single instance (Mieder 2010: 410–14).

7. Doyle, Mieder, and Shapiro, *The Dictionary of Modern Proverbs* (2012), documents the first recorded use of the proverb "last, hired, first fired" as being as early as 1918.

8. One may only guess about whether or not King had Randolph's message to the Committee on Labor and Public Welfare in mind when he uses the proverb "last hired, first fired" the very same year in what would be regarded as one of King's many landmark speeches. King says: "We've been pushed around so long; we've been the victims of lynch mobs so long; we've been the victims of economic injustice so long—still the last hired and the first fired all over this nation" (Mieder 2010: 345).

CHAPTER FOUR: "WORDS ARE BUT WIND":
THE PROVERBS AND PROVERBIAL SAYINGS OF BOB DYLAN

1. See more on Alabama and Mississippi as epicenters of racial violence in chapter seven.

2. "Police and vigilantes murdered about 125 civil rights activists and supporters, and the police and FBI killed at least thirty-four Black Panthers. More than two hundred people . . . lost their lives during the 'protest riots' of the 1960s" (David Michael Smith. *Endless Holocausts: Mass Death in the History of the United* States, Monthly Review Press, 2023, 264).

3. Dylan wrote hundreds of songs which incorporate proverbs, but chapter four will focus solely on songs which pertain to social justice. For more on proverb use in some of Dylan's other work see Raymond Summerville, Words Are but Wind': The Proverbs and Proverbial Expressions of Bob Dylan," in *Proverbium: Yearbook of International Proverb Scholarship* 36 (2019): 371–406. See also Betsy Bowden, *Performed Literature Words and Music by Bob Dylan* (1982).

4. This Kennedy proverb is also addressed in chapter seven.

WORKS CITED

Abrahams, Roger. "British West Indian Proverbs and Proverb Collections." *Proverbium* 10 (1968): 239–43.
Amistad Research Center. "Theater Legend and Friend Remembered." Tulane University. http://www.amistadresearchcenter.org. Accessed 12 July 2020.
Anderson, Jervis. *A Philip Randolph: A Biographical Portrait*. Harcourt Brace Jovanovich, 1972.
Andrews, William L. *The Literary Career of Charles W. Chesnutt*. Louisiana State University Press, 1980.
Andrews, William, and Henry Louis Gates Jr., eds. *The Portable Charles W. Chesnutt*. Penguin, 2008.
Arora, Shirley L. "The Perception of Proverbiality." *Proverbium* 1 (1984): 1–38.
Ashton, Susanna, and Bill Hardwig, eds. *Approaches to Teaching the Works of Charles W. Chesnutt*. Modern Language Association of America, 2017.
Bailey, Anne C. *The Weeping Time: Memory and the Largest Slave Auction in American History*. Cambridge University Press, 2017.
Ball, Jared A., and Todd Steven Burroughs, eds. *A Life of Reinvention: Correcting Manning Marable's Malcolm X*. Black Classic Press, 2012.
Barker, Derek. *Too Much of Nothing*. Red Planet Books, 2018.
Bauldie, John. *The Chameleon Poet: Bob Dylan's Search for Self*. Route, 2021.
Bay, Mia. *To Tell the Truth Freely: The Life of Ida B. Wells*. Hill and Wang Publishing, 2009.
Bay, Mia, and Henry Louis Gates, eds. *Ida B. Wells, The Light of Truth: Writings of an Anti-Lynching Crusader*. Penguin Books, 2014.
Blackmon, Douglas. *Slavery by Another Name: The Re-Enslavement of Black People in America from the Civil War to World War II*. Random House, 2008.
BlackPast, B. *Frederick Douglass, Men of Color, To Arms!*. 2007. https://www.blackpast.org/african-american-history/1863-frederick-douglass-men-color-arms/. Accessed 10 May 2019.
BlackPast, B. *Henry Highland Garnet, "An Address to The Slaves of the United States."* 2007. https://www.blackpast.org/african-american-history/speeches-african-american-history/1843-henry-highland-garnet-address-slaves-united-states/. Accessed 10 May 2019.
Blake, John. *Children of the Movement*. Lawrence Hill Books, 2004.
Blake, John. "Black in America 2." CNN, 4 July 2020. https://www.cnn.com/2008/US/04/04/mlk.children.movement/index.html. Editorial.
Bond, Julian. *Julian Bond's Time to Teach: A History of the Southern Civil Rights Movement*. Beacon Press, 2021.

Bond, Julian. "Consensual Leadership." *Explorations in Black Leadership*. University of Virginia. www.blackleadership.virginia.edu/28QR. Accessed 23 December 2023.

Bowden, Betsy. *Performed Literature: Words and Music by Bob Dylan*. Indiana University Press, 1982.

Bowden, Betsy. "A Modest Proposal, Relating Four Millennia of Proverb Collections to Chemistry Within the Human Brain." *Journal of American Folklore* 109 (1996): 440–49.

Bowie, David. "As the World Falls Down." *Labyrinth*, July 1986. https://genius.com/David-bowie-as-the-world-falls-down-lyrics.

Boyd, Herb, and Ilyasah Al-Shabazz, eds. *The Diary of Malcolm X: El-Hajj Malik El Shabazz, 1964*. Third World Press, 2013.

Breitman, George, ed. *By Any Means Necessary: Speeches, Interviews, and A Letter by Malcolm X*. Pathfinder Press, 1970.

Breitman, George, ed. *Malcolm Speaks: Selected Speeches and Statements*. Grove Press, 1990.

Breitman, George, ed. *The Last Year of Malcolm X: The Evolution of a Revolutionary*. Pathfinder Press, 1992.

Brodhead, Richard H., ed. *The Journals of Charles W. Chesnutt*. Duke University Press, 1993.

Brown, Donald. *Bob Dylan: American Troubadour*. Rowan and Littlefield, 2014.

Browning, Gary, and Constantine Sandis, eds. *Dylan at 80*. Imprint Academic, 2021.

Brunvand, Harold Jan. *American Folklore: An Encyclopedia*. Garland Publishing, 1996.

Bryan, B. George, and Wolfgang Mieder. *A Dictionary of Anglo-American Proverbs & Proverbial Phrases: Found in Literary Sources of the Nineteenth and Twentieth Centuries*. Peter Lang, 2005.

Burns, Robert. 1795. "A Man's a Man for A' That." In *An Introduction to the Scottish Poet*. www.forathat.com. Accessed 21 December 2019.

Burton, Richard, trans. *The Arabian Nights*. Baker &Taylor Publishing Group, 2011.

Bynum, Cornelius L. *A. Philip Randolph, and the Struggle for Civil Rights*. University of Illinois Press, 2010.

Byrd, Dustin J., and Sayed Javed Miri, eds. *Malcolm X: From Political Eschatology to Religious Revolutionary*. Brill Press, 2016.

Carmichael, Stokely. *Stokely Speaks: From Black Power to Pan-Africanism*. Lawrence Hill, 1971.

Carmichael, Stokely, and E. Michael Thelwell. *Ready for Revolution: The Life and Struggles of Stokely Carmichael*. Scribner, 2003.

Carpenter, Damian A. *Lead Belly, Woody Guthrie, Bob Dylan, and American Folk Outlaw Performance*. Routledge, 2018.

Carter, Jimmy. "Our Nation's Past and Future." Address accepting the presidential nomination at the Democratic National Convention in New York City, 1976. http://www.presidency.ucsb.edu/ws/?/pid=25953.

Charron, Katherine Mellon. *Freedom's Teacher: The Life of Septima Clark*. University of North Carolina Press, 2009.

Chesnutt, Charles W. Various speeches. In *Charles W. Chesnutt: Essays and Speeches*, edited by Joseph R. McElrath, Robert C. Lietz III, and Jesse S. Crisler, 1–12. Stanford University Press, 1881.

Clark, Septima Poinsette. "Champions of Democracy" [brochure]. Highlander Folk School, 1957.
Clark, Septima Poinsette. *Echo in My Soul*. E. P. Dutton & Company, 1962.
Clark, Septima Poinsette. "Citizenship and Gospel." *Journal of Black Studies* 10, no. 4 (1980): 461–66.
Clark, Septima Poinsette, and Mary A. Twining. "Voting Does Count: A Brief Excerpt from a Fabulous Decade." *Journal of Black Studies*, vol. 10, no. 4 (1980): 445–47.
Clark, Steve, ed. *February 1965, The Final Speeches: Malcolm X*. Pathfinder Press, 1992.
Collins, Joseph. "Septima Clark—Liberation Through Education." *Infinitefire.org*. Accessed 15 December 2020.
Collins, Patricia Hill. *On Lynchings: Ida B. Wells-Barnett*. Humanity Books, 2002.
Cone, James H. *Martin & Malcolm & America: A Dream or A Nightmare*. Orbis Books, 1991.
Corcoran, Neil. *Do You Mr. Jones?: Bob Dylan with the Poets and Professors*. Vintage, 2010.
Cossu, Andrea. *It Ain't Me, Babe: Bob Dylan and the Performance of Authenticity*. Paradigm Publishers, 2012.
Cott, Jonathan., ed. *Bob Dylan: The Essential Interviews*. Simon & Schuster, 2017.
Crisler, Jesse S., Robert C. Leitz III, and Joseph R. McElrath, eds. *An Exemplary Citizen: Letters of Charles W. Chesnutt, 1906–1932*. Stanford University Press, 2002.
Davidson, James West. *"They Say": Ida B. Wells and the Reconstruction of Race*. Oxford University Press, 2007.
Davila, Lauren. "Public Memory of the Domestic Slave Trade in Charleston, South Carolina Streets." https://avery.cofc.edu/public-memory-of-thedomestic-slave-trade-in-charleston-south-carolina-street-by-lauren-davila/. Accessed 26 June 2023.
Davis, Daniel S. *Mr. Black Labor: The Story of A. Philip Randolph, Father of the Civil Rights Movement*. E. P. Dutton, 1972.
DeCaro, Louis A. *On the Side of My People: A Religious Life of Malcolm X*. New York University Press, 1996.
DeCaro, Louis A. "'The Enemy of My Enemy': Malcolm X and the Legacy of John Brown." In *Malcolm X: From Political Eschatology to Religious Revolutionary*, edited by Dustin J. Byrd, and Sayed Javed Miri, 179–94. Brill Press, 2016.
DeCosta-Willis, Miriam. *The Memphis Diary of Ida B. Wells*. Beacon Press, 1995.
Donne, John. 1839. *The Works of John Donne*, edited by Henry Alford. John W. Parker, 1839.
Doyle, Charles Clay. *Doing Proverbs and Other Kinds of Folklore*. University of Vermont, 2012.
Doyle, Charles Clay, Wolfgang Mieder, and Fred R. Shapiro. *The Dictionary of Modern Proverbs*. Yale University Press, 2012.
Dunaway, King David, and Molly Beer. *Singing Out: An Oral History of America's Folk Music. Revival*. Oxford University Press, 2010.
Dundes, Alan. "On the Structure of the Proverb." In *The Wisdom of Many: Essays on the Proverb*, edited by Wolfgang Mieder and Alan Dundes, 43–64. Garland Publishing, 1981.
Duster, Alfreda M. *Crusade for Justice*. University of Chicago Press, 1970.
Duster, Michelle. *Ida B. the Queen: The Extraordinary Life and Legacy of Ida B. Wells*. Atria/One Signal Publishers, 2021.

Dylan, Bob. *Tarantula*. Scribner, 2008.
Dylan, Bob. *Bob Dylan Lyrics: 1962–2012*. Simon & Schuster, 2016.
Dylan, Bob. *The Philosophy of Modern Song*. Simon & Schuster, 2022.
Edlis Café. *Bob Dylan's Hibbing*. Edlis Café Press, 2019.
"Ella Baker." *SNCC Digital Gateway*, SNCC Legacy Project and Duke University. http://SNCCdigital.org. Accessed 23 December 2023.
Epstein, Mark Daniel. *The Ballad of Bob Dylan: A Portrait*. HarperCollins, 2011.
Fabian, Johannes. *Power and Performance: Explorations Through Proverbial Wisdom and Theatre in Shaba, Zaire*. University of Wisconsin Press, 1990.
Finnegan, Ruth. "Proverbs in Africa." In *The Wisdom of Many: Essays on the Proverb*, edited by Wolfgang Mieder and Alan Dundes, 10–42. Garland Publishing, 1970.
Fradin, Dennis B., and Judith B. Fradin. *Ida B. Wells: Mother of the Civil Rights Movement*. Clarion Books, 2000.
Gallen, David. *Malcolm X as They Knew Him*. Carroll & Graf Publishers, 1992.
Gans, Terry. *Surviving in A Ruthless World: Bob Dylan's Voyage to Infidels*. Red Planet Books, 2020.
Garland, Phyl. "A. Phillip Randolph: Labor's Grand Old Man." *Ebony*, vol. 24, no. 7 (1969): 31.
Gates, Henry Louis, Jr. *Stony the Road: Reconstruction, White Supremacy, and the Rise of Jim Crow*. Penguin Press, 2019.
Giddings, Paula J. *Ida, A Sword Among Lions: Ida B. Wells and the Campaign Against Lynching*. Harper Collins Press, 2008.
Gilmour, Michael J. *Tangled Up in the Bible: Bob Dylan & Scripture*. Continuum Press, 2004.
Goldman, Peter. *The Death and Life of Malcolm X*. University of Illinois Press, 2013.
Gray, Michael. *Outtakes On Bob Dylan: Selected Writings, 1967–2021*. Route, 2021.
Greaves, William, director. *Ida B. Wells: A Passion for Justice*. California newsreel, 1989.
Gussow, Adam. *Beyond the Crossroads: The Devil & The Blues Tradition*. University of North Carolina Press, 2017.
Hajdu, David. *Positively 4th Street: The Life and Times of Joan Baez, Bob Dylan, Mimi Baez Farina, and Richard Farina*. Farrar, Straus, and Giroux, 2011.
Haley, Alex. *The Autobiography of Malcolm X*. Grove Press, 1992.
Hall, Jacquelyn. Interview with Septima Clark. *Southern Oral History Program Collection*, 1976.
Hall, Jacquelyn Dowd. "The Long Civil Rights Movement and the Political Uses of the Past." *Journal of American History* 91, no. 4 (2005).
Hamilton, Alexander. 1780. "Constitution of Massachusetts." Yale Law, *Avalon Project*, 2019. http://avalon.law.yale.edu/18th_century/fed79.asp#1T. Accessed 10 May 2019.
Hampton, Timothy. *Bob Dylan: How the Songs Work*. Zone Books, 2019.
Harder, Kelsie B., Stewart A. Kingsbury, and Wolfgang Mieder. *A Dictionary of American Proverbs*. Oxford University Press, 1992.
Harlan, Louis R., ed. *The Booker T. Washington Papers*, vol. 3. University of Illinois Press, 1974.
Harris, Trudier. *Selected Works of Ida B. Wells-Barnett*. Oxford University Press, 1991.
Hawkins, Robert. "Brotherhood Men and Singing Slackers: A. Philip Randolph's Rhetoric of Music and Manhood." In *Reframing Randolph: Labor, Black Freedom, and the*

Legacies of A. Philip Randolph, edited by Andrew E. Kersten and Clarence Lang, 101–28. New York University Press, 2015.

Heermance, Noel J. *Charles W. Chesnutt: America's First Great Black Novelist*. Archon Books, 1974.

Hentoff, Nat. "The Crackin,' Shakin,' Breakin' Sounds." In *Younger Than That Now: Collected Interviews with Bob Dylan*, 13–30. Thunder's Mouth Press, 1964.

Herren, Graley. *Dreams and Dialogues in Dylan's "Time Out of Mind."* Anthem Press, 2021.

Heylin, Clinton. *Bob Dylan: Behind the Shades Revisited*. William Morrow Books, 2001.

Heylin, Clinton. *Revolution in the Air: The Songs of Bob Dylan, 1957–1973*. Constable, 2009.

Heylin, Clinton. *Still on the Road: The Songs of Bob Dylan, Vol. 2, 1974–2008*. Constable, 2010.

Heylin, Clinton. *No One Else Could Play That Tune: The Making and Unmaking of Bob Dylan's 1974 Masterpiece*. Route, 2019.

Heylin, Clinton. *The Double Life of Bob Dylan: A Restless, Hungry Feeling, 1941–1966*. Little, Brown, and Company, 2021.

Holsaert, Faith S., et. al., eds. *Hands on the Freedom Plow: Personal Accounts by Women in SNCC*. University of Illinois Press, 2010.

Hoskyns, Barney. *Small Town Talk: Bob Dylan, The Band, Van Morrison, Janis Joplin, Jimi Hendrix, and Friends in the Wild Years of Woodstock*. Da Capo, 2016.

Howard-Pitney, David. *Martin Luther King, Jr., Malcolm X, and the Civil Rights Struggle of the 1950s and 1960s: A Brief History with Documents*. Bedford/St. Martins, 2004.

Ibekwe, Patrick. *Wit and Wisdom of Africa: Proverbs from Africa and the Caribbean*. Africa World Press, 1998.

Ingate, Matthew. *Together Through Life: My Never Ending Tour with Bob Dylan*. Matador, 2022.

Izzo, David Garrett, and Maria Orban, eds. *Charles Chesnutt Reappraised: Essays on First Major African American Fiction Writer*. McFarland & Company, 2009.

Jackson, Andrew. 1837. "Farewell Address." *University of Virginia-Miller Center*, millercenter.org. Accessed 4 February 2020.

Jeffries, Hasan Kwame. *Bloody Lowndes: Civil Rights and Black Power in Alabama's Black Belt*. New York University Press, 2009.

Jennings, Peter. *The Wit and Wisdom of Bob Dylan: Dylan Quotes*. Castle Printing, 2017.

"John M. O'Neal." *SNCC Digital Gateway*, SNCC Legacy Project and Duke University. http://www.sncclegacyproject.org. Accessed 12 July 2020.

Johnson, Cedric. *Revolutionaries to Race Leaders: Black Power and the Making of African Politics*. University of Minnesota Press, 2007.

Johnson, Cedric. "Luminous Exposures: Gordon Parks, Stokely Carmichael, and the Birth of Black Politics." In *Gordon Parks, Stokely Carmichael and Black Power*, edited by Lisa Volpe, 28–33. Steidl/Gordon Parks Foundation/The Museum of Fine Arts, Houston, 2022a.

Johnson, Cedric. Interview by Lisa Volpe. YouTube, 8 December 2022. https://www.gordonparksfoundation.org/education/art-x-activism/lisa-volpe-x-cedric-johnson. Accessed 25 December 2023.

Johnson, Cedric G. *After Black Lives Matter: Policing and Anti-Capitalist Struggle*. Verso, 2023.

Joseph, Peniel E. *Waiting 'Til the Midnight Hour: A Narrative History of Black Power in America*. Henry Holt Press, 2006.

Joseph, Peniel E. *Stokely: A Life*. Basic Civitas Books, 2014.
Joseph, Peniel E. *The Sword and the Shield: The Revolutionary Lives of Malcolm X and Martin Luther King, Jr.* Basic Books, 2020.
Kemp, Louie. *Dylan and Me: 50 Years of Adventures*. Westrose Press, 2019.
Kersten, Andrew E. *A. Philip Randolph: A Life in the Vanguard*. Rowan & Littlefield Publishers, 2007.
Kersten, Andrew E., and Clarence Lang, editors. *Reframing Randolph: Labor, Black Freedom, and the Legacies of A. Philip Randolph*. New York University Press, 2015.
Kersten, Andrew E., and David Lucander, eds. *For Jobs and Freedom: Selected Speeches and Writings of A. Philip Randolph*. University of Massachusetts Press, 2014.
King, Martin Luther, Jr. *Where Do We Go from Here: Chaos or Community?* Harper & Row, 1967.
Kirshenblatt-Gimblett, Barbara. "Toward a Theory of Proverb Meaning." In *The Wisdom of Many: Essays on the Proverb*, edited by Wolfgang Mieder and Alan Dundes, 111–21. Garland Publishing, 1981.
Knowles, Elizabeth. *Oxford Dictionary of Phrase and Fable*. 2nd ed., Oxford University Press, 2005.
Latham, Sean, ed. *The World of Bob Dylan*. Cambridge University Press, 2021.
Leffler, Phyllis. *Black Leaders on Leadership: Conversations with Julian Bond*. Palgrave Macmillan, 2014.
Leigh, Spencer. *Bob Dylan: Outlaw Blues*. McNidder and Grace, 2020.
Litovkina, Anna T., and Wolfgang Mieder. *Old Proverbs Never Die, They Just Diversify*. University of Vermont, 2006.
Little, Malcolm. *The End of White World Supremacy*. Merlin House, 1971.
Long, Michael G., ed. *Race Man: Julian Bond: Selected Works, 1960–2015*, City Light Books, 2020.
Lowcountry Digital History Initiative (LDHI). "Remembering Individuals, Remembering Communities: Septima P. Clark and Public History in Charleston." http://ldhi.library.cofc.edu/exhibits/show/septima_clark/virtual-tour/106-coming-street. Accessed 15 December 2020.
The Lumberjack. 1913. New Orleans, Louisiana. www.marxist.org. Accessed June 2021.
"Lynchings by Year and Race, 1882–1968." *University of Missouri-Kansas City, Law School*. http://law2.umkc.edu/Faculty/projects/ftrials/shipp/lynchingyear.html. Accessed 26 January 2020.
Maggio, John, director. *A Choice of Weapons: Inspired by Gordon Parks*. HBO, 2021.
Marable, Manning. *A Life of Reinvention*. Penguin Press, 2011.
Marable, Manning, and Garrett Felber, eds. *The Portable Malcolm X Reader*. Penguin, 2013.
Marcus, Greil. *Like A Rolling Stone: Bob Dylan at the Crossroads*. Public Affairs, 2006.
Marcus, Greil. *Bob Dylan: Writings, 1968–2010*. Public Affairs, 2010.
Marcus, Greil. *The Old, Weird America: The World of Bob Dylan's Basement Tapes*. Picador, 2011.
Marcus, Greil. *Folk Music: A Bob Dylan Biography in Seven Songs*. Yale University Press, 2022.
Margotin, Philippe, and Jean-Michel Guesdon. *Bob Dylan All the Songs: The Story Behind Every Track*. Black Dog & Leventhal, 2015.

Marqusee, Mike. *Chimes of Freedom: The Politics of Bob Dylan's Art*. New Press, 2003.
Marshall, Lee. *Bob Dylan: The Never-Ending Star*. Polity Press, 2007.
Marshall, Scott. *Bob Dylan: A Spiritual Life*. BP/WND Books, 2017.
Martin, Roland S. *White Fear: How the Browning of America is Making White Folks Lose Their Minds*. BenBella Books, 2022.
Marx, Karl. 1818–83. *The Communist Manifesto*. Pluto Press, 1996.
McClendon, H. John, III, and Stephen C. Ferguson II. "On the Dialectical Evolution of Malcolm X's Anti-Capitalist Critique: Interrogating His Political Philosophy of Black Nationalism." In *Malcolm X: From Political Eschatology to Religious Revolutionary*, edited by Dustin J. Byrd and Seyed Javad Miri, 37–90. Brill Press, 2016.
McDougal, Dennis. *Bob Dylan: The Biography*. Turner Publishing, 2014.
McElrath, Joseph R., and Robert C. Lietz, III., eds. *"To Be an Author": Letters of Charles W. Chesnutt, 1889-1905*. Princeton University Press, 1997.
McElrath, Joseph R., Robert C. Lietz III, and Jesse S. Crisler, eds. *Charles W. Chesnutt: Essays and Speeches*. Stanford University Press, 1999.
McKenzie, Peter K. *Bob Dylan: On A Couch & Fifty Cents a Day*. MKB Press, 2021.
McMurry, Linda O. *To Keep the Waters Troubled: The Life of Ida B. Wells*. Oxford University Press, 1998.
McWilliams, Dean. *Charles W. Chesnutt and the Fictions of Race*. University of Georgia Press, 2002.
Meade, Robert D. *Patrick Henry: Practical Revolutionary*. Lippincott Press, 1969.
Meeks, Catherine, and Nibs Stroupe. *Passionate for Justice: Ida B. Wells as Prophet for Our Time*. Church Publishing, 2019.
Messenger, John C. "The Role of Proverbs in A Nigerian Judicial System." *Southwestern Journal of Anthropology* 15, no. 1 (1959): 64–73.
Mieder, Wolfgang. *American Proverbs: A Study of Texts and Contexts*. Peter Lang Publishing, 1989.
Mieder, Wolfgang. *Proverbs Are Never Out of Season: Popular Wisdom in the Modern Age*. Oxford University Press, 1993.
Mieder, Wolfgang. *The Politics of Proverbs: Traditional Wisdom to Proverbial Stereotypes*. University of Wisconsin Press, 1997.
Mieder, Wolfgang. *"No Struggle, No Progress": Frederick Douglas and His Proverbial Rhetoric for Civil Rights*. Peter Lang, 2001.
Mieder, Wolfgang. *Proverbs: A Handbook*. Greenwood Press, 2004.
Mieder, Wolfgang. *"Yes We Can": Obama's Proverbial Rhetoric*. Peter Lang, 2009.
Mieder, Wolfgang. *"Making a Way Out of No Way": Martin Luther King's Sermonic Proverbial Rhetoric*. Peter Lang, 2010.
Mieder, Wolfgang. "'Keep Your Eyes on the Prize': Congressman John Lewis's Proverbial Odyssey for Civil Rights." *Proverbium* 31 (2014): 331–93.
Mieder, Wolfgang. *"Right Makes Might": Proverbs and the American Worldview*. Indiana University Press, 2019.
Mieder, Wolfgang. *Proverbial Rhetoric for Civil and Human Rights by Four African American Heroes*. University of Vermont, 2020.
Mieder, Wolfgang. *The Worldview of Modern American Proverbs*. Peter Lang, 2020.

Mieder, Wolfgang. *Dictionary of Authentic American Proverbs*. Berghahn Books, 2021.

Mieder, Wolfgang, Stewart A. Kingsbury, and Kelsie B. Harder. *A Dictionary of American Proverbs*. Oxford University Press, 1992.

Miles, K. G. *Bob Dylan in the Big Apple: Troubadour Tales of New York*. McNidder and Grace, 2021.

Miles, K. G., and Jeff Towns. *Bob Dylan and Dylan Thomas: The Two Dylans*. McNidder and Grace, 2022.

Miller, Calvin Craig. *A. Philip Randolph and the American Labor Movement*. Morgan Reynolds Publishing, 2003.

Moore-Wilson, Shirley Ann, and Quintard Taylor, eds. *African American Women Confront the West, 1600–2000*. University of Oklahoma Press, 2008.

Morrow, Andrew John. "Malcolm X: Message to Humanity." In *Malcolm X: From Political Eschatology to Religious Revolutionary*, edited by Dustin J. Byrd and Seyed Javad Miri, 211–26. Brill Press, 2016.

Moskalenko, Sophia, and Clark McCauley. *Radicalization to Terrorism: What Everyone Needs to Know*. Oxford University Press, 2020.

Moye, Todd J., *Ella Baker: Community Organizer of the Civil Rights Movement*. Rowan & Littlefield Publishers, 2013.

Natambu, Kofi. *The Life and Work of Malcolm X*. Alpha Books, 2002.

Neary, John. *Julian Bond: Black Rebel*. Willam Morrow and Company, 1971.

Newman, Martin. *Bob Dylan's Malibu*. EDLIS Café Press, 2021.

Nkrumah, Kwame. *The Axioms of Kwame Nkrumah: Freedom Fighter's Edition*. International Publishers, 1967.

Ogden, Mary Macdonald. *Wil Lou Gray: The Making of a Southern Progressive from New South to New Deal*. University of South Carolina Press, 2016.

Parks, Gordon. *A Choice of Weapons*. Minnesota Historical Society Press, 1966.

Parks, Gordon. "Stokely Carmichael: Young Man Behind an Angry Message." *Life*, 19 May 1967: 76A–84.

Parks, Gordon. "Whip of Black Power." Draft manuscript for *Life*, 1967. gordonparks-foundation.org/publications/Gordon-parks/Stokely-carmichael-and-black-power. Accessed 23 December 2023.

Parks, Gordon. *To Smile in Autumn*. University of Minnesota Press, 2009.

Payne, Les and Tamara Payne. *The Dead Are Arising: The Life of Malcolm X*. Liveright Publishing Corporation, 2020.

Perry, Bruce. *Malcolm: The Life of a Man Who Changed Black America*. Station Hill Press, 1991.

Pfeffer, Paula F. *A. Philip Randolph Pioneer of the Civil Rights Movement*. Louisiana State University Press, 1990.

Pichaske, David. *Song of the North Country: A Midwest Framework to the Songs of Bob Dylan*. Continuum Press, 2010.

Pickens, Ernestine Williams. *Charles W. Chesnutt and the Progressive Movement*. Pace University Press, 1994.

Prahlad, Anand Sw. *African-American Proverbs in Context*. University Press of Mississippi, 1996.

Prahlad, Anand Sw. *Reggae Wisdom: Proverbs in Jamaican Music*. University Press of Mississippi, 2001.

Ransby, Barbara. *Ella Baker & the Black Freedom Movement: A Radical Democratic Vision*. University of North Carolina Press, 2003.

Ricks, Christopher. *Dylan's Visions of Sin*. HarperCollins, 2005.

Rogovoy, Seth. *Bob Dylan: Prophet, Mystic, Poet*. Scribner, 2009.

Ronson, Mick. "When the World Falls Down." *Heaven and Hull*, July 1994. https://genius.com/Mick-Ronson-when-the-world-falls-down-lyrics.

Rosenbaum, Ron. "The Diamond Voice Within." In *Younger Than That Now: Collected Interviews with Bob Dylan*, 109–59. Thunder's Mouth Press, 1978.

Rotolo, Suze. *A Freewheelin' Time: A Memoir of Greenwich Village in the Sixties*. Aurum, 2009.

Russell, Jessica, Hilda Little, and Steve Jones Sr. *The Life of Louise Norton Little: An Extraordinary Woman, Mother of Malcolm X, and His Seven Siblings*. Our Hidden Gem, 2021.

Sanders, Daryl. *That Thin, Wild Mercury Sound: Dylan, Nashville, and the Making of Blonde on Blonde*. Chicago Review Press, 2018.

Santino, Jack. "Miles of Smiles, Years of Struggle: The Negotiation of Black Occupational Identity Through Personal Experience Narrative." *Journal of American Folklore* 96 (1984): 393–412.

Sawyers, June Skinner. *Bob Dylan's New York*. History Press, 2022.

Scaduto, Anthony. *Bob Dylan*. Tolmitch, 2016.

Scaduto, Anthony. *The Dylan Tapes: Friends, Players, and Lovers Talkin' Early Bob Dylan*. University of Minnesota Press, 2022.

Schechter, Patricia A. "All the Intensity of My Nature": Ida B. Wells, Anger, and Politics. *Radical History Review* 70 (1998): 48–77.

Schechter, Patricia A. *Ida B. Wells-Barnett, and American Reform, 1880–1930*. University of North Carolina Press, 2001.

Seitel, Peter. "Proverbs A Social Use of Metaphor." In *The Wisdom of Many: Essays on the Proverb*, edited by Wolfgang Mieder and Alan Dundes, 122–39. Garland Publishing, 1981.

Shakespeare, William. 1599. *The Tragedy of Hamlet, Prince of Denmark*. MIT. http://shakespeare.mit.edu/hamlet/full.html. Accessed 11 May 2019.

Shelton, Robert. *No Direction Home: The Life and Music of Bob Dylan*. 2nd ed., Backbeat Books, 2011.

Siebert, J. Rudolf. "Malcolm X—A Martyr of Freedom." In *Malcolm X: From Political Eschatology to Religious Revolutionary*, edited by Dustin J. Byrd and Sayed Javed Miri, 131–78. Brill Press, 2016.

Silkey, Sarah L. *Black Woman Reformer: Ida B. Wells, Lynching, and Transatlantic Activism*. University of Georgia Press, 2015.

Simmons, Ryan. *Chesnutt and Realism: A Study of Novels*. University of Alabama Press, 2006.

Simpson, John. *The Concise Oxford Dictionary of English Proverbs*. Oxford University Press, 1982.

Sims, Angela D. *Ethical Complications of Lynching: Ida B. Wells's Interrogation of American Terror*. Palgrave MacMillan, 2010.

Smith, David Larry. *Writing Dylan: The Songs of a Lonesome Traveler*. Praeger, 2005.
Smith, Michael David. *Endless Holocausts: Mass Death in the History of the United States Empire*. Monthly Review Press, 2023.
SNCC Legacy Project. "Septima Clark." SNCC. http://www.sncclegacyproject.org. Accessed 15 December 2020.
Sounes, Howard. *Down the Highway: The Life of Bob Dylan*. Grove Press, 2011.
Speake, Jennifer. *Oxford Dictionary of Proverbs*. 6th ed., Oxford University Press, 2015.
Spencer, Neil. "The Diamond Voice Within." In *Younger Than That Now: Collected Interviews with Bob Dylan*, 171–85. Thunder's Mouth Press, 1981.
Spitz, Bob. *Dylan: A Biography*. W. W. Norton & Company, 1991.
Star, Larry. *Listening to Bob Dylan*. University of Illinois Press, 2021.
Sterling, Dorothy. *Black Foremothers: Three Lives*, 2nd ed., Feminist Press at the City University of New York, 1988.
Summerville, Raymond. "'Words Are but Wind': The Proverbs and Proverbial Expressions of Bob Dylan." *Proverbium: Yearbook of International Proverb Scholarship* 36 (2019): 371–406.
Sussman, Mark. "Chesnutt as Cultural Critic." In *Approaches to Teaching the Works of Charles W. Chesnutt*, edited by Susanna Ashton and Bill Hardwig, 85–90. Modern Language Association, 2017.
Taylor, Archer. 1931. *The Proverb*. Harvard University Press, 1962, 1985.
Taylor, Archer. "The Wisdom of Many and the Wit of One." In *The Wisdom of Many: Essays on the Proverb*, edited by Wolfgang Mieder and Alan Dundes, 3–9. Garland Publishing, 1981.
Taylor, Archer, and Bartlett Jere Whiting. *A Dictionary of American Proverbs and Proverbial Phrases, 1820–1880*. Harvard University Press, 1958.
Taylor, Cynthia. *A. Philip Randolph: The Religious Journey of an African American Labor Leader*. New York University Press, 2006.
Taylor, Quintard. *In Search of the Racial Frontier: African Americans in the American West, 1528–1990*. W. W. Norton & Company, 1999.
Terborg-Penn, Rosalyn. *African American Women in the Struggle for the Vote, 1850–1920*. Indiana University Press, 1998.
Thomas, Richard F. *Why Bob Dylan Matters*. HarperCollins, 2017.
Thompson, Mildred I. *Ida B. Wells-Barnett: An Exploratory Study of an American Black Woman, 1893–1930*. Carlson Publishing, 1990.
Thoreau, Henry David. *Walden or Life in the Woods*. Wisehouse, 1854.
Ture, Kwame, and Charles Hamilton. *Black Power the Politics of Liberation in America*. Vintage Books, 1967.
Urban, Wayne J., *Black Scholar: Horace Mann Bond (1904–1972)*. University of Georgia Press.
Volpe, Lisa. Lecture | "Gordon Parks, Stokely Carmichael and Black Power." YouTube, Museum of Fine Arts, Houston, 7 January 2023. https://www.youtube.com/watch?v=ZwYqggXtz68.
Volpe, Lisa, ed. *Gordon Parks, Stokely Carmichael and Black Power*. Steidl/Gordon Parks Foundation/Museum of Fine Arts, Houston, 2022.
Wainstock, Dennis D. *Malcolm X: African American Revolutionary*. McFarland & Company, 2009.

Walker, Eugene. Interview with Septima Clark. *Southern Oral History Program Collection*, 1976.

Warren, Robert Penn. "Septima Poinsette Clark." In *Who Speaks for the Negro? Archival Collection*. https://whospeaks.library.vanderbilt.edu/interview/septima-poinsette-clark. Accessed 15 December 2020.

Weissman, Dick. *Which Side Are You On? An Inside History of the Folk Music Revival in America*. Continuum, 2005.

Welky, David. *Marching Across the Color Line: A. Philip Randolph and Civil Rights in the World War II Era*. Oxford University Press, 2014.

Wells, Ida B. Various speeches. In *Ida B. Wells, The Light of Truth: Writings of an Anti-Lynching Crusader*, edited by Mia Bay and Henry Louis Gates Jr., 19–20. Penguin Books, 1885.

Whitaker, Mark. *Saying it Loud: 1966–The Year Black Power Challenged the Civil Rights Movement*. Simon & Schuster, 2023.

Whiting, Bartlett Jere. "The Nature of the Proverb." In *Harvard Studies and Notes in Philology and Literature* 14 (1932): 273–307.

Whiting, Bartlett Jere. *Modern Proverbs and Proverbial Sayings*. Harvard University Press, 1989.

"Willie Ricks." *SNCC Digital Gateway*, SNCC Legacy Project and Duke University. http://SNCCdigital.org. Accessed 12 July 2020.

Wilson, F. P. *Oxford Dictionary of English Proverbs*. 3rd ed., Oxford, 1970.

Work, Monroe N. "Geechee and other Proverbs." *Journal of American Folklore*, no. 32 (1919): 441–44.

Wright, Richard., *Black Power: A Record of Reactions in a Land of Pathos*. Harper & Brothers, 1954.

INDEX

A&T Four (student protestors), 129
African American labor movement, 75, 82
All-African People's Revolution Party, 167–70, 194–95
Allen, Louis, murder of, 160
Allen, Richard, 78
antiproverb, 42, 58, 186
apartheid (African), 147
apartheid (American), 100
Arabian Nights, The, 41–42
"Atlanta Compromise" (Washington), 88
Avery Normal Institute, 112–13, 118

Back to Africa movement, 27, 74, 136
Baez, Joan, 6, 99
Baker, Ella Josephine, 115, 120, 125, 129, 182, 192, 197–200
"Ballad of Hollis Brown" (Dylan), 99
Bembry, John Elton, 138
Black Codes, 19, 50
Black diaspora, 167, 195
Black Panther Party, 104, 175, 193–94
Black power, 10, 204
Black Power (Carmichael and Hamilton), 177, 186
blaxploitation era, 190
"Blowin' in the Wind" (Dylan), 99, 101–2
Bond, Horace Mann, 199
Bond, Julian, 175, 199
Bowden, Betsy, 105, 158
Brown, John, 97, 143
Browne, Sir Thomas, 60

Brownsville Affair, 62
Brown v. Board of Education, 190
Bulwer-Lytton, Edward, 64
Bundy, LeRoy C., 34
Burns, Robert, 39

Cable, George, 65, 72
Carmichael, Stokely, xi, xiv, 3, 6, 10–11, 115, 154–96
Carter, Jimmy, 102–3
Chaney, James, murder of, 194
Charles, Robert, 26–28
Chesnutt, Charles Waddell, 48–73
Chicago World's Fair, 29
Choice of Weapons (film), 201
Choice of Weapons (Parks), 201
Citizenship Education Program, 120, 134
Clark, Septima Poinsette, x, xiv, 3, 6, 109, 110–35
Colonel's Dream (Chesnutt), 49
colonialism, 144, 154, 163, 167, 176, 188; anticolonialism, 149
Colored American Day/Negro Day, 30
Conjure Woman (Chesnutt), 49
convict lease system, 44, 49
cotton, 19
Cox, Courtland, 179–80
Crusade for Justice (Wells), 28
Curran, Philpot, 45

Daniels, Jonathan, 168–69
"Death of Emmett Till, The" (Dylan), 105

Douglass, Frederick, xiii, 4, 14, 25, 28, 30–31, 33, 36, 45, 49, 57–59, 77, 83, 86–87, 93, 102, 145, 186
Du Bois, David, 183–84
Du Bois, W. E. B., 51, 74. *See* Washington/Du Bois debate
Durham, North Carolina, xi, 6, 63, 161
Dylan, Bob, xi, xiv, 3, 6, 8, 95–96, 97–109

Ellison, Ralph, 107–8, 201
Esau (Bible), 67
escapism, 70
Europe, 36–43, 78, 80, 149, 161, 167, 188–89
Evers, Medgar, 108, 140, 144
Executive Order 8802, 91

Fair Employment Practices Committee, 75, 90–91
Farmer, James, 181–82
Fayetteville State University, 49. *See also* State Colored Normal School
Finnegan, Ruth, 85
Fortune, T. Thomas, 26, 29, 35, 37
forty acres and a mule, 49, 168
Fox, George, 117, 200
Freedman's Bureau, 48–49
Freedom Schools, 168, 173
Freewheelin' Bob Dylan, The (Dylan), 99
Fugitive Slave Law, 48

Garnet, Henry Highland, 83, 87–88
Garvey, Marcus, 13, 36, 74, 136
General Federation of Laborers of the Land of Israel, 88. *See also* Histadrut
Ghana, 142, 154, 157, 161–62, 167, 171; coup, 162, 167
Grandfather Clause, 50
Gray, Victoria, 115
Green, Nancy (Aunt Jemima), 29
Golden Rule, 16, 52–54, 59, 122, 199
Goodman, Andy, murder of, 194
Guinea, 6, 10, 154, 167, 169, 171, 184

Haiti, 30, 111
hajj (spiritual journey), 142

Hamer, Fannie Lou, 177, 197
Handbook of Revolutionary Warfare (Nkrumah), 167
Highlander Folk School, 88, 98, 116. *See also* Garnet, Henry Highland
Histadrut, 88
Holly Springs, Mississippi, 18–21
Hoover, Herbert, 34–35
Horton, Myles, 6, 9, 98, 116, 118, 128, 130
House Behind the Cedars (Chesnutt), 49
Howard, Oliver Otis, 48
Howard, Ruth, 186
Howard School, 48–49
Howard University, 10, 162, 174, 191
humanism, 172
Hunter, Charles N., 63
"Hurricane" (Dylan), 105

imperialism, 104, 144, 154, 167, 195
institutional racism, 155, 173, 203
"It's Alright, Ma (I'm Only Bleeding)" (Dylan), 99

Jacob (Bible), 67
Jamaica, xiii, 36, 136, 154
Jamestown (colony), 55
Johns Island, 112–16, 121
Johnson, Cedric G., 97
Johnson, June, 177
Johnson, Lilian Wyckoff, 119
Johnson, Robert, 100
Jones, Junebug Jabbo, 173–76, 183, 195
Jordan, Vernon, 198

Kennedy, Bobby, 140, 160, 165
Kennedy, John F., 106, 141, 163
King, Coretta Scott, 93
King, Martin Luther, xiii, 5, 14, 74, 78, 94, 120, 132, 140, 145, 156, 186, 201
Ku Klux Klan, 100, 128, 136–37, 164, 190, 194

Lawless, Elaine J., x
Learning Tree (Parks), 201
Leffler, Phyllis, 199
Leopard's Spots, The (Dixon), 61–62

Lincoln, Abraham, 14, 18, 123–24, 186
Lincoln's Legal Loyal League (4-L's), 20
Liuzzo, Viola Fauver, death of, 98
Liverpool, England, 39
"Lonesome Death of Hattie Carroll, The" (Dylan), 105
Lovejoy, Jordan, xi
Lowndes County Freedom Organization, 169, 186, 193
Luther, Martin, 78
lynching, 13

Macaulay, Thomas Babington, 55
Mahoney, Bill, 179
Malcolm X, 135, 136–53, 159–63, 201, 203
Malcolm X Liberation University, 6, 161
March on Washington for Jobs and Freedom, 6, 8, 74, 84–87, 140
Marrow of Tradition (Chesnutt), 47, 49, 67, 70–72
Marx, Karl, 152
McDowell, Calvin, lynching of, 13
Meredith, James, March Against Fear, 155
Messenger, xi, 80, 83, 86, 90–91
Mississippi Freedom Democratic Party, 178, 186
Mississippi Summer Project, 160, 166
Mob Rule in New Orleans (Wells), 26
Morrison, Toni, 176–77
Moss, Thomas, lynching of, 13, 29, 33
Mugwump Progressive, 50–51
Muhammed, Elijah, 138, 142
"Murder Most Foul" (Dylan), 106

neo slavery, 43
Neuberger, G., 163
Nkrumah, Kwame (Osagyefo), 6, 10, 159, 161–62, 167–69, 170, 194
Non-Violent Action Group, 173–74, 179
Normal School Literary Society, 56
"North Country Blues" (Dylan), 99

Oberlin and Wellington Rescue Case of 1858, 48
O'Neal, John M., 173–74

"Only a Pawn in Their Game" (Dylan), 108
"Oxford Town" (Dylan), 106

Pan-Africanism, 167, 172
Parks, Gordon, 197–204
Parsons Weekly Blade (Labette County, Kansas), 37
Pickens, Ernestine Williams, 50, 70
plantation mentality, 43
Poinsette, Joel Roberts, 111
Prahlad, Anand, ix–xiii, 4–5, 76, 167
progressive era, 49, 57
Protestantism, 50, 52, 55, 78, 200
proverb, 17, 52, 76, 114, 154
proverb master, 4–5, 95, 135, 196
proverb song, 102
Pythagorean Theorem, 180–81

race man, 20
racial prognostication, 57
radical interracialists, 12
Randolph, Asa Philip, 3, 5–8, 13–14, 73, 74–98
Ready for Revolution (Carmichael), 153, 156, 178
Ready from Within (Clark), 135
realist (literary), 70
Reconstruction, 12–14, 43, 49, 63, 79, 84, 93, 168, 187
Reed, Herbert, 174–75
Richardson, Gloria, 180
Rustin, Bayard, 93

Schwerner, Mickey, murder of, 98, 194
sexism, 37–38
Shaw University (Rust College), 20–21, 182, 192, 198
"Shock Treatment Speech" (Warring), 128
Smile in Autumn (Parks), 200
socialism, 80, 83, 171
Society for the Recognition of the Brotherhood of Man, 36
Southern Christian Leadership Conference, 120, 125, 129, 188
Southern Horrors (Wells), 14, 25–26

Special Field Order No.15, 168
State Colored Normal School, 49, 53
Stewart, Will, lynching of, 13
Stokely Speaks (Carmichael), 161, 166, 172, 176, 187
Student Nonviolent Coordinating Committee, 6, 10, 95, 98, 120, 125, 129, 134, 150, 155, 163, 172–74, 179, 188
"Subterranean Homesick Blues" (Dylan), 103–5

tactical invisibility, 124
Thelwell, Ekwueme Michael, 176
Thiers, Louis Adolphe, 56
Times They Are A-Changin', The (Dylan), 106
Touré, Ahmed Sékou, 6, 10
Treaty of Cambridge, 180
Trinidad, 154, 157, 179, 189
Turnbow, Hartman, 177–78
Tuskegee Institute, 13, 88

Vietnam, 8, 95, 100, 104, 166, 203
visionary pragmatism, 12

Voice That Could Stir an Army (Parker), 197
Volpe, Lisa, 202–4

Warren, Robert Penn, 122–24
Warring, Elizabeth, 127–28. *See also* "Shock Treatment Speech" (Warring)
Washington, Booker T., 51, 74, 81, 88, 114. *See also* Washington/Du Bois debate
Washington/Du Bois debate, 67–68, 74
Weathermen/Weather Underground Organization, 104
Wells-Barnett, Ida B., 3, 6, 12–47
West India, 154, 180–83
"Whip of Black Power" (Parks), 203
Wife of His Youth (Chesnutt), 49
Willard, Francis E., 43–44
Wilmington Massacre of 1898, 46–47, 70–72

Young Women's Christian Association, 114, 127–28

Zimbabwe, 166
Zionism, 163

ABOUT THE AUTHOR

Photo courtesy of the editor

Raymond Summerville earned an MA in English and African American literature from North Carolina Agricultural and Technical State University and a PhD in English with a concentration in folklore, oral tradition, and culture from the University of Missouri–Columbia. His research interests include diaspora studies, postcolonial studies, African American literature, American history, and all subjects related to folkloristics including African American folklore and paremiology. He currently teaches at Fayetteville State University in North Carolina in the Department of English: Literature, Teaching, Pre-Law, and Professional Writing.

www.ingramcontent.com/pod-product-compliance
Lightning Source LLC
Chambersburg PA
CBHW022011220426
43663CB00007B/1045